Shyam Benegal

Sangeeta Datta is a film historian, lecturer, critic and documentary film-maker. She runs a London-based film society 'In Focus' which promotes South Asian Cinema in the UK. A member of FIPRESCI International, she has worked with Indian film-makers Basu Bhattacharya and Rituparno Ghosh. She has also worked closely with the National Film Theatre, promoting Indian film programmes in London, the latest being 'A Tribute to Shyam Benegal' in 2002.

Datta undertook a post-doctoral project on Indian cinema at the University of Sussex. She holds a PhD in English from Jadavpur University, Calcutta, and has taught English and Film Studies at St Xavier's College, Mumbai. A frequent cultural commentator for the Indian and British media, Datta lives in London with her husband and two sons. Her film *The Way I See It* (on Indian women film-makers) has been screened in film festivals across the world and is also part of the curriculum for Film Studies.

OTHER LOTUS TITLES

Anil Dharker — *Icons: Men & Women Who Shaped Today's India*
Ajit Bhattacharjea — *Sheikh Mohammad Abdullah: Tragic Hero of Kashmir*
Aitzaz Ahsan — *The Indus Saga: The Making of Pakistan*
Ajay Mansingh — *Firaq Gorakhpuri: The Poet of Pain & Ecstasy*
Alam Srinivas & T.R. Vivek — *IPL: The Inside Story*
Aruna Roy — *The RTI Story: Power to the People*
Ashis Ray — *Laid to Rest: The Controversy of Subhas Chandra Bose's Death*
Bertil Falk — *Feroze: The Forgotten Gandhi*
Harinder Baweja (Ed.) — *26/11 Mumbai Attacked*
Harinder Baweja — *A Soldier's Diary Kargil: the inside story*
Ian H. Magedera — *Indian Videshinis: European Women in India*
Kunal Purandare — *Ramakant Achrekar: A Biography*
Lucy Peck — *Agra: The Architectural Heritage*
Lucy Peck — *Delhi a Thousand Years of Building: An INTACH-Roli Guide*
Maj. Gen. Ian Cardozo — *Param Vir: Our Heroes in Battle*
Maj. Gen. Ian Cardozo — *The Sinking of INS Khukri: What Happened in 1971*
Madhu Trehan — *Tehelka as Metaphor*
Moin Mir — *Surat: Fall of A Port Rise of A Prince Defeat of the East India Company in the House Of Commons*
Monisha Rajesh — *Around India in 80 Trains*
Noorul Hasan — *Meena Kumari: The Poet*
Prateep K. Lahiri — *A Tide in the Affairs of Men: A Public Servant Remembers*
Rajika Bhandari — *The Raj on the Move: Story of the Dak Bungalow*
Ralph Russell — *The Famous Ghalib: The Sound of my Moving Pen*
Rahul Bedi — *The Last Word: Obituaries of 100 Indian who Led Unusual Lives*
R.V. Smith — *Delhi: Unknown Tales of a City*
Salman Akthar — *The Book of Emotions*
Sharmishta Gooptu — *Bengali Cinema: An Other Nation*
Shrabani Basu — *Spy Princess: The Life of Noor Inayat Khan*
Shahrayar Khan — *Bhopal Connections: Vignettes of Royal Rule*
Shantanu Guha Ray — *Mahi: The Story Of India's Most Successful Captain*
S. Hussain Zaidi — *Dongri to Dubai*
Sunil Raman & Rohit Aggarwal — *Delhi Durbar: 1911 The Complete Story*
Thomas Weber — *Going Native: Gandhi's Relationship with Western Women*
Thomas Weber — *Gandhi at First Sight*
Vaibhav Purandare — *Sachin Tendulkar: A definitive biography*
Vappala Balachandran — *A Life In Shadow: The Secret Story of ACN Nambiar – A Forgotten Anti-Colonial Warrior*
Vijayan Bala — *The Complete Indian Sports Quiz Book*
Vir Sanghvi — *Men of Steel: India's Business Leaders in Candid Conversation*

FORTHCOMING TITLE

Brij Mohan Bhalla — *Kasturba Gandhi: A Biography*

Shyam Benegal

Sangeeta Datta

LOTUS COLLECTION
ROLI BOOKS

To Babafor introducing me to world cinema through film society screenings
To Ma and Mashifor nurturing my love for good stories…
To Chikoo and Jijo to know more about a great master and his craft.

Lotus Collection

First published in 2002 by the British Film Institute
First published in India in 2003
This paperback edition 2008
Second impression, 2020

The Lotus Collection
An imprint of
Roli Books Pvt. Ltd.
M-75, G.K. II Market, New Delhi 110 048
Phone:
E-mail: info@rolibooks.com
www.rolibooks.com
Also at Bengaluru, Chennai, & Mumbai

Published by arrangement with British Film Institute
21 Stephen Street, London W1T1LN

For sale in India, Pakistan, Myanmar, Bhutan,
Bangladesh, Sir Lanka and Nepal only

ISBN: 978-81-7436-651-1

Typeset in Minion by Roli Books Pvt. Ltd. and
printed at Repro India, Mumbai.

Contents

Foreword

I have known Shyam Benegal on and off for around 30 years, ever since he was particularly kind to me when I first came to India on a rather vague mission to understand Indian cinema and possibly proclaim it to a world which still sometimes seems to know very little about it, except in terms of clichés. This was before I saw any of his films. And when I finally sat down in front of Ankur, I realised that here was a pretty special film-maker, in the world as well as Indian terms. Since then, he has always struck me as an international figure, securely Indian, but well able to transcend any barriers of nationality because of his wide interests and an insatiable curiosity about most things outside India. Certainly he is greatly respected and liked everywhere he goes – an ambassador for India almost without parallel in the cultural field.

As a film-maker pure and simple, it can be said with some accuracy that no director since Satyajit Ray has done more for Indian film than Shyam Benegal. His first few films provided a huge marker for other young directors of what was once hopefully called the Indian parallel cinema. And the fact that he made his films in Hindi, the language of what the West rather insultingly calls Bollywood, yet spoke of social and political commitment in terms much more firmly grounded in reality than Bollywood was able, made his success all the more notable. If it wasn't for the lightning bolts of *Ankur*, *Nishant*, *Manthan* and *Bhumika*, many other films we now celebrate as highpoints of the parallel cinema might never have been made. Benegal's continued persistence in increasingly difficult times for the serious film-maker has encouraged countless others. And it should be said that personally he has always found time to give advice to any who asks, whether he knows them or not.

Added to all this, which would surely be enough for most people, Benegal's films on Indian history, whether cultural or political, are models of their kind, showing that his commitment is not confined to fiction but securely based on fact as well as imagination. But I have no wish to seem like a hagiographer, since Benegal would probably admit that in some senses he has failed in his task to broaden the West's view of Indian film and to push those who distribute and exhibit them in India itself towards more audacious policies. Goodness knows he has tried. But your average Western audience are still largely ignorant of the scope and power of the best of Indian cinema, apart perhaps from a cursory knowledge of Satyajit Ray. And there are many Indians who have never had a regular chance to see the best either. Any Indian film-maker of note must have been plagued by pessimism at one time or another during the last decades of the twentieth century. But Benegal has never let such thoughts deter him. He is incapable of giving up, and that is one of his prime virtues. Long may his courage and persistence shore up those of others.

Derek Malcolm

Acknowledgments

I would like to acknowledge my thanks to the following.

My friends in India who helped during my research trip in May–June 2001.

In Bombay: Shabana Azmi and Javed Akhtar for their generous hospitality, feedback and advice; Rajan Kothari, Khalid Mohamed, Sudhir Nandgaonkar, Govind Nihalani, Om Puri, Maithili Rao, Bhawana Somayaa and Shama Zaidi for extending interviews.

Shyambabu, who generously gave his time as we talked through hot, languid afternoons in his office in Everest Building over the bustling street in Tardeo, boosted periodically by the glasses of sugary tea the local chai-wallah brought in; and Raj Pius and other staff members in Shyam Benegal's well-organised office, who helped with the photographs, press cuttings and video tapes.

In Pune: P. K. Nair and Anil Zankar for their comments; the National Film Archives where I reviewed many of Benegal's films; and special thanks to Shashidharan and Aarti Karkhane for providing research material.

In Kolkata: Amiya and Jasodhara Bagchi, Samik Bandopadhyay and the late Subrato Mitra for their comments.

In London: Nasreen Munni Kabir, Girish Karnad and Avtar Panesar for their interviews; Derek Malcolm for the foreword and an illuminating discussion we had with Gierson and Uma da Cunha during the mayor's lunch at Cannes; Kitty Cooper and Pamela Cullen for brief but useful discussions; Mukulika Banerjee, Kaushik Bhowmick and Sudipta Kaviraj, who read the chapters at various stages and made useful suggestions; and friends Seema Anand, Mukulika (again), Rachel and Michael Dwyer, Naman Ramachandran, Vipul Sangoi and Cary Sawhney for their continuing support.

In Boston: Satrajit Ghosh and Katrien Vander Straeten for procuring the DVDs.

The BFI for offering funds to support the research trip; and Andrew Lockett for his editorial support, advice and patience.

Finally, family and friends, especially Soumilyo and my sons Soumik and Souvid, who pitched in often to help. Last but not least, Dipali, for holding fort when I was away.

Images courtesy of The National Film Archives, Pune; Shyam Benegal Sahyadri Films, Bombay; Hyphen Films, London.

Preface

I grew up in India during the exciting developments of parallel cinema, the women's movement and street theatre of the late 1970s and 1980s. Shyam Benegal's films were formative influences in defining the parameters of good cinema and shaping the way a generation of educated middle-class youth learned to look at life. His trilogy and *Bhumika* (1977) provided the context for much debate and discussion during university days in Calcutta. Later, when I was teaching at St Xavier's College, Bombay, Shyambabu (as he is commonly addressed) would often agree to introduce his films to my students of Indian film. I also wrote on his films in newspapers and journals in India.

While at Sussex in 1997 at a special conference on 50 years of Indian independence, I programmed *Bhumika*, and Shyambabu was invited as a guest speaker from India. In 1998, when I was shooting for my documentary on women film-makers, *The Way I See It*, every director referred to Benegal's films. As Shabana Azmi said, 'The yin and the yang are perfectly balanced in Shyam!' In the end, he was the only man I interviewed for the film.

In 1999, I was in Jaipur for the shooting of *Zubeidaa* (2000) as Benegal's guest. The set in Ram Niwas Mahal bore witness to the director's meticulous eye for detail and historical accuracy. The walls had been decorated and painted with intricate motifs, old sepia – coloured photographs of royal hunts were up on the wall, a portrait of the prince (played by Manoj Bajpai) dominated one end of the room. Shyambabu was directing Rekha and Karishma Kapoor, setting the actors at ease even as he corrected accents and dialogue delivery. After every take, the actors would crowd around the monitor to watch the replay and receive the director's approval. As cinematographer Rajan Kothari got ready to light the next sequence, Shyambabu pulled up a chair on the terrace and lit his trademark Dunhill cigarette. A spotboy ran up with glasses of hot tea as Shyambabu proceeded to tell me about that period of Indian history when princely lands were confiscated by the state. He discussed the next day's festival sequence with the local musicians who would be singing in it. The air was relaxed: here was a master in perfect control of his world. The meals reflected the perfect democracy of this unit – all the members of the cast and crew assembled around a giant table in the sprawling gardens on which lunch was served by the caterer brought from Bombay.

Throughout my six years in London, I have been painfully aware of the rapidly declining interest in alternative or independent cinema and the celebration of the kitsch in Bollywood. Our film society In Focus was set up to offer a forum for South Asian cinema and film-makers in the United Kingdom. We have screened films which do not enjoy the normal commercial distribution channels. In fact, the reason I proposed a book on Benegal was to keep a critical discourse alive on realistic, socially meaningful cinema – a premise fast losing space to the gloss and fantasy of the mainstream. It is important for students of Indian cinema to remain aware that there is a long and rich legacy of realistic films which document the nation's historical, political and cultural aspects.

The book was written in a short time frame, a prospect which seemed rather difficult as Benegal's oeuvre is large. It is based on film analysis and extensive interviews with the director and with his cast, crew and critics. The research required viewing and analysing more than 23 films (including the long documentaries), most of which are not readily available. Fortunately, between Benegal's own office and the National Archives, I did manage to see them all. Then there were several interviews and discussions with Benegal's cast and crew, fascinating reconstructions of those heady days in the 1970s and 1980s. Whether in India or in the United Kingdom, everyone unanimously agreed on the significance of this film-maker and the place he occupies in the annals of Indian cinema. The enthusiasm with which every respondent spoke only echoes Shyambabu's lucidity and objectivity about his own work.

Author's note

In the book, I refer to Shyambabu as 'Benegal' and as 'Shyam' in Chapter 2 (which covers his early years). All unacknowledged quotes from the director are from interviews I held with him in Bombay (May–June 2001) and London (October 2001). All unacknowledged translations are mine. Following Benegal's filmography from his office, I have used the date of release for his films. Most of the dates for other films are from the *Encyclopaedia of Indian Cinema* which lists films by year of production.

Introduction

> ... political cinema will only emerge when there is a need for such a cinema.
>
> *Shyam Benegal*

Today, Shyam Benegal is considered the father of parallel, or new wave cinema in India.[1] Indeed, the history of this politically conscious film movement with realist premises more or less coincides with Benegal's career span close to 30 years commencing in 1974. So central to the movement is Benegal's work that could be said to have forged an aesthetic: an aesthetic of an 'alternative cinema' (another name for parallel cinema) or of a realist Hindi cinema that reflects his socially conscious yet deeply humanistic mind.

Benegal's films offer an 'alternative' history of India, as well as an example of film-making practice from the margins. This is a history that challenges assumptions about national progress and provokes considerations of the consequences of this development. When revisiting all of Benegal's 20 feature films while writing this book (see Filmography), what struck me powerfully was the unarguable historical and cultural significance of this body of work. These films may be read as a cinematic rendition of the story of a nation in continuous transition. Now 55 years after Independence, while a younger generation celebrates consumer culture, Benegal still draws attention to caste and gender inequalities – those basic, unavoidable realities of Indian life that are airbrushed out of the rosy images conjured up by Bollywood for the benefit of a global market. And Benegal has been doing this right from his first film. *Ankur* (1974) made use of the background of peasant revolt in Southeast India, while his latest project about the controversial leader Subhas Chandra Bose looks at the nationalist movement and the problems of leadership in the freedom fight.

Constantly drawing upon voices from the margins, Benegal's films articulate concerns about national identity, life on the periphery and gender/caste/class issues – from the peasant movements of the 1970s to the rural development drive and its conflicts to the untold stories of the handloom weaver, the low-caste farmer and the performing woman. Yet whether it is caste, gender or community that serves as the broader parameter of a Benegal film, at the core of each lie deeply humanist narratives that reach beyond their specific settings. Strongly delineated individual characters are set in a recognisable social milieu. The credibility of the narrative is underlined by the definite relationship between the character and his or her environment. And by exploring characters caught in the flux of change, Benegal offers sharp analyses of the underlying socioeconomic

Benegal with Shabana Azmi and Smita Patil at the Cannes Film Festival, 1976.

forces that affect the people who inhabit these worlds. Benegal's people appear in recognisable dilemmas and are given a reality by a repertory of strong dramatic actors that breathe life into the roles.

Benegal has discovered some of the best acting talents in Indian film, a veritable gallery of dramatic actors whose names have become synonymous with parallel cinema – Shabana Azmi, Smita Patil, Naseeruddin Shah, Anant Nag, Om Puri and others. These performers appear and reappear as in a repertory company, exhibiting unique strengths and talents from film to film and in the works of other parallel cinema directors. Benegal has been compared to a conductor of an orchestra, one who draws out a collective performance with an invisible baton. One of his strongest points is his ability to gather people and keep them in a repertory of films, while maintaining a democratic spirit in the unit. Benegal's production schedules usually last between four and six weeks, during which time he prefers to take his entire unit on location to interact with local people and improvise with the script.

A commentary on 'modernity' and social change, Benegal's work is also the product of an individual perspective present from the beginning of his career. He has been absorbed in exploring the concept and contradictions of change and its effect on human relationships and social structures. For example, when he first moved to Bombay in 1963, Benegal turned down the offer to assist his cousin Guru Dutt in his productions. He was convinced that those were not the films he wanted to make: 'People make films according to individual sensibilities. The existing formal style was not suitable – I had no wish to work on design-made films. But eventually all work is part of the same river.'

Benegal's oeuvre also reveals an interesting alternation between narrative experiments and social concern films. His style of film-making places him in the parallel cinema genre, although Benegal himself is impatient with arbitrary categorising of cinema. It is easy to see why. Although he began with independent producers, Benegal has also had his work produced by cooperatives and state ministries. He has been described as a maker of development films in the Nehruvian vision, but the surprising variety of his work belies this statement. His increasing restlessness with narrative styles has taken his oeuvre beyond realistic linear drama, and his familiarity with literature has often led to delightful experiments in narrative style and craftsmanship such as *Kondura/Anugraham* (1977) and *Suraj Ka Satwan Ghoda* (1992).

In choosing to tell stories of the oppressed, Benegal represents (quite literally) the 'subaltern subject' in cinema, a figure of importance in the revival of revisionist history and cultural studies – and in whom is embodied the idea of looking at history from below.[2] In October 1988, during the *Guardian* lecture at the National Film Theatre in London, Benegal said:

> These themes of economic disparity, caste system – after a while I saw them no longer in a linear way, but in a much more complex manner. I asked am I just sloganeering – surely there is a deeper reality. These themes have metamorphosed into something else, not only do I look at the 'other', but somewhere I start looking at myself and my own relationship to my environment.[3]

Almost always Benegal offers drama about power struggles, whether it is the peasant struggling to reclaim his land or the woman who rebels against social norms. *Ankur* and *Nishant* (1975) were directly cited in the history of peasant revolt in Southeast India. He uses the Indian Mutiny of 1857 as the backdrop for an unusual story of a Pathan and an Anglo-Indian girl in *Junoon* (1978). Muslim identity is explored in *Mammo* (1994) through a deeply sensitive and understated story of a Pakistani refugee in Bombay.

Benegal is also both famed and remarkable as a male director who places women at the centre of so many of his films. He has

Benegal (centre) with actor Amol Palekar, cameraman Govind Nihalani and long-time collaborator Shama Zaidi on the set of Bhumika.

unceasingly raised questions about gender exploitation in a patriarchal society. His work radically challenges middle-class morality and received notions of womanhood as ideal wife and mother, sometimes drawing censorious responses as he did with *Ankur* and *Bhumika* (1977). Mainstream industry wallahs condemned his subjects as un-Indian, whereas feminists alleged that his female characters were portrayed too much as victims. Yet the very credibility of his characters – so often doubly marginalised by caste and gender – invests them with deep dignity. In the *Guardian* lecture at London's National Film Theatre in October 1988, when speaking to Derek Malcolm, Benegal highlighted another aspect of his empathy by pointing to the problems posed by virtuous female stereotypes for the 'woman' in Indian society: 'Her virtue is in being the good mother, wife, sister – a set of essential roles woman has to play – which is a terrible kind of oppression; a glorification not allowing the woman any choice.'[4] His strong female characterisation links up with Benegal's biggest strength – his unerring, intuitive casting eye – discovering some of the best acting and technical talents in the industry. Just as Nargis and Nutan became epitomes of mainstream female stories, in his films Benegal created parallel cinema icons, Shabana Azmi and Smita Patil, two actors who became icons of 1970s/1980s feminism for an entire generation in India.

Smita Patil died prematurely in 1986 at the zenith of her career, after power-packed performances in Benegal's *Bhumika* and *Mandi* (1983), and also in Jabbar Patel's *Umbartha/Subah* (1981). Smita's death was a great loss to Benegal; according to him, Smita was just beginning to grow as an actress. Shabana Azmi's very powerful debut in *Ankur* won her a national award and international fame at the Berlin Film Festival. Her film work and subsequent career as social activist, member of the upper house of Indian Parliament and UN goodwill ambassador of population and development were largely shaped by the ideology of Benegal's early films. Azmi has talked about how the roles she enacted made it impossible for her later to do films which showed women as stereotypes or in a derogatory fashion. Furthermore, while making my documentary on women filmmakers (*The Way I See It*, 1999), all of the directors interviewed unanimously acknowledged Shyam Benegal's women-oriented films.[5] Working against the grain of mainstream entertainment films, Benegal's rare perspective consciously avoids the prevalent male gaze in order to give a focus to the subjectivity and sexuality of female characters:

> It has been a growing awareness of women's centrality to life and society, although I do not subscribe to the Western concept of feminism. I didn't consciously choose to portray women characters; it is my predilection. Indian women – if they have to survive and function – are forced to become strong and resilient. A lot of demands are made on them; they use strategies to keep alive and survive. I hate to represent women simply as victims, the sati syndrome [women as self-sacrificing martyrs] that warms the cockles of our hearts in paternalistic society. We need to see things not with the filter of what is given but to see things as they are ....

Benegal at the Karlovy Vary Film Festival, 1982.

Benegal's career in context

Shyam Benegal has had a prolific career, having made about 900 films (shorts, advertising films and documentaries) before he made *Ankur*, his first feature. Over 28 years, there have been 20 features and several television series, including the epic *Discovery of India*. The features are perhaps surprising in their variety, from the politically inflected early films to brilliant narrative experiments. Benegal's later work has not always matched the cinematic vision of the earlier works that led the *International Film Guide* to cite him as one of the five best directors in the year 1979.[6] In the 1970s, Benegal was being fêted internationally for his work, but by the mid-1980s he was accused of being too pragmatic, making films with careless speed. With the 1990s marking a revival of interest in his work, his career path has followed the trajectory of parallel cinema itself, and as such his films represent key historical/cultural texts about India and should be viewed from that perspective. In what follows, I will try to offer a sketch of the various contexts for understanding Benegal's work: the earlier work of major directors; the particular importance of Satyajit Ray; and lastly the reshaping of the commercial Hindi industry from the 1970s to the present.

Where does Benegal stand in relation to his predecessors? In the 1950s and 1960s, the four big directors in Bombay films were Mehboob, Raj Kapoor, Bimal Roy and Guru Dutt. Benegal's oeuvre comes closest in some respects to the concerns of Bimal Roy, with their mutual interests in class and gender themes and the linking of film and literature. More frequently, Benegal has been considered a successor to Satyajit Ray. Ray's *Pather Panchali* (1955) was one of the formative influences on Benegal's ideas about cinema. And there is much to link the two afterwards (see pp. 9, 205–15). Ray worked with literary sources and his film treatment also used literary devices; Benegal worked with theatre collaborators and literary and journalistic sources. There is, however, a tradition of realist films before new cinema even within the Bombay industry which Benegal draws upon, represented by the reformist films of Prabhat Studio (*Duniya Na Maaney*, 1937; *Aadmi*, 1939), Bombay Talkies (*Achut Kanya*, 1935) and the modernist themes of New Theatres (*Mukti*, 1937). Two film-makers, Mehboob Khan (*Aurat*, 1940; *Roti*, 1942) and Bimal Roy (*Do Bigha Zameen*, 1953; *Sujata*, 1959; *Bandini*, 1963), can claim strong realistic credentials with films that touched upon vital social issues.[7] This tradition itself can also be considered a development of the aesthetic principles of the Indian People's Theatre Association (IPTA) formed in 1943 by progressive writers, playwrights and film people.[8] In their depiction of rural poverty and women's exploitation, these Bombay films paved a way that Benegal in a manner followed, in his choice of real-life rural stories and female protagonists.

Both Mehboob and Bimal Roy offered melodrama with good music. Likewise, too, Benegal has made use of music very effectively in almost all his films, contrary to some notions of realist cinema. The music, though, has often been of a different kind to that used in mainstream cinema. His use of folk songs and music in *Ankur*, *Nishant*, *Manthan* (1976) and *Bhumika*; memorable thumris in *Sardari Begum* (1996); and the evocative score of *Zubeidaa* are now part of popular memory. The influence of Ray's *Pather Panchali* is strongly evident in Benegal's use of rustic theme music in *Ankur*. In his effort to place his stories in specific contexts, he has used regional Hindi dialects and folk music from various regions, including Andhra Pradesh, Gujarat, Maharashtra and Bengal. Turning away from the fantasy song-and-dance sequences of popular cinema, Benegal has instead drawn on authentic regional music through his long-term collaborator Vanraj Bhatia. The music in his early films did not enjoy the marketing channels available now in the gigantic music industry, but the soundtracks for *Sardari Begum* and *Zubeidaa* successfully plugged into the promotion network for film music. In addition, on another linguistic level, Benegal has explored the fringes of the official Hindi language in its regional inflections, thus retaining access to a larger audience compared to some other regional film-makers:

> Language is such an important aspect of human culture, it helps reveal aspects of a particular culture. I have used Dakhni in *Ankur*, dialect of Saurashtra in *Manthan*, Urdu in *Junoon*, Konkani elements in *Bhumika*, Bengali in *Aarohan*. It helps locate characters in a more organic manner.

He is probably the only film-maker in India who has consistently made films with stories outside the region in which he lives. While building on the tradition of those earlier film-makers, he has also extended their concerns more deeply and widely throughout the great variety of regional and national subcultures, dialects and traditions.

It is Satyajit Ray, however, who has perhaps the largest claim to being both precursor and mentor for Benegal. A realist who made most of his films in Bengali, Ray was the focus of an illuminating documentary made by Benegal discussed later in this book (see pp. 205–12). Even before Ray, the influence of Italian neo-realism in Indian cinema was already evident in Bimal Roy's *Do Bigha Zameen* (*Two Acres of Land*, 1953), but it found its most brilliant manifestation in Satyajit Ray's Bengali film *Pather Panchali* (*Song of the Road*). In fact, Ray's Apu trilogy (*Pather Panchali*; *Aparajito*, 1956; *Apur Sansar*, 1959) remains a masterful exercise in cinematic actualisation documenting hugely significant social transitions, as the village boy Apu moves to the big city for education and employment. When referring to the trilogy, Madhava Prasad said that it 'inaugurated the project of representing the nation, and charting the emergence of India'.[9]

The tension between modernity and tradition negotiated by the characters in Ray's trilogy is very much the same dynamic presented in Benegal's first trilogy of *Ankur*, *Nishant* and *Manthan*. As well as being an important model, Ray (who continued to make films until 1991) was a contemporary of Benegal for no less than 17 years. In 1973, Ray made *Ashani Sanket* (*Distant Thunder*), depicting events that led to the Bengal famine of 1943. This film very much resembles Benegal's *Ankur* (in production the same year) in its use of realistic treatment within a melodramatic structure. Though perhaps not so overtly political as Benegal's work, Ray's last film of his Calcutta trilogy, *Jana Aranya* (*The Middleman*, 1975), which followed *Pratidwandi* (*The Adversary*, 1970) and *Seemabaddha* (*Company Limited*, 1971), was perhaps the closest he came to a political statement during the Emergency. The two directors continued to overlap in certain ways. Ray's Hindi film *Sadgati* (1981), based on Premchand's famous story about untouchability, was his most direct contribution to the realist rural stories of oppression developed by Benegal. In his essay 'Four and a Quarter', Ray wrote with great appreciation about the narrative dramas *Ankur* and M. S.

Sathyu's *Garam Hawa* (1973), barely concealing his impatience with the stylised films of Mani Kaul and Kumar Shahani:

> Story apart, *Ankur* has enough qualities to make one look forward to Benegal's future with keen anticipation. For one thing he shows great confidence in the handling of two major elements of filmmaking: acting and camera. Shabana Azmi who plays the farmhand's wife … firmly establishes herself as one of our finest dramatic actresses.[10]

And like other directors of the time, Ray cast some of the same repertory actors from Benegal's 'stable' – Shabana Azmi in *Shatranj Ke Khiladi* (1977), Smita Patil and Om Puri in *Sadgati*. In *Ghare Baire* (*Home and the World*, 1984), the Bengali director examined the women's question in the nationalist setting of the first Bengal partition. The influence of Ray's *Charulata* (1964), a classic portrait of female subjectivity was evident in Benegal's *Bhumika*, a fiery woman's quest for autonomy.

Ray's career eventually came to a close with another trilogy consisting of *Ganashatru* (1989), a localised adaptation of Ibsen's *An Enemy of the People*; *Shakha Proshakha* (*Branches of a Tree*, 1990); and *Agantuk* (*The Stranger*, 1991). These treatments of the collapse of moral values and family structures, and his critique of middle-class society within these films, articulate a humanism and a concern with ethics which is also evident throughout Benegal's career, but perhaps most evident in later films such as *Samar* (1998) and the last trilogy on Muslim women (*Mammo*, *Sardari Begum*, and *Zubeidaa*). It is no surprise, therefore, that Benegal's documentary *Satyajit Ray* (1984) reveals the two directors very much as contemporaries, kindred spirits and colleagues with much in common.

Benegal's popularity in the West is second only to Ray's. Beginning with the stirring impact of *Ankur* in the Berlin Film Festival and its European distribution, Benegal's films travelled widely to international festivals and markets. The eloquent director became one of the best cultural ambassadors of India worldwide.

Benegal and popular cinema

Looming over Benegal's shoulder throughout his career has been the unavoidable presence of the powerful Indian commercial film industry, against which his practice could be said to have defined itself. As *Ankur* went into production in 1973, the hugely successful teen romance *Bobby*, directed by Raj Kapoor, appeared on screens across the country. At the same time, Prakash Mehra's *Zanjeer* (*Chains*) marked the introduction of Amitabh Bachchan as the angry young man. Nasir Hussain's *Yaadon Ki Baraat* (1973), a vendetta/lost-and-found story, was hugely successful in 1974 when *Ankur* was released. Both teen romance and the vendetta films provide stark contrasts to Benegal's work. Bachchan's vigilante films valorised violence and reduced female characters to stereotypes

Shyam Benegal directs on location for Antarnaad.

Benegal with cameraman V. K. Murthy on location for Antarnaad.

as the archetypal mother or glamour object. This has never been Benegal's way. His *Nishant* (*Night's End*), which explores feudal oppression and peasant revolt, taps into some of the same energy arising from the unrest of the period, but does so in an entirely different way. Benegal's treatment of female characters was and is remarkable in this context. There were other contrasts, too. The family values represented by Yash Chopra's *Kabhi kabhie* (1976), with its romance, weddings, song and dance, seem a world away from Benegal's searing analysis of the tragic consequences of superstition and sexual repression in *Kondura/Anugraham* (1977).

By the late 1980s, both Chopra's romances[11] and parallel cinema faced difficulties. Video piracy and satellite channels threatened cinematic releases. Parallel cinema films floundered because of serious deficiencies in the distribution and exhibition system. In 1989, Benegal launched his epic television series *Bharat Ek Khoj* (*Discovery of India*), a 52-part serial which involved five years of continuous work. Based on Nehru's

Benegal speaks at the Delhi premiere of The Making of the Mahatma (1996).

Discovery of India, the series explored 3000 years of Indian history. Benegal returned to films in 1991, by which time a sea change had taken place in the industry. Pirated videos and satellite television had taken away the audience from cinema halls. In Benegal's own words, 'When I got back, it was like waking up from Rip Van Winkle's slumber. Everything has changed. Non-traditional cinema had lost its entire audience to television.'[12]

As the 1980s ended and the 1990s began, there was further change. The story of the angry young man had given way to a new generation of lush romance and melody, signalled first by Sooraj Barjatya's *Maine Pyar Kiya* (1989). This rich boy/poor girl story brought back the Indian joint or extended family that was a forerunner of musical blockbusters such as *Hum Aapke Hain Koun ...!* (1994) and *Dilwale Dulhania Le Jayenge* (1995).

The foundations continued to shift in the 1990s. The realist aesthetic of earlier parallel cinema was largely absorbed into popular cinema. Shekhar Kapur's *Bandit Queen* (1994) was based on the socio-realist genre – the dialect of bandit country, the prolonged rape scene directly traceable to Benegal's *Nishant*. Film-makers such as Mani Rathnam, Priyadarshan and Ram Gopal Varma clearly use the style of parallel film-makers and concede their debt to this style of cinema. Ram Gopal Varma openly acknowledges Benegal's films (in particular *Kalyug*, 1980) as a primary influence on his form and treatment of *Satya* (1999), a gritty drama depicting the Bombay underworld. Sudhir Mishra made his contribution with the powerful film *Dharavi* (*Quicksand*, 1991), while Mani Rathnam (perhaps the director most associated with this trend) made *Roja* (1992), a mainstream patriotic love story exploring the terrorist problems in Kashmir. It started a trend for politically controversial films which presented issues more forcefully and blended art-house conventions with action, large-scale romance and patriotic sentiment (e.g. *1942: A Love Story*, 1994). Benegal, meantime, continued to make films of a different kind. In the face of this new tide of chauvinist film-making (e.g. *Border*, 1997; and *Mission Kashmir*, 2000), Benegal's *Mammo* stands out as a deeply understated drama about the tragic repercussions of partition and communal violence.

The biggest impact on this kind of cinema has been liberalisation and the proliferation of television. In 1991, the liberalisation of the economy generated an unprecedented range of goods encouraging consumerism, celebration of youth culture and the global outlook projected by film and pop stars. Globalisation brought about radical changes in lifestyles and mindsets, leading to declining interest in social or political issues and in development initiatives. By the end of the twentieth century, most narrative and stylistic experiments seemed to have been subsumed by the triumph of the musical epitomised by Sooraj Barjatya's *Hum Aapke Hain Koun ...!*, which launched the now hackneyed plotline of family weddings, rituals and festivities. The film celebrated consumerism and Hindu values (divine intervention in the plot), negating any space for the realities of gender or class conflict. The glamour and opulence of spectacle, founded on the structuring principle of the North Indian wedding, grew with every successive film in this genre: Aditya Chopra's *Dilwale Dulhania Le Jayenge*, Sanjay Leela Bhansali's *Hum Dil De Chuke Sanam* (1999), Karan Johar's *Kabhi Khushi Kabhi Gham* (2001). The younger generation of film-makers now appear far removed from the national ideals, political ideologies and dilemmas of previous generations. Consumerism is fast levelling any voice of dissent in Bombay films with so much of its diaspora audience now beyond national borders and across the seas. Sentiment towards parental love and duty signals a revival of a patriarchy now subsumed uncritically into conformist ideals and the celebration of the comforts of postmodern globalisation.

Benegal himself is openly critical about films being reduced to mere entertainment and their complete lack of context. 'Hindi films have created this pan-Indian industry which relates not to any specific culture. They have created their own culture. Today it is merely the story of the family, the Indian family and its traditions, which define the film – and you can take this and set it down anywhere.' There is still a place for other stories and other ways of telling them. Benegal remains the leading exemplar of the countermovement that survived into the 1990s and beyond, with his portrayals of real people and concerns, as opposed to the escapist fantasy world offered in Bollywood films. *Samar* examines the deep-seated prejudices concerning caste in contemporary India, and *Hari Bhari* (2000) deals with the lack of reproductive control for Indian women in the twenty-first century. With *Zubeidaa*, however, even Benegal played the mainstream game. The director cast Bollywood actress Karishma Kapoor and used A. R. Rahman's music to ensure access to a wider audience, but he still retained a typical focus on a female protagonist. In the past, Benegal had maintained that marketing and distribution of the film were not the director's concerns. Ironically, lack of marketing and distribution were the principal failures of state-supported cinema (Film Finance Corporation/National Film Development Corporation).

Several proposals for art-house cinema outlets in the cities never materialised. Early corporate structures also failed in their marketing strategy (Plus Channel was unable to distribute *Sardari Begum* and other productions successfully in cinemas; Pritish Nandy Communications failed to distribute *Samar*). Benegal now acknowledges that, in the new global market, product packaging and branding are important and that a director needs to participate actively in the distribution and release of a film, as he did with *Zubeidaa*'s release. The posters read: 'Zubeidaa – the story of a princess'; however, at its core, this was another powerful story of a woman's search for a place in society. The subject remained trademark Benegal, bearing out his intent of continuing to make films in which he believes. Despite this, he has been criticised recently both for crossing over to the mainstream and for working with the government to make films.

Although new cinema has been pronounced dead by some, Benegal continues to make films reflecting his own sensibility. Benegal himself considers this decline in parallel cinema and comments:

> Every movement has a certain peaking state, then it plateaus and starts to erode. Because these are really vanguard motions, directional movements, after which the job is done in many ways. If it is worth it, then it gets absorbed into the mainstream. See for instance today's film-makers like Rathnam, Priyadarshan and Varma – their films offer accessible entertainment and connect to life. They would not have been possible without the influence of our kind of realism.

One problem encountered in my research has been that of accessing primary material. To enable film students to study his remarkable oeuvre, more of Shyam Benegal's films should be urgently released on DVD. The few titles internationally available on this format are *Ankur*, *Nishant*, *Bhumika*, *Mandi*, *Trikaal* (1985), *Zubeidaa* and *Hari Bhari*, but this is not enough. Part of the aim of the book is therefore to encourage everyone to look more deeply into this impressive body of work. A very high percentage of Benegal's work (and all the films discussed in this book) do merit attention and should in the future become the subject of further release.

It has not been possible to discuss every film in detail, so the structure of the book and the focus of the chapters have involved selecting what I consider to be the most important themes and films. In Chapter 1, I have tried to position Benegal in the context of the entire history of the new cinema movement in India. In Chapter 2, Benegal's early years and his career up to his debut feature film are discussed. Chapter 3 focuses on the first rural trilogy that placed Benegal on the national map and gave him a place in world cinema. Chapter 4 examines Benegal's women-oriented films, while Chapter 5 looks at Benegal's historical films and his reinterpretation of the Mahabharata epic. His films about the dispossessed are examined in Chapter 6. The last trilogy – narratives about the lives of contemporary Muslim women – is explored in Chapter 7. Chapter 8 analyses his masterpiece in narrative experimentation, *Suraj Ka Satwan Ghoda*, and ends by discussing two of Benegal's significant documentaries. The origins of this discussion lie in the birth of new cinema and the political and historical events that led to its appearance in the 1970s.

1

Parallel Cinema in India

The work of Benegal is central to the history of Indian alternative cinema. This cinema has many names, including new cinema, Indian new wave, parallel cinema, realist cinema and even regional cinema, and there are good cases for using any and all of these terms. While in many respects I prefer to use the term 'parallel cinema', I shall also below refer to the movement as 'new cinema', which as a term captures some of the freshness and the excitement of a new development in the immediate postcolonial context of the 1950s.

Just how useful are these labels of 'new' or 'parallel' cinema anyway? These are categories that somehow embrace a diversity of film-makers, techniques, approaches, aims and intentions. Many consider Satyajit Ray to be the pioneer of this school, the history of which dates back to the 1950s. If we consider the 1960s, then film-makers as diverse as Mrinal Sen, Ritwik Ghatak and Mani Kaul – with their differing ideologies, views and structures – would need to be accommodated.

A defining relationship is that of the movement's position in relation to the commercial cinema industry. Whereas the terms 'new' and 'alternative' serve to underline divergences from popular cinema, the term 'parallel' cinema instead suggests a genre of cinema which runs *alongside* the mainstream. It has been argued that the sensibility and ideology of the educated and trained film-maker drove this parallel cinema, reaching out to a liberal middle-class viewer who shares his or her progressive notions. To the commercial film-maker, such notions of cinema are elitist. This is borne out further by comments from film critics such as Chidananda Dasgupta, who affirms:

> The difference between art cinema and commercial cinema in India is simply the difference between good cinema and bad – between serious films and degenerate 'entertainment'. The new cinema in India is a creation of an intellectual elite that is keenly aware of the human condition in India.[1]

Such arguments have only served to underscore the high art versus popular culture debate and polarise it further. By describing popular cinema as the slum's eye view of national politics, Ashish Nandy has reinforced the same oppositional discourse of high art and mass culture.[2] The success of some of Benegal's films (e.g. *Ankur*) does, however, suggest a more complicated picture than this and a more complex interaction with audiences than the elitist–populist debate suggests. Likewise, the production histories of a number of the films (sponsored in part or in whole by cooperatives or other collective bodies) also testify to a fuller engagement with non-middle-class communities on the part of the film-makers than critics allow. Lastly, the impact of parallel cinema aesthetics on the mainstream suggests a legacy of mutual influence alongside a history of contrast.

These categories and their counterparts of 'popular', or 'mainstream', or 'Bollywood', cinema are anything but watertight. In practice, parallel and mainstream cinema have overlapped and intertwined in response to the same changing social contexts from the 1950s to the present.

Indian cinema as an institution

When India gained independence soon after World War II in 1947, the war had already affected both the economy and the format of popular cinema in India. The breakdown of the three influential studio production companies, Bombay Talkies, Prabhat and New Theatres, marked a shift in ideology away from the reformist zeal that characterised cinema of the 1930s and early 1940s. One example of that zeal had been *Achut Kanya* (Prabhat, 1936), while other films such as *Mukti* (New

Theatres, 1937) addressed the conflict between changing social values. By 1947, however, postwar profiteers had turned into fly-by-night producers, and the market was awash with unaccounted money. This economy fuelled the star system by offering unprecedented amounts of money to stars. By the 1950s, films were sold by the dominant stars of the time, not by production banners. Against this background, film-makers such as V. Shantaram, Mehboob Khan, Bimal Roy and Guru Dutt who worked in mainstream cinema still continued to explore relevant social issues in their works. Mehboob's *Aurat*, later reworked as *Mother India* (1957), and Bimal Roy's *Sujata* and *Bandini* were particularly significant in exploring the ideology of womanhood and creating strong, individual female characters.

The S. K. Patil Film Enquiry Committee submitted its report in 1951. Commenting on all aspects of cinema, it noted the shift from the studio system to individual entrepreneurship. Strongly critical of the black market and the star system, the report recommended state investment in film production and the setting up of a film institute and film archives. These proposals were supported by some film-makers critical of popular cinema who foregrounded the aesthetics of film or used the cinematic form for social comment. During this time, there was a concerted effort by the state to institutionalise cinema. Soon after Nehru formed his government in 1952, the first International Film Festival of India was held in Bombay, Madras and Calcutta by the Films Division. For the first time, the Indian film industry had an opportunity to watch a large number of films from across the world. The films of Vittorio De Sica made a tremendous impact, and neo-realism had a lasting influence on Indian film-makers. The same year, Indian film industry representatives visited Hollywood at the invitation of the Motion Picture Association of America.

International recognition of Indian cinema then began to gather pace. In 1953, Bimal Roy's *Do Bigha Zameen* (*Two Acres of Land*), showing the direct influence of Italian neo-realism, received a special mention at Cannes and the Social Progress award at the Karlovy Vary Festival. In 1954, the first national film awards were instituted, and P. K. Atre's Marathi feature *Shyamchi Aai* (1953) was awarded the best feature film. The same year, Raj Kapoor's *Awaara* (1951) proved a major hit in the Soviet Union. Prior to this, the socialist Indian People's Theatre Association's film *Dharti Ke Lal* (1946) had received widespread distribution in the Soviet Union in 1949.

In 1955, Satyajit Ray's *Pather Panchali* (*The Song of the Road*) was released, triggering Ray's international success. It was premiered at the Museum of Modern Art in New York. In 1959, the film ran for seven weeks at the Fifth Avenue Playhouse, New York, breaking a 30-year record for foreign films in the United States.[3] Ray's film showed the influence of neo-realism in his use of outdoor locale, available light and amateur actors. The Bengali-language film made under considerable financial constraints finally generated money for the West Bengal Government. Its economic success persuaded the central government to review the Film Committee recommendations of 1951, which it had so far ignored.

In 1955, Nehru made his famous speech at the Avadhi Congress calling for a 'Socialistic pattern of society'. This formed the basis of what came to be defined as the 'Nehruvian' vision of the secular state, citizenship, egalitarianism, education and technological progress. Nehru's focus on children as the 'future of the nation' worked as a potent metaphor for the optimism of a young nation. The Children's Film Society was set up in the same year to target young audiences. Later, Benegal was to make his children's film *Charandas Chor* (1975) for this society. His prodigious work in the documentary field testified to his version of Nehruvian idealism.

By 1956, Indian films were being showcased at various international forums, such as the Edinburgh, Karlovy Vary and Berlin film festivals. Ray's *Aparajito* (*Unvanquished*, 1956) won the Golden Lion at Venice, and Sombhu Mitra's *Jagte Raho* (1956) won the first prize at Karlovy Vary in 1957. The first Indo-Soviet co-production, *Pardesi* (co-directed by K. A. Abbas and Vassili M. Pronin), was made the same year. Ritwik Ghatak's *Ajantrik* (1957) was shown at Cannes in 1958.

The Federation of Film Societies was founded in 1959, with Satyajit Ray as president. Twelve years prior to that, Ray had launched the Calcutta Film Society along with critic Chidananda Dasgupta and other friends. This launched a national network, operating on a moderate scale even today, which provided access to world cinema and a forum for debate for enthusiasts in cities and small towns.

'Times of great ferment ...'

Within the same period (1950–70), the new democracy also busied itself in the business of nation building. Left-led peasant movements in Kerala, Andhra Pradesh and Bengal; student uprisings (the Naxalite movement) in Calcutta; border conflicts with Pakistan and China; riots and conflicts around state reorganisation; the North–South language and culture debate; acute food shortages leading to grain importation from America – these were some of the strongest challenges to the new nation. In keeping with the Nehruvian socialist and secular vision, progress was constructed through structured planning (five-year plans), technological advances (iron and steel plants, dams which were hailed by Nehru as temples of the future), and a celebration of regional diversity and didacticism through educational programmes on radio and television. The official attempt was to construct an image of integrated India progressing towards modern times. A nation in transition, however, manifested its discontents in conflicts and ruptures which belied the promise of this idea of India.[4]

By the late 1960s, there was political upheaval across the country, particularly in the East and Southeast. In 1967, widespread armed peasant insurgency in the Naxalbari district

Benegal among the weaver community in a village in Andhra Pradesh shooting Susman.

of Bengal grew against the landlords. The Naxalite rebellion took a new turn in 1970 with student uprisings in Calcutta. Corruption in education, unemployment and the class divide were all leading to the collapse of the democratic dream. In some Naxalite pockets in the state of Andhra Pradesh, peasants redistributed land among themselves. Protest against feudal structures, caste, class and community divides was becoming increasingly strident. As Benegal himself puts it, 'Those were times of great ferment ... I was deeply influenced by the peasant struggle.' The Indo-Pakistan War in 1971 resulted in the liberation of East Pakistan and the creation of Bangladesh. New cinema was therefore born in the immediate context of political strife and protest.

Against this gradually unfolding context, the government implemented the 1951 Film Committee recommendations and, in 1960, started the Film Finance Corporation (FFC) to give low-interest loans to selected projects. The FFC was modelled on

Britain's National Film Finance Corporation, offering funds for quality films. In 1960, the National Film Institute was founded in Pune on the former Prabhat Studio premises. Professionally trained actors and technicians were to be made available to the industry for the first time. Students gained access to a wide range of world cinema. Film-maker Ritwik Ghatak took on the directorship. His students included K. K. Mahajan, Mani Kaul and Kumar Shahani, who later became influential film-makers in their own right. The same year, the Institute for Film Technology was set up in Madras.

Government-sponsored cinema was to create a new tradition. Supported heavily by film critics in the press, this movement privileged cinema as an art form and declared realism as its manifesto. The movement was born with inherent contradictions: it had to be specific and particular in its code of realism and yet universal enough to appeal to a wider audience outside the country while also being entertaining enough to reach the Indian masses. The Indian Motion Picture Export

Benegal with cinematographer V. K. Murthy on location for Antarnaad. *Local villagers form part of the cast.*

Corporation (IMPEC) was formed in 1963. A manifesto for an Indian new cinema movement was issued by Mrinal Sen and Arun Kaul in 1963, advocating a state-sponsored cinema for new directors.

In the 1960s, popular cinema was preoccupied with romance, family structures and the nuances of urban–rural values. In this context, Mrinal Sen's iconoclastic *Bhuvan Shome* (financed by the FFC) may be said to have launched the Indian new cinema in 1969. The unusual theme (a railway bureaucrat enters a simple village girl's life) and the treatment set up an ironic conflict between city/village sensibilities. Although Ray's Bengali films were already popular in the West, they were far less well known in Indian regions outside Bengal. And *Bhuvan Shome* made a big impact just as innovations in Bengali cinema by directors such as Ray, Ghatak and Sen were brought to the Hindi-speaking, pan-Indian audience for the first time. Equally significant were Mani Kaul's *Uski Roti* (1969) and Basu Chatterjee's *Sara Akash* (1969) – the latter was even a commercial success. Soon there were directors in Kerala and Karnataka who defined their individual style in contrast to popular cinema. By the 1970s, more film-makers in Bombay had pledged to move away from mainstream fare and attempted to redefine cinematic form. Tracing the aesthetic debate surrounding new cinema, Sumita Chakravarty writes that one way in which 'film-makers may contest the hegemony of the commercially based, profit-driven popular cinema was to search for alternatives in the name of a higher calling to the art of the motion picture'.[5] This 'good' cinema was termed '*Samantar*', or 'parallel cinema', by journalist Arvind Mehta, and the coinage gained currency in the Hindi journal *Madhuri*, a publication of *Times of India* in 1970. Mehta's argument was that this new cinema could coexist in a parallel trajectory to popular cinema. The term 'parallel' very soon became common parlance among critics. Both the English-language and regional press lent massive support to this realistic cinema.

Subaltern histories

Sumita Chakravarty has suggested that the reason that new cinema did not make its mark on the international scene was a 'lack of a vital communication with or articulation of a larger national experience'.[6] Many of these films were based on true incidents or drawn from journalistic or literary sources. She further opines that, unlike neo-realism, French new wave, or Latin American third cinema aesthetics, India's new cinema was neither revolutionary enough nor culturally distinct enough to influence aspiring film-makers elsewhere. That is not, however, the whole story. It can be argued that new cinema did emerge out of a sociopolitical critical context, and the film-makers were expressing the national experience in their own way. In the case of Benegal, his body of work can be located in the context of third cinema, postcolonial hybridity and subaltern studies – intellectual developments that have made their mark worldwide. The manifesto for subaltern studies was published by Ranajit Guha in his essay, 'On Some Aspects of the Historiography of Colonial India', published in *Subaltern Studies* (1981). Guha critiques the tradition of elite histories:

> What clearly is left out of this un-historical historiography is the politics of the people. For parallel to the domain of elite politics there existed another domain of Indian politics in which the principle actors were … the subaltern classes and groups constituting the mass of the labouring population and the inter-mediate strata in town and country – that is, the people.[7]

In his preface, Guha defines the subaltern as inferior rank and presents its history and society as all that is involved in the culture informing the subaltern condition – whether in terms of class, caste, age, gender or office.

> We recognise of course that subordination cannot be understood except as one of the constitutive terms in a binary relationship of which the other is

> dominance, for 'subaltern groups are always subject to the activity of ruling groups, even when they rebel and rise up'.

It is this dialectic that informs Benegal's cinematic texts and can be seen to operate within this paradigm of subaltern histories. In his narratives, Benegal privileges subaltern subjectivities – the low-caste peasant woman, the film actress, performing women, Muslim, Christian and Dalit histories and identities. Benegal draws the viewer into the dramatic conflict of characters who live on the periphery of the nation-state. It is almost as if the film-maker reveals the underbelly or hidden text of the nation in his oeuvre. Over 28 years, his films have continued to express concern about human rights in an unequal society and to possess a reformist zeal for improving the condition of the oppressed.

Parallel cinema therefore can be viewed as a modernist project, as an agent of social change with the film-maker firmly entrenched within the premise of nationhood, capturing the contradictions of changing society. A dialectic structure can be seen to operate between the master narrative of mainstream cinema and the 'other' of parallel cinema articulated by a group of film-makers who would work outside the dictates of commercial cinema. The film-makers turned away from the star system, concentrating on well-trained, relatively unknown actors. They also rejected obviously commercial ingredients such as song-and-dance and action sequences. The collective commitment to culture-specific realism (urban/rural; class/caste/gender; national/regional) nurtured what one could also define as an authentic or responsible cinema.

The trend, then, was to reject the studio system and shoot in outdoor locales, in available light, very often in the rural hinterlands, in and around villages. The search for rural subjects resulted in entire units travelling for four to six weeks, enhancing team spirit and controlling costs. This trend of shooting rural people's lived reality is cleverly critiqued by

Mrinal Sen in *Akaler Sandhaney* (*In Search of Famine*, 1980), in which a film unit arrives in a village to shoot a realist film about the Bengal Famine.

Film-maker Girish Karnad says the reasons for this 'ruralist drive' were primarily the influence of Ray's trilogy and the literary works (mostly novels) on which many parallel films were made. He also attributes this move to a post-independence belief that the 'real India' was in the villages. Most important, however, was the low cost of shooting in a village where locations and crowd scenes could be organised for little or no money.

Parallel cinema

Initially, the government required guarantees, and hence extended support only to established film-makers whose work had been commercially successful. By 1971, the official directive to the FFC was to support independent film-making. Film was to be 'an effective instrument for the promotion of national

(L to r) Playback singer Preeti Sagar, Shyam Benegal, Smita Patil and music director Vanraj Bhatia on the set of Bhumika.

culture, education and healthy entertainment ... by granting loans for modest but off beat films of talented and promising persons in the field'.[8] The licensing policy of the 1970s reduced the number of Hollywood imports to India; cinemas thus had screen time to offer to new cinema products. The agreement for import of American films was allowed to expire that year, and the number of foreign films dwindled from more than 100 films in 1972 to 26 in 1974. Film-maker Govind Nihalani, Shyam Benegal's cinematographer for 11 films, identifies this as a significant factor in creating space for an audience for parallel cinema. The exhibitors filled their cinemas by offering screen time to these new films in the cities, where they found a ready English-speaking, middle-class audience.

The government had set up institutes for training and funding state-supported cinema which established a new tradition of film-making in which authenticity and realism were key terms. Independent film-makers such as Shyam Benegal (who came from the advertising world) began work around this time, working outside the parameters of both the commercial and state-sponsored cinema. There appeared to be a collective move against the illusionist and fantastical character of the Bombay film. Benegal comments:

> Until cinema in the 60s – apart from Bengal and Kerala there was no split yet in Hindi cinema because of the many crises in the post-independence era. But then the formula became too hard, marketable ingredients became specific, the director was left inexpressive if he was working with stereotypes. The split happened then ... [9]

Twenty-five years after independence, caste and class issues were still very much part of everyday reality in the interior of the country, certainly in rural India. The urban populace was slowly becoming disillusioned with promises held out by the state. As in literature and theatre, cinema also was to be inflected with the idiom of protest.

Shyam Benegal and Govind Nihalani, his cinematographer for eleven films.

Shyam Benegal and Govind Nihalani on location for Bhumika.

Hindi-language films which experimented with form and content are considered milestones of new cinema. Film-makers such as Kumar Shahani (*Maya Darpan*, 1972) and Mani Kaul (*Uski Roti*) who were influenced by the French new wave took a formal aesthetic approach. Others highlighted social issues: M. S. Sathyu confronted the dilemma of partition and migration in *Garam Hawa* (*Hot Winds*, 1973), Saeed Mirza made films on the predicament of urban minorities (*Albert Pinto Ko Gussa Kyon Aata Hai*, 1980), Basu Bhattacharya explored marital relationships in the city (*Anubhav*, 1971). Shyam Benegal dramatised peasant conflict in his two early films *Ankur* (*The Seedling*) and *Nishant* (*Night's End*). Govind Nihalani further explored this theme in *Aakrosh* (*Cry of the Wounded*, 1980). Regional films, many of them based on class and caste conflict, peasant movements, the partition trauma and urban politics, include those by Mrinal Sen, Ritwik Ghatak, Goutam Ghosh (Bengali), G. Aravindan and Adoor Gopalakrishnan (Malayalam), Girish Karnad, B. V. Karanth, Girish Kasaravalli (Kannada), Jabbar Patel (Marathi) and Ketan Mehta (Gujarati). These film-makers were using film as an instrument for social commentary and change. A Nehruvian vision of a socialist pattern of society and a commitment to development informed Benegal's early films; some of his contemporaries were more radical in their call for change. The films partook of those wider social movements just as new cinema had begun to influence and shape the development of film institutions.

There are two principal reasons that this form of cinema turned into a national aesthetic programme with Satyajit Ray and Mrinal Sen in Calcutta/Bengal, Adoor Gopalakrishnan and Aravindan in Kerala, and Girish Karnad and B. V. Karanth in Karnataka. These were the formulation of an enlightened audience on the one hand and the arrival of new directors/ actors/technicians from the Film Institute of India emboldened with a socialist view of the state on the other. By the time *Ankur* was made, an extended debate between the formalists such as

Anant Nag and Shabana Azmi in Ankur.

Kaul and Shahani and the realist film-makers such as Benegal and Sathyu was in place. While Benegal and Karnad were seen as city-bred boys travelling to villages to document experiences beyond their own, the realists expressed impatience with self-indulgent film-makers whose intentions never matched the films they made. Benegal himself was criticised as the commercial film-maker trying to make rural films. His consistent work and resilience explain his survival in the industry for almost 30 years while many other experimental film-makers have disappeared as one-film wonders.

When Benegal's *Ankur* was released in 1974, critics hailed the arrival of new cinema. Aruna Vasudev explains that before *Ankur*, 'new modes of perception and technique for both film-makers and audience were still hazy and barely formulated. In the context of its time *Ankur* was a major step.'[10] After the initial years of experimentation, Benegal's film appeared to crystallise the aesthetics of new cinema, represent the culmination of a cultural movement and define its critical parameters. These film-makers were hailed as the pioneers of a cinema offering a different aesthetic and ideological vision, breaking away from the studio-controlled, market-driven, entertainment-based cinema of Bombay. Lauded by critics, *Ankur* also proved a commercial success, starting what the *Encyclopaedia of Indian Cinema* calls 'middle of the road cinema, of the independently financed, commercially designed art-house movie, a genre that soon began to dominate state sponsored film and television'.[11] Derek Malcolm has explained this notion of middle cinema as 'films that communicate with the audience and pay for themselves (through box-office returns)'.[12]

New cinema was being hailed as a breakthrough even while the political environment in India remained restless and volatile. After years of planning and development, the socialist dream seemed to have collapsed. The promises made by the state had proved elusive. The nation was stirred by four wars, internal party conflicts and student/peasant movements protesting against age-old power structures and the urban divide from the rural reality of India.

Developments continued to gather pace in the 1970s, and more films with a new cinema aesthetic were released. In 1974, the Film Festival was turned into an annual event. The Film Institute of India was registered as an autonomous society and merged with the television training centre to become the Film and Television Institute of India (FTII). In 1980, the FFC and the Film Export Corporation were merged to form the considerably expanded National Film Development Corporation.

The impetus for new cinema had continued to grow throughout the 1970s. Noted playwright and Benegal's script collaborator Girish Karnad made his second film, *Kaadu* (Kannada, 1973), drawing upon the skills of Benegal's cinematographer Govind Nihalani and actor Amrish Puri. In 1975, when Benegal made *Nishant* (*Night's End*), a rich canvas of political films was also being made, including Mrinal Sen's *Chorus* (1974), a black comedy about unemployment in

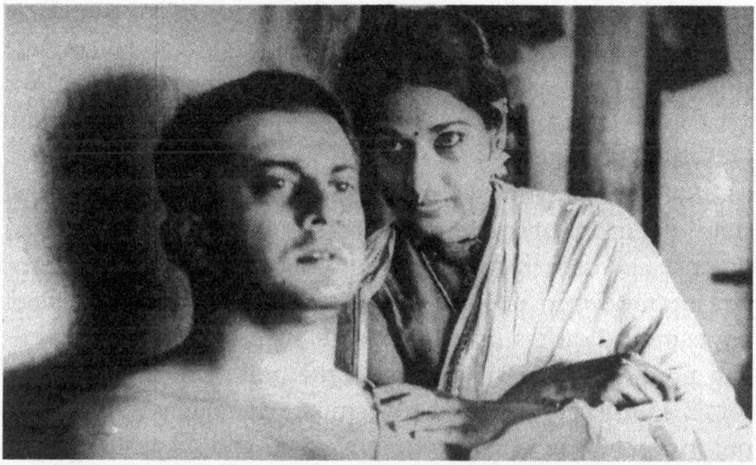

Victims of superstition: Anant Nag and Vanishree in Kondura/Anugraham.

Calcutta. In the same year, Basu Chatterjee's *Rajanigandha* (*Tube Rose*) featured the story of a working woman's dilemma of choosing between the two men in her life. The reception of this film by a wide middle-class audience consolidated the 'middle cinema' and established the claim that low-budget films could be commercially successful. Bimal Roy's unit members Hrishikesh Mukherjee and Gulzar became important directors of this middle cinema, blending realistic cinema with sufficient sentiment to capture larger audiences.

Benegal's next major feature, *Manthan*, produced by a cooperative of farmers in Gujarat, dealt with development and change in society. The film was used as an education tool in India and in several countries across the world, including China, where it was broadcast on television. Collective film-making was in vogue and included work by Mani Kaul, Saeed Mirza and other FTII students in such films as *Ghashiram Kotwal* (director Jabbar Patel, 1978). These years marked a high point for regional parallel cinema, with Mrinal Sen's *Mrigaya* (*The Royal Hunt*, 1976), Adoor Gopalakrishnan's *Kodiyettam* (*The Ascent*, 1977), Govinda Aravindan's version of the epic Ramayana, *Kanchana*

Seeta (*Golden Seeta*, 1977) and Benegal's *Kondura*/*Anugraham* (1977), which dealt with the tragic consequences of superstition and sexual repression.

The Emergency

In 1975, Prime Minister Indira Gandhi declared an internal state of emergency, after being accused of corrupt electoral practice and debarred from holding elective office for six years. Drastic measures followed in the face of increasingly strident opposition. Leaders opposed to the government, intellectuals and political workers were jailed, the press was censored and forcible sterilisation and slum-clearance campaigns were carried out in Delhi, resulting in widespread fear and suspicion among the masses.

During the Emergency, the FFC was attacked for its 'art-film' policy because not even half of the funds disbursed for 30 feature films in 1969 had been recovered. Of the 16 completed films, ten had not been successful at the box office. The fact that this had a lot to do with the failure of marketing/exhibition strategy was largely ignored. Certain criteria for future film funding included 'Indianness' and human interest themes and characters with which the audience could identify. The FFC was criticised for overlooking 'that films are primarily a means of entertainment and [that] unless the films financed provide good entertainment' they would be rejected by the masses. By 1978, state-owned cinemas had been built in Punjab, Kerala and Uttar Pradesh. Other states adopted financing of rural and semi-rural cinemas; by 1980, there were 6000 cinemas and another 4000 touring cinemas. The need for small art-house cinemas in the cities, however, was not met. In 1980, the first colour television broadcast marked the shift to colour and commercialisation.

In the 1970s, popular cinema also shifted to an idiom of protest. The collapse of state-controlled law and order created a series of narratives centred on the vengeance-seeking hero. In commercial Hindi films, the vigilante or angry young man (personified by Amitabh Bachchan) precipitated more violent and action-oriented films. The scriptwriter duo Salim–Javed is considered responsible for the construction of this persona. In films such as Yash Chopra's *Deewar* (1975), the archetypal heroic mother and the good son/bad son of Mehboob's *Mother India* were reworked into a crisis-ridden world of urban corruption.

Reiterating their position on the urgent need for better cinema, the Forum for Better Cinema was launched by independent film-makers in 1980. The Report on National Film Policy advocating the establishment of a film academy in line with the academies for literature, theatre and dance was ignored by the government. The Indian Academy of Motion Picture Arts and Sciences founded the next year proved to be a short-lived project. Official support for new cinema and increasing Western interest in Indian films resulted in a three-part touring package to the United States the same year. This package included pre-Ray films, a Ray retrospective and a new cinema package, but the impact was fleeting in the international arena.

Audiences, marketing and distribution

In the early 1970s, when new cinema was on the rise, Satyajit Ray questioned the audience targeted by parallel cinema.

> I understand that the new filmmakers are pinning their faith on the perceptive minority and the hunt is to track them down and turn them into patrons of the proposed art theatres … My own belief is that they (viewers) are all around us, within easy reach and in enough numbers to make a two-*lakh* proposition pay, waiting for the right kind of off-beat movie to turn up.[13]

Critical debate generated among the middle class and the press resulted in the grouping of film-makers into two camps: the populist and the alternative. This bifurcation proved damaging to the new movement fighting off accusations of elitism from the mainstream industry.

What were the characteristics of parallel cinema that ensured at least its critical success? Benegal offers an insight into this issue when he describes mainstream cinema as:

> A kind of Procrustean bed that shaped its content to fit its form. On the one hand it had the magpie-like ability to accumulate a great deal of variety to the entertainment it offered, but on the other hand the compulsion to picturize songs and dances in every film tended to circumscribe the subject matter of the films themselves. Often this form was a hindrance to cinematic self-expression.[14]

The new cinema film-makers turned away from formulaic, sentimentalised melodrama, from the stereotyped representations of the hero and glamorous heroine, from the pleasures of spectacle as in song and dance, and action, and from mandatory happy endings. Adapting the realist aesthetic, they cast new actors with no glamour attached to play recognisable characters in a specific milieu. Following the European neo-realists, they opted out of studio environments and set their narratives in realistic settings – in most cases, rural locales. The economics of taking small units out into remote areas also suitably matched the ideology of new cinema.

Parallel cinema film-makers experimented with form, technique and content, often working in different directions. Mani Kaul and Kumar Shahani were experimenting with the cinematic form and deconstructing temporal and linear structures of narrative; they were slotted as art film-makers. Others such as Mrinal Sen in Bengal were making overtly political cinema. Set in the political unrest of 1970s Calcutta, Sen's Calcutta trilogy (in Bengali) was immediately compared to Latin American films. Sen made the famous statement 'Calcutta is my El Dorado' in this context.

Achieving a clever balance between art and commerce, it was Shyam Benegal who quickly appeared at the zenith of the new movement. Cloaked in the new cinema ideology, Benegal offered independently financed, engaging, character-driven narratives set in specific sociopolitical contexts. Realism in his films was a product of new social forces and relationships, depicting action which was contemporary, an ideology which was secular and, at the same time (like Ray's films), universal. Benegal has commented about his stand against tradition and orthodoxy:

> A passive acceptance of life is of no interest to anyone, let alone a creative man. A dynamic society is always changing, and the duty of every creative film-maker is to locate and identify those catalytic elements which cause a change in society.[15]

Parallel cinema therefore had an uncompromising realistic creed. In Benegal's words, 'My films reflect my own sensibilities, and my purpose is to tell stories that are part of people's experiential reality.' Changing society, however, as opposed to picturing a society in change, is a tall order. The paradox of parallel cinema can be defined as one of an art sponsored by a capitalist state – an art which is necessarily bound by market forces that might serve to lessen its impact. As Chakravarty states, the argument then moves to a rarefied space in which 'the integrity and personal vision of the artist (is placed) against the imitative-exploitative propensities of commercial filmmakers.'[16]

The biggest problem for new cinema government-sponsored films was distribution. While government funds were made available to aspiring film-makers, there was no infrastructure to market those films and recover investments. By 1982, 84 of the 130 commissioned films had not been distributed and were still on the shelf. The NFDC has actually co-financed more than 250 films, but many of them have not found distribution in India. This led to a bifurcation of art films (branded as 'festival films') from commercial films. A suggestion to build smaller cinemas (200–300 seats) to attract art-house audiences was never taken up seriously by the government. As a result, most state-sponsored films languished in cans for want of suitable exhibition and marketing. The critical need to provide adequate cinemas for art-house films to sustain an art-house audience was recommended by the Film Policy Committee, but never seriously addressed by state officers.

Benegal, who served as Board Director of the National Film Development Corporation (NFDC) between 1981 and 1987, is severely critical of the bureaucratic nature of the institute. He says with some sadness that:

> the NFDC never fulfilled the promise, the culture in which it took shape. Unlike corporate organisations like ABCL or Yashraj Films, the NFDC did not learn to become self reliant – to buy, sell and distribute films. Secondly they needed to define the parameters of a good film – to determine the new kind of cinema in the system. They should have created small theatres to support arthouse cinema but instead the states built theatres where there was no demand. Also they could not deal with the unaccounted money system prevalent in Bollywood.

Although Benegal later worked with the NFDC and state ministries, he did also work with the 'system', or at least part of it. His producer Blaze Films was the largest distributor of advertising films in India. Its distribution network reached the interior towns and semi-rural areas as well. Large, diverse audiences across the country saw *Ankur* and *Nishant*. The assumption that new cinema catered to only the urban middle class did not prove entirely true when it came to Benegal's first trilogy.

These films also found an export market. Benegal found a Swiss distributor for the European market, and Contemporary Films, Ray's distributors in the United Kingdom, bought his films.[17] As time passed, though, conditions in all parts of the industry were to change.

Into the 1980s

Between 1981 and 1985, some classic art-house films were made with the support of state funds, including Ketan Mehta's *Mirch*

Masala (1985) and Prakash Jha's *Damul* (1984). Mrinal Sen's *Khandhar* (*The Ruins*, 1983) marked his departure from political cinema. Blaze productions financed Benegal to make *Mandi*, his darkly humorous ensemble film about a brothel in Hyderabad. Satyajit Ray's *Ghare Baire* (*Home and the World*, 1984) examined the women's question in the nationalist setting of the first Bengal partition. In 1986, as Benegal made *Susman* for the weaver's cooperative (Apex Society of Handloom and Association of Co-operatives), Mrinal Sen made *Genesis*, partly financed by European television channels. In regional cinema, Aravindan's *Oridathu* (1986) made a nostalgic return to village life, while Adoor Gopalakrishnan's *Anantaram* (*Monologue*, 1987) experimented with subjective storytelling.

By the mid-1980s, a much harsher climate stalled the progress of new cinema. Doordarshan, India's state-owned television, opened its doors to private producers, and the hugely popular, glossy soap operas took away the cinema audience. Alongside this existed rampant video piracy. The video player allowed family audiences to view films at home, violently affecting the domestic and overseas market. For the Indian audience abroad, watching Hindi videos over the weekend with family and friends fed into the nostalgia culture of the diaspora. In the United Kingdom, for example, cinemas rapidly closed in community areas such as Southall and Kings Cross in London. Video rights were sold cheaply to the distributors for fear of piracy. Girish Karnad analyses the changing cinema audience in a review article:

> Of the 734 Indian films released in 1984 only one was in the super hit category as against six the previous year. When the empty theatres started filling up again, it was evident that the urban audience was cleft into two clear halves – the middle class stayed loyal to television, the urban poor returned to the movies. Soon most of the 'parallel' filmmakers were to follow the audiences and move to television.[18]

Not only did television offer work to the parallel cinema actors, but also the medium allowed experimentation with realist drama (e.g. Saeed and Aziz Mirza's pioneering series *Nukkad* and *Circus*). This in turn provided the backdrop for much of the cinema of the 1990s. The superstar Shahrukh Khan was given his first significant roles in television. Shahrukh's entry into television via parallel film-makers such as Kundan Shah (*Kabhi Ha Kabhi Na*, 1993) and Mani Kaul (*Idiot*, 1991) traces another trajectory from small screen to cinema (e.g. Shahrukh's home production *Phir Bhi Dil Hai Hindusthani* [*Yet the Heart is Indian*, 1999], directed by Saeed Mirza).

Satellite channels and cable television brought home cinema to the viewer. At present in India, there are about 80 channels celebrating consumer culture and offering a confusing choice to viewers. The middle-class audience, who were the primary patrons of new cinema, opted to stay at home instead of going to the cinema. The low-budget social drama gradually moved to the small screen. With economic liberalisation, American films again flooded the market. Cinema time was not so easily available to the parallel film-makers. The NFDC was unable to offer a coherent vision or an organised marketing and distribution system to the film-makers it commissioned. Many films simply remained in their cans to be pulled out only occasionally to be sent to film festivals. Still, the impact of new cinema continued to be felt, and Benegal's work influenced a range of women directors who made films at this time.

In 1980, Sai Paranjpaye made her first feature, *Sparsh*, about a widow who falls in love with a blind school principal. This film flagged an exciting decade of women's films based on humanitarian issues or female-oriented subjects. Almost all women film-makers of this period (Sai Paranjpaye, Vijaya Mehta, Aparna Sen) acknowledged Benegal as the inspiration for their choice of subjects and treatment. Kalpana Lajmi trained in Benegal's unit before directing her first film. The theme of female sexuality in Lajmi's *Ek Pal* (1985) and Aparna Sen's *Paroma* (1985) had its roots in Benegal's influential treatment of women protagonists.[19] In 1980, Benegal's cinematographer Govind Nihalani had made his debut with a classic Tendulkar script, *Aakrosh* (*Cry of the Wounded*), which was based on a real-life case in which a tribal man is accused of murdering his wife. The film worked on the same premise of fictional reconstruction of stories of oppression as seen in Benegal's *Ankur* and *Nishant*. In 1980, Mrinal Sen made *Akaler Sandhaney* (*In Search of Famine*, Bengali), in which a small film unit arrive in a village to make a film about the 1942 famine. The film-within-film structure and the ethics of exploiting poverty for art were to be explored and re-energised by Benegal in his award-winning *Samar*. Parallel cinema film-makers – most of them fresh FTII graduates – delivered several masterpieces in 1980, including Rabindra Dharmaraj's realist drama about slum life, *Chakra* (*Vicious Circle*); Saeed Mirza's film about minority identity, *Albert Pinto Ko Gussa Kyon Aata Hai* (*What Makes Albert Pinto Angry*); and Ketan Mehta's remarkable use of folk theatre and fable in his debut, *Bhavni Bhavai* (*A Folk Tale*). Benegal's *Kalyug* was his interpretation of a complex family saga based on the epic Mahabharata, but reconfigured to the present with a narrative of industrial rivalry and crime in Bombay. And wider strengths of the movement shone, too. The repertory actors in Benegal's art-house films, Shabana Azmi, Smita Patil, Naseeruddin Shah and Om Puri, were cast extensively by other film-makers of the time – Mrinal Sen, Ketan Mehta, Govind Nihalani, Saeed Mirza and also Ray.

The popular parallel cinema of the 1980s was signified by films such as Govind Nihalani's *Ardh Satya* (*Half Truth*, 1983) and Mahesh Bhatt's *Arth* (*Meaning*, 1982). The extraordinary success of these films allowed the absorption of parallel cinema language into mainstream cinema. *Ardh Satya* was a landmark film launching the popular film career of Om Puri and triggering a spate of action-filled angry cop films. *Arth* featured parallel cinema actors Shabana Azmi, Smita Patil and Kulbhushan Kharbanda in a film about female autonomy. Its success was largely due to the feminist theme and the highly publicised rivalry between the two female leads. Benegal's most popular films in the 1990s such as *Zubeidaa* probably fit into the early space created by such experiments and crossovers in the 1980s.

The revival of popular cinema

By the 1990s, there was still further change. Popular cinema reinvented itself in the 1990s, according to film-maker Govind Nihalani in his lecture at the Nehru Centre in London:

> Also Bombay cinema hit back with a renewed confidence. With increasing liberalisation the ceiling in foreign exchange was lifted which meant film producers could go abroad to shoot song sequences in the Alps and in the Scottish highlands. The discovery of the international market for Hindi films (in the UK and the US), and the fact that Bombay films were pitted against Hollywood products, resulted in slicker and technically polished films which demanded colossal budgets.[20]

The marketing strategy for films includes music sales and huge promotion drives on television. Market-driven entertainment demanded big star casts. This has escalated the Hindi film budget so that today it can easily reach as much as a few million dollars or even a reported 50 crores ($10.3 million) in the case of the 2002 remake of *Devdas* (director Sanjay Leela Bhansali). In contrast, Benegal's last film, and probably his most expensive, *Zubeidaa*, was made at the cost of 4 crores ($825,000). Yet 2001's big release from the Yashraj house, Karan Johar's *Kabhi Khushi Kabhi Gham*, had a staggering budget 42 crore rupees ($8.7 million). The celebration and integration of the rich Hindu Indian family and its traditional values are incorporated into the film's publicity line, 'It's all about loving your parents.' Youth culture and conformist traditional values (arranged marriages, colourful social weddings, concepts of duty, refining romance) in the commercially popular Yashraj and Barjatya productions have effectively erased differences in specific cultures and histories, or any commitment to reform.

When corporate companies such as ABCL and Plus Channel were floated in the 1990s, it seemed to offer some hope for organised business.[21] Plus Channel commissioned 12 films by film-makers, including Benegal, Sai Paranjpaye, Sudhir Mishra, Aruna Raje and others. But poor distribution strategies gave the films very short cinema runs. Subsequently, however, they have been telecast several times on satellite channels. For *Sardari Begum*, for example, first screening rights were given to Star TV. With the proliferation of channels, parallel cinema gained a new lease of life. Almost all new cinema titles were broadcast on television. In fact, most of contemporary middle-class memory of new cinema comes from television.

According to Benegal, the commercial viability of the Hindi film depends on the marketing of music, reasonable success in overseas markets and the sale of television rights. In this context, the domestic market cannot recover the financial investment in a film and its promotion, and yet Benegal has always managed to raise funds from unconventional sources. *Hari Bhari* was funded by the Ministry of Family Welfare and *Samar* (1998) by the Ministry of Human Development. His own big-budget film was *Zubeidaa*, in which he cast the leading heroine of Bombay cinema, Karishma Kapoor, and worked with ace music-maker A. R. Rahman. Benegal has been both hailed and criticised for this crossover into mainstream territory. The fact remains, however, that in *Zubeidaa* he was still able to tell his story and rework his interest in women's voices, in history and in cultural context into a more commercially viable marketing structure – which is what any film-maker would want. As Benegal puts it, 'In this Tower of Babel, one has to find a way to be seen and heard with the kind of films one makes.'

As the movement floundered and government support declined with the move to liberalisation, alternative cinema aesthetics became absorbed into mainstream cinema. Shekhar Kapur's *Bandit Queen* was based on the socio-realist genre. The bandit country dialect showed this influence, while the prolonged rape scene appeared to have come directly out of Benegal's *Nishant*. Film-makers such as Mani Rathnam, Priyadarshan and Ram Gopal Varma clearly use the style of parallel film-makers. Mani Rathnam's *Bombay* (1995), set in the 1993 Bombay riots, combined romance and patriotism, as well as a realistic style of riot violence. Ram Gopal Varma openly acknowledged Benegal's films – in particular, *Kalyug*, Benegal's finest film according to him – as a primary influence on his form and treatment of *Satya* (1998), a gritty drama of the Bombay underworld. The themes of new cinema have also been reworked elsewhere in the hybridised world of contemporary cinema. For example, Raj Kumar Santoshi's *Lajja* (2001) may have been a multiple star product, but it still combined four narratives on the oppression of women. Small-budget Hindi films such as Madhur Bhandarkar's *Chandni Bar* (2001), about Bombay beer bar dancers, and Mahesh Manjrekar's *Astitva* (2000), about a middle-class woman's sexual choice, also draw upon and to some extent continue the tradition of new cinema. Regional cinema also featured new talent such as Rituparno Ghosh in Bengal and Kavita Lankesh in Karnataka.

Another interesting development of this globalisation process has been the initiative by South Asian diaspora directors to make English-language films reach an international audience. The success of Deepa Mehta's *Fire* (1996) and *Earth* (1998), and Nagesh Kukunoor's *Hyderabad Blues* (1999), was followed by Dev Benegal's *Split Wide Open* (1999), Kaizad Gustad's *Bombay Boys* (1998) and Sunhil Sippy's *Snip!* (2001). This appeared to be a second coming of new cinema, culminating in the extraordinary international reception of Mira Nair's *Monsoon Wedding* (2001). As Benegal himself analyses, 'We are getting globalised – becoming players in the international arena of cinema, working in the opportunity area with English-language films.'

2

The Formative Years

Family background

Shyam Benegal was born in Trimulgherry, a cantonment town (for the British Army) about 15 kilometres from Hyderabad, on 14 December 1934. Hailing from the Saraswat Brahmin community, the Benegal family originates from South Kanara in Karnataka, where an unwritten west-coast dialect, Konkani, is spoken. Benegal locates his Hyderabad household in a lower middle-class background.

The world of images has been a familiar one since childhood. His father, Shridhar Benegal, was a film photographer with a little studio in the cantonment town. He was a professional photographer, a very good painter and interested in most visual arts. Shridhar Benegal also possessed a 16mm hand-cranked camera (Paillard Bolex) and a passion for home movies. With a three-gauge projector, films could be screened on 16mm, 8mm and 9.5mm. The elder Benegal had ten children, with a child born in the family every two years. He would film one child from the day of birth until the next one was born. Commenting humorously on his large family – six sisters and four brothers – Shyam Benegal says, 'It was like a club.' At the age of six, he was presented with a Magic Lantern, which led to a growing fascination with the moving image. Young Shyam would retreat under a large four-poster bed with his brother into this magic world of shadows. Family films were Benegal's childhood entertainment. He remembers after-dinner screenings on a three-gauge projector, when family members and friends would watch his father's films on festivals, fairs, picnics and army parades. The children were later invited to discuss and comment on them. His father had a collection of silent films which included the films of Buster Keaton and Laurel and Hardy. There was also a large collection of five-minute 8mm and 16mm films marketed by Castle Films. The children also watched longer nature films on topics such as how the Earth began, the Jurassic Age, the Palaeolithic Age and other science subjects.

Shyam developed an early feel for the medium as he learnt how to wash film and scratch in his own ideas. These experiments were also carried out under the big bed and viewed on the Magic Lantern. At 68, he reminisces:

> This was my entertainment as a child, from as long as I can remember. Father was a fairly authoritarian kind of figure as far his family was concerned. And had definite ideas about what his children should do. He had this notion that we had to be taught what we needed to learn, and what we wanted to learn we would learn ourselves. So he didn't place too much emphasis on formal education, he was a liberal humanist basically, very Gandhian in his thinking. All of us were taught to spin as children. We had several *charkas* (spinning wheels) at home, the thread we would exchange for cloth at the Khadi Bhandar (cooperative stores for handspun cloth). I never wore any other fabric except khadi till I went to college. This was true for the entire family – father was very particular about it. He also read Ruskin and there was a great deal of stress on living with nature.
>
> My eldest brother and sister were put into a Gurukul (residential Hindu school with traditional teaching methods) in Hyderabad in Begumpet. Father pulled them out in a few years and put them directly in an English medium school. He can be called a nineteenth-century liberal. He was very insistent about formal education for his daughters and invested money on the daughters, not on the sons. He paid for the daughters through school and college; the boys were left entirely on their own after their matriculation (school leaving). The six daughters were seen through college because he felt that women should be able to fend for themselves – it was very important for him. He said boys will be able to deal with things on their own ...

Shyam's father had lived in Delhi between 1916 and 1920, during the time of Asaf Ali and Annie Besant, and he was involved in the Home Rule movement which preceded the Civil Disobedience Movement led by Gandhi in 1921. After an incident in which he allegedly slapped a British officer, a warrant was issued for his arrest. Shridhar escaped from Delhi and settled in Hyderabad, opening his little studio in the cantonment town. Benegal's parents married in the early 1920s. There was a considerable age difference between his father and his mother. His mother, Saraswati, was the only girl in her village school. Her father had admitted her because her elder brother was headmaster in that school. Married at 14, she had to leave her village and family in Konkan to join her husband in Hyderabad.

Shyam started school a few months after the outbreak of World War II. After starting at St Anne's Convent School and spending an unhappy year at the Wesley High School (run by Protestant missionaries), he moved to a secular nationalist school called Mahbub College High School. He matriculated from here in 1951. The young boy felt the repercussions of significant political developments within the confines of his own home. One of his cousins was very close to the prominent nationalist leader Subhas Chandra Bose and, later on, a member of Bose's party, Forward Bloc. He would visit their Hyderabad home very often to collect country-made weapons to carry back to Calcutta. The eldest brother, Sudarshan, an artist, was working with their uncle B. B. Benegal, who had a commercial art studio in Calcutta. Sudarshan came under the influence of the communist movement and would send books for his brothers to read. These included books by Eisenstein and Pudovkin. Shyam especially remembers an uncle whose family was born in Burma and lived in Rangoon. After the Japanese occupied the city, he walked all the way back to Calcutta with his mother. He was very seriously ill and came to their home to convalesce. This uncle, Benegal Dinkar Rao, was a strong influence on Shyam and central to the formulation of his interest in literature and science. The uncle's wide-ranging interests included films; he would often take Shyam and his brother Sadanand to see films in the local cinema. The cantonment cinema, Garrison, which screened Hollywood and British films, was a stone's throw away from their house.

Benegal talks fondly of the time spent with his uncle Dinkar:

> My interests in astronomy and literature were developed because of him. Even when I was a child he never thought it odd to give me adult books to read like Hardy's novels; he would explain what I did not understand and was a great one in improving my vocabulary and language. He would play dictionary games with us.
>
> Uncle Dinkar would take us to see films much against my father's wishes. My father was of the opinion that fiction films were generally not good for anyone. The only films that he took the entire family to were the social reform films of Prabhat and New Theatre. Twice a month he would book a box in the cinema halls for the family. Otherwise all this illicit watching of movies was with my uncle.

Later, very much as in the *Cinema Paradiso* (Guiseppe Tornatore, 1988) story, both Shyam and his brother befriended the projectionist in the Garrison cinema and managed to see every change of films from the peep hole in the projection booth. The boys put a little wedge in an unused door to the hall and watched films from there. The young Shyam discovered Tyrone Power, Errol Flynn, William Wyler, Billy Wilder and John Huston from these films. The projectionist would also give them the extra cuttings from films, which the boys would take home and view in 8mm on their Magic Lantern.

Shyam has vivid memories of horror films such as *Cat People* (1943), *Return of Frankenstein* (1935) and others such as *Jesse James* (1939), *Green Years* (1946), *How Green Was My Valley* (1941) and *Rebecca* (1940).

> I became interested in books which were adapted into films. After watching *The Lost Horizon* [1937] and then a *Tale of Two Cities* [1935], I

> read about Napoleon and the French Revolution and developed an abiding interest in many things. I got absolutely hooked on films from that time; my eldest brother subscribed to the *Penguin Film Review*, which eventually became the *Sight and Sound*. He would read them and send them to Hyderabad so we had a huge collection. My brother also sent books by Eisenstein and Pudovkin. I remember the first time Karel Reisz's book came out, on technique of film editing, which had a tremendous impact on my mind. For the first time I got an insight into how films were actually made. I keep telling my technicians even now that they should read the book.

During his last years in school and throughout college life, Shyam was reading a great deal on film. By then he had decided that he would be a film-maker, in fact a writer-director. Fascinated by the form, by the world that could be created by the movies, he was also fascinated by the art of storytelling. His first Russian film was the *Childhood of Maxim Gorky* (1938) – Gorky's trilogy was made into films by Mar Donskoi. *Battle of Stalingrad* and *Fall of Berlin* (both 1949) were other films that were shown in Hyderabad by the Communist Party at special screenings. He followed the films of Elia Kazan (seeing *On the Waterfront* [1954] 12 times), John Ford and Howard Hawks.

Benegal talks of the stimulating political arguments at home:

> In the political atmosphere at home, here was my father a staunch Gandhian, my eldest brother in Calcutta with communist leanings, then my second brother was a member of the RSS [Rashtriya Sevak Sangh, the right-wing Hindu fundamentalist group] who would attend annual RSS conventions – a complete oddball in this atmosphere. We would have wonderful dinner-time conversations, my brother and father would exchange strong opinions on their political beliefs. If my oldest brother would come to visit from Calcutta, he would dismiss my second brother's right-wing beliefs.

The coexistence of Gandhian and Marxist ideas in a liberal

household was not seen as a contradiction. At an early age, Shyam became interested in the Indian National Army. Dinkar's brother Ramesh was chosen by Subhas Chandra Bose as one of a group of six Indian boys to be sent for flight training to Japan. These six were part of a group of 35 known as Tokyo cadets in the INA history. They stayed in Japan during World War II. Ramesh, who actually flew over Nagasaki the day after the bombings, faced a trial after he returned to India. He was interned on Butcher Island (off Bombay), where the INA prisoners were held by the British. In 1946, Shyam and his older brother were sent to Bombay to bring him to Hyderabad. Ramesh came back broken in health with chronic malaria – the British had treated the prisoners very badly. It took him five years to recuperate before he could join the Indian Air Force, in which he played a strategic role during the Indo-Pakistan War. Shyam's life-long fascination with Subhas Chandra Bose's career has led to a feature film on the nationalist hero which is currently in pre-production. Benegal says:

> My childhood was very enjoyable, it was also a time of great ferment, a lot of ideas were floating about. When India became independent, two things happened, the British Army left, which meant that my father's custom was gone. He went through a very bad time. In 1946, our home was auctioned publicly even while we were still living in the house. A shattering experience for someone like me who was about 11 at that time. I realised we were actually very poor. Then we had to move to another house bought by my oldest brother because my father could not have afforded anything. The influence of school became more predominant. I joined *morchas* [processions] and student movements – we wanted Hyderabad to join the Indian Union in 1947. We were beaten back with tear gas and lathi charges. I came back with my eyes swollen because of the tear gas.

In 1948, the Razakar movement started. The Razakars were a paramilitary group of Muslim fundamentalists who decided to help the Nizam.[1] Shyam remembers feeling threatened when the

Razakars were committing atrocities – burning up property, parading women naked. This was before political action in Hyderabad. On the other hand, the communists were very active; the communists' vehicles were stationed close to where the Benegal family was staying in Bhongli district. At night this area was ruled by the communists. The Nizam had lost hold over nine of the districts of Telengana at the time of the peasants' insurrection. In 1948, the Indian Army came in and forced the Nizam to surrender. The Communist Party of India (CPI) refused to call off the Telengana insurrection, so the peasants – who earlier fought the Razakars and Nizam's army – continued to fight the Indian Army.

After 1948, life became more stable. Around this time, Shyam was given two books as a gift which made a deep impression on him, *Letters from a Father to a Daughter* and *Glimpses of World History* by Nehru. Eventually he was to read *Discovery of India*, the book which he adapted for the television mega-series *Bharat Ek Khoj* (1986–91). Benegal recalls:

> *Glimpses* suddenly extended my view (like cinema had done) beyond my immediate environment. The sort of discussions that adults used to have, extended my awareness beyond my immediate life, which I see as a great boon because very few children had that sort of exposure. Today with television, kids have the chance to see images beyond their lives every day. At that time where was this opportunity? In that sense I think I certainly treasure a lot of things that happened in my childhood.

Discovering film

Shyam attended a youth conference at which he heard Nehru speak of the power of cinema and the subliminal influence of audiovisual images. From that time he became totally fascinated by the medium and read everything he could lay his hands on. At that time, Guru Dutt (who became an influential film-maker in the 1950s), a cousin, would spend summer vacations with the Benegals in Hyderabad. Guru Dutt was then training with dancer Uday Shankar at the India Culture Centre in Almora.[2] Shyam looked forward to his cousin's visits, when he would hold dance performances on the terrace. His younger brother and many other cousins came for vacations as they had a fairly large house. That is how, at the age of 12, Shyam made his first film, called *Chuttiyon Mein Mouj Mazha* (*Fun in the Holidays*), with his father's 16mm camera and inspired by his interest in comic books. His older brother helped him. Benegal remembers with some amusement:

> It had all sorts of little trick things. Train arrives at platform, all my cousins getting off the train, and then the train would go in reverse. The story was very simple, the cousins go for a picnic, one child gets lost and we go seeking the lost child. That was basically the story of the film. This was seen by the family. This house had a large peepul tree – the oldest in the neighbourhood. I used this in my children's film *Charandas Chor* later.[3]

By now, Shyam was seeing films of particular directors, absconding from school for Thursday matinees. There is also the now legendary story of the young schoolboy cycling through a cyclone to reach the cinema for a favourite film. Once, when the matinees were not doing well, Shyam found himself alone in the cinema hall. The cinema manager refused to run the film unless there were at least five tickets sold, as the electricity costs had to be covered. Shyam promptly ran back to school, collected four friends and brought them to the cinema hall. The film the boys saw that afternoon was Vittorio De Sica's *Bicycle Thieves* (1948).

From Mahbub College High School, Shyam went on to study economics at Nizam's College, Osmania University. He remembers some special friends very fondly. Vaitheshwaran, a much older friend, was part of the Telengana movement. He joined college with Shyam, who was greatly impressed and influenced by this Marxist ideologue. Shyam recalls how Vaitheshwaran came first in the national IAS exams, but was refused a job by the Indian Government because he was part of the Moral Re-Armament (MRA) group which was supported by the CIA. Several postgraduate lectures given by Krishna Menon opened up the world to him in a very interesting way. There were other international economists such as Chettijagan (from British Guyana) and Professor Myers, who came for visiting lectures. The latter assisted Mahalanobis in drafting the Second Five-Year Plan which led India to industrialisation.

Nizam's College was an interesting, stimulating place, one where Shyam was involved in several extracurricular activities, as editor and short story writer for the college magazine and president of the English union in college. Around this time, Yale University donated a whole section of American literature to Osmania University library. Shyam was introduced to American literature, as well as French, German and Russian literature (fiction, poems, novels). He went through the entire collection of books methodically, exhausting one section after another during the holidays. His favourite writers were Steinbeck,

Surya (Anant Nag), the landlord pleads with Lakshmi (Shabana Azmi) in Ankur. *Benegal wrote the story in his college days.*

Hemingway, Rilke and Thomas Mann. He was by now directing plays in college and acting in his own theatre production of T. S. Eliot's *Murder in the Cathedral.*

During discussions with other friends, the young Shyam gradually realised that the kind of films he wanted to make was at variance with others. Mehboob's *Aurat* (1940), Vittorio De Sica and Satyajit Ray's films, Bimal Roy's *Do Bigha Zameen* (1953), Sombhu Mitra's *Jagte Raho* (1956) – all had made a tremendous impact on his formative mind. These were the kind of films he wanted to make. He was writing scripts and short stories, but there was no opportunity to make films in Hyderabad. His short story *Ankur* was written during this time, which he carried around for 14 years before making it into a film. Shyam was also closely following Guru Dutt's film career in Bombay. Guru Dutt produced and directed films through the 1950s: *Mr and Mrs '55* (1955), *CID* (produced by Guru Dutt and directed by Raj Khosla, 1956), *Pyaasa* (1957) and *Kaagaz Ke Phool* (1959). His success had made Shyam's family more open to the idea of a film career. Shyam was clear, however, that he did not want to make films in the Guru Dutt style. After the first International Film Festival in 1952, some of the films that had been included in the festival were subsequently shown commercially. That is how Benegal first saw De Sica's *Bicycle Thieves* when it arrived in Hyderabad on the commercial circuit. There were several other films, neo-realist films such as Giuseppe De Santis's *Bitter Rice* (1948) which were a revelation and very different from what the public was accustomed to seeing.

As university champion, Benegal was in Calcutta for the state swimming championships. While there, he spent time with his uncle B. B. Benegal, a commercial artist who had an office in Dharamtalla Street. This uncle had been very helpful to his cousin Guru Dutt, who met the artist brothers Uday Shankar and Ravi Shankar through him.[4] Shyam later met Ravi Shankar through his cousin Guru Dutt – he even used Shankar's music for an award-winning advertisement. He

Satyajit Ray's Pather Panchali *had a profound influence on the young Shyam Benegal.*

describes his first viewing of Satyajit Ray's *Pather Panchali* as 'a complete revelation – mind blowing'. For the first time, he saw it was possible to make the sort of films he wanted to make. Like Ray, who had started the Calcutta Film Society soon after returning to Hyderabad, Shyam started his own film society in 1956. This was rather pretentiously called The Culture Group and organised art exhibitions and poetry readings, in addition to Sunday screenings (along with other painters, Shyam exhibited his paintings as well). Benegal talks of his first communication with Ray:

> We would have screenings on Sunday mornings. Screenings would be followed by discussions in an Iranian café called Khursheed. I wrote to Satyajit Ray asking him for *Pather Panchali*. By that time Ray had made *Aparajito* [1956] and *Parash Pathar* [1957]. I showed some of his later films before I left Hyderabad. We also showed a series of neo-realist films, Eisenstein's *Ivan the Terrible* [1945] and a whole lot of other Russian films.

Our society was not yet part of any national network, I would write directly to film-makers and producers.

Mainstream for me was basically four or five directors – Mehboob, Guru Dutt, Bimal Roy and Raj Kapoor. They constituted mainstream cinema for me. I did not care for any other film-makers. Later I was also very impressed with Basu Chatterjee's *Sara Akash* [1969] and Mani Kaul's *Uski Roti* [1969].

Pather Panchali was so different from anything that I had seen before. Compared to the artificiality of Hindi films, Indian films in general, *Pather Panchali* seemed so real, so experientially true. That hit me, like I had felt about the Italian neo-realists – *Miracle of Milan* [1951], *Bicycle Thieves*, *Shoeshine* [1946]. The photography – I was completely taken by the look of the film.

My cousin Guru Dutt was making films in Bombay. But I didn't know how I could start with my films. I didn't have enough money to travel to Bombay. So when I finished college I taught for a while. I was given a one-way third-class ticket to Bombay by a friend, whose brother worked in the Indian railways. This was the end of 1958, and I was looking for work in Bombay. Guru Dutt asked me to join his directorial department as his assistant, but that did not interest me. Luckily I found a job as a copywriter within three days!

Through a friend's contact, Shyam joined the National Advertising Agency as a copywriter on a very low salary, but he valued the job for one experience. The boss asked him to take trunkloads of commercials (of Vicks Vaporub) to different cities of Assam – Guwahati, Tezpur, Jorhat, all the way up to north Assam. It was winter, and he was given a plane ticket, a luxury at that time. He was travelling to different cities by road. From Jorhat, he travelled in an army convoy to Kohima and was shot at. When he reached Kohima, it was fraught with incendiary activity. He stayed with people who were supporters of the separatist leader A. M. Phizo and learnt more about their points of view.

Soon after in Bombay, Shyam joined Lintas as a copywriter

Benegal interviews Ray for his documentary on the life and work of his senior colleague

for six months, then moved swiftly to the film department where he immediately started to write scripts and make advertising films. 'And it has been like that ever since,' reminisces Benegal, 'There were some award-winning films, about 14 – Lux toilet soap, Hima peas, Rexona, and all the toothpaste you can think of! Textile companies, a film with Leela Naidu for Finlay fabrics, Lux toilet soap (which were then endorsed by glamorous film stars). I was making ad films for two reasons: one that I was good at them, but more than that it was helping me train as a film-maker.' He was experimenting with different styles, for instance, shooting a slow-motion ad film for Kolynos toothpaste accompanied by Ravi Shankar's music.

In his first year, 1959, he had made 150 films. When he left advertising, Shyam had already made more than 1000 films. He continues to talk of his perception of films:

> I had a certain view of cinema because I was seriously interested as a movie buff. More than that I was reading and studying a lot of material and books on film-making. I felt existing Indian cinema did not allow you to express

> yourself and connect film-making to the environment in which you lived. I felt we should make films that are closer to our sense of reality, closer to the Indian experience, closer to the kind of lives we lead. So that was the main intention from the very beginning.
>
> Both advertising and film have everything to do with communication, trying to speak to people to persuade them. Advertising is in the service of a product. While a film, according to me, must provide an artistic experience to the audience and have a kind of social communication. The film-maker should be aware of the values he is projecting. It is important to me that a film should provide what one might call a worthwhile experience, that which gives you an insight into life. Then it is worthwhile doing it, or else it is simply money-making.

The most valuable lesson learnt from advertising films was economy of expression, the dense concentration of information about characters and their context that Benegal is able to offer in any single scene and which remains one of his most outstanding strengths as a film-maker. In 1962, Shyam received an offer to make a Gujarat documentary about the Mahi Dam project in the Khera district. This was produced by Vinci Wadia (of Wadia Movietone), who was trying to set himself up as a distributor at that time.[5] Two documentaries were made: *Child of the Streets* was seen by Louis Malle, who was visiting Bombay and much appreciated. Shyam and Malle were to become friends as a result. Early documentaries included one on Indian classical music and one on steel. The Indo-Soviet production *Nehru* (1983) and his *Satyajit Ray* (1984) are considered milestones in his documentary career.

Benegal's boss at Lintas, Alyque Padamsee, was the father of English-language theatre in Bombay. Leading Hindi playwright Satyadev Dubey was also a close friend. It was inevitable that Shyam would become involved with theatre in one way or another. When Padamsee learnt that Shyam knew the art of make-up, he immediately employed him backstage. It was here that Shyam met Nira Mukherji. A graduate from Miranda House in Delhi, Nira had just returned from a management job in London and was helping out in Padamsee's productions. This backstage romance led to marriage in 1963. The couple moved into their South Bombay apartment on Peddar Road, where they live even today. Nira worked in the art department for *Kondura* and has been informally involved in all of Shyam's productions. Their daughter Pia has worked as costume designer in Shyam's films, starting with *Antarnaad* in 1991 (also *Sardari Begum*; *Hari Bhari*; *Zubeidaa*). Both Nira and Pia are Shyam's present partners in his production company Shyam Benegal Sahyadri Films.

Shyam was also a painter and a poet in his younger days. He exhibited his work with other artist friends in the film society in Hyderabad. His sister Lalita Lajmi recalls how, after he moved to Bombay, they would often paint together using the same models and he would read self-composed poems. His niece Kalpana Lajmi remembers him as a surrogate father figure who introduced her family to Western music and enriched her perception of literature and theatre. Shyam says, 'It is from theatre that I learnt the art of *mise-en-scène* and methods of working with actors.' South Bombay in the 1970s was a charged and energised centre for bright, young talents involved in theatre. From this arose the early collaborations with theatre practitioners Vijay Tendulkar (story), Satyadev Dubey (script/dialogues and acting) and Girish Karnad (script and acting). It also explains the director's dependence on stage actors, as well as his ability to draw remarkable performances from his cast. Almost all of his lead actors have won national awards and other prestigious prizes.

Girish Karnad, playwright, film-maker, actor and collaborator in Benegal's early career, recalls meeting Benegal in Bombay on the eve of his (Karnad's) play performance of *Tughlaq* (1970, directed by Alyque Padamsee):

> Shyam's house was the salon of the young, bright people in south Bombay. You must credit his wife Nira's management of the social side of his career.

> In Shyam's house, we would go to have a drink, eat and have scintillating conversations about anything under the sun – he was then the whizz kid of the advertising world, he had read widely, he knew about everything, he is the 'know-all', with an absolute visual memory!
>
> In Bombay, one source of creativity was Shyam, the other was Satyadev Dubey, whose theatre group was extremely active in Hindi and Marathi. Vinod Doshi of the Walchand Hirachand industrialist group had given Dubey an apartment for his rehearsals. We would live there, rehearse, eat, drink and fight. This apartment in Tardeo was close to Shyam's apartment in Peddar Road. It is between these two creative points that I would swing.
>
> I was making my third feature, *Kaadu*, in 1973 when Shyam suggested that I take his cameraman Govind Nihalani for my film. Shyam was getting close to 40 and was extremely restless about making a feature film. Soon after he got the Bijlanis to back his project, they were the big advertisement kings holding the entire advertisement monopoly in theatres for 30 years until television came into the picture.[6]

This familiarity with the moving image and passion for cinema, the witnessing of major changes in society (independence and peasant revolts), an inherent love for history and literature, a childhood which allowed the coexistence of Gandhian ideals and Marxist principles and, finally, the move to Bombay and fresh experiments in new cinema – the stage was set for the film-maker who would combine his social concerns and his narrative ideas, whose name would soon be synonymous with good cinema.

Though not dwelt on elsewhere in this book, it is worth mentioning that Benegal's lifelong interest in learning, education and children dates back to his childhood and upbringing. Benegal occasionally taught mass-communication techniques between 1966 and 1973 at Bhavan's college in Bombay. Between 1970 and 1972, he studied children's television under the Homi Bhabha Fellowship and worked for a few months as an associate producer with WGB Boston in the United States. He also spent some time with the Children's

Television Workshop (*Sesame Street*) in New York and worked briefly in the United Kingdom with children's programmes on the BBC. In 1975, he made his own children's film *Charandas Chor* and created 29 learning modules for the satellite television experiment for rural children. *Charandas Chor* was produced by the Indian Children's Film Society. Basing his story on a classic folk play by Habib Tanvir, Benegal used a number of theatre actors from the Chattisgarh district and cast debutante Smita Patil as the princess in the folk tale. The black-and-white comedy was about a thief and his accomplice who keep evading the police in a village.

Shyam Benegal later took on an active role in shaping film education as chairman of the Film and Television Institute of India from 1980–83 and 1989–92. Deeply committed to social integration in India, he was part of the National Integration Council 1986–89 and the National Council of Art. The Government of India has conferred on him two of its most prestigious awards: Padma Shri in 1976 and Padma Bhushan in 1991.

Benegal's television work has been considerable and influential. *Yatra*, a 15-part serial on the Indian railways, was made in 1986. *Kathasagar* (1986–91), a 10-part series of international stories, was made for Doordarshan, India's state-owned television network. His magnum opus was the 52-part series *Bharat Ek Khoj* based on Jawaharlal Nehru's *Discovery of India.* Televised over five years from 1986 to 1991, this series covered 3000 years of Indian civilisation and has remained a seminal education programme on Indian history and culture.[7]

3

The Rural Trilogy: Winds of Change

Ankur (*The Seedling*, 1974)

Shyam Benegal touted the story of *Ankur* for 14 years, knocking on the doors of several producers who turned down his proposal. Many of them had the same question for him: 'Who wants to see a film about a landlord and his mistress?' He finally secured independent financing from Blaze Films, the largest distributors of advertising films in India. Mohan Bijlani and Freni Varavia were far-sighted producers who convinced him to make the film in Hindi and not in the regional language of Telegu, which was the director's original plan.

Soon after World War II, Bijlani realised the importance of advertisements in cinema halls – his company, Blaze, made advertisement films and slides which reached the furthest corners of the country. Benegal had already made commercials for the company which was to back his subsequent works as well. Set firmly within the realist aesthetic, *Ankur* deals with feudal oppression in the microcosmic rural world of a village in Andhra Pradesh. The film contains explicit references to the peasants' movement, initially led by the CPI (M) (Communist Party of India [Marxist]), which acquired a national dimension following the failure of the 1971–72 harvests. Shyam had written the script in his college years, basing it loosely on a true story.

An absentee zamindar's (landlord's) son, Surya (Anant Nag), is despatched to the village to look after his father's land. The film opens with a procession of village women approaching their shrine. It is a religious festival, and the camera focuses on one woman who prays for a child. The next scene opens in a small town in which the feudal landlord lives; he is a patriarch whose word is uncontested both at home and in the outside world. We catch a glimpse of the landlord's mistress and her son, who have come to town to deliver the harvest crop. The landlord's wife has accepted this a long time ago. The one who chafes impatiently is Surya, the landlord's son. He has finished high school and now wants to study further. His father believes that he has no need for further education. Surya reluctantly relents to an arranged marriage with a young girl who will join him at the farm when she comes of age. Surya is sent to the village to oversee the family estates.

Surya arrives with all the arrogance of a city person. The farmhouse in which he must live is a shambles; the low-caste peasant woman Lakshmi (Shabana Azmi) cleans the house. Her mute husband, Kishtaya (Sadhu Meher), is jobless and addicted to alcohol. Surya displays liberal ideas when he eats food cooked by the untouchable Lakshmi and sends off the village priest who protests. Free from his domineering father, he exercises his power in the village and stops village women from collecting water at his tank. He also cuts off the water supply to his half-brother's fields. He threatens to drive out of the village anyone who steals from his fields.

The viewer is offered an inside view of Lakshmi's little hut across the fields. Living on the verge of poverty, Lakshmi steals grain from her master's storeroom – her survival instincts are stronger than any moral qualms. She is anxious that Kishtaya's drinking habits will bring them shame. Lakshmi has a strong sense of pride, even as she struggles to go through her daily life. In one scene, the drunk Kishtaya passes by dozing on a bullock cart; Lakshmi walks home purposefully with the grocery she purchases. On several occasions, she rises to her husband's defence – she will not have anyone speak ill of him. Kishtaya is caught stealing from the landlord's fields. As the village constable had threatened earlier, he is shaven and paraded around the village on a mule. Unable to bear his humiliation, the mute peasant disappears without notice.

Surya now has Lakshmi in his space. The long corridor suggesting the distance between them is bridged as he asks her to move into his house. A faint glimmer of understanding flits across Lakshmi's face. Her dilemma is projected onto another village woman who is tried for adultery by the village panchayat (court). Promising to take care of her forever, Surya enters into an illicit relationship with Lakshmi. In the morning, Lakshmi is seen sharing her master's bed. Surya lies in bed, and the camera moves back, out of the room into the passage, to frame Lakshmi who is putting on her clothes. She is worried about local gossip and also that her master's wife will join him soon. Surya assures her that there is nothing to fear. Despite his earlier display of progressive views, Surya's claim on Lakshmi is a replay of his father's ownership of the village woman Kaushalya. Lakshmi is burdened by her caste and gender – a few economical strokes lay bare the gender exploitation which lies deeper than the caste and class issues.[1]

Surya now asks Lakshmi to tell him about her life. Unable to provide Lakshmi with any dowry, her mother had her married to Kishtaya. Lakshmi feels deeply indebted to Kishtaya and is fiercely protective of him. Kishtaya was a potter, and they had seen days of prosperity. With the demand for plastic goods, the potter lost his trade. Lakshmi's brief statement points to the economic changes that are destroying traditional livelihoods.

Soon after, Surya's new wife (Priya Tendulkar) joins him in the village. She has heard gossip about her husband and the other woman. She gradually pushes Lakshmi out of the home, back to her hut across the field. Despite Lakshmi's illicit liaison and theft, the viewer's sympathy for her only increases as the oppressive schema unfolds. When Lakshmi discovers she is pregnant, Surya asks her to abort the baby. Lakshmi refuses, as she has always wanted a child. 'Must I only feel shame and not you?' she asks in a powerfully understated scene. Inverting the oppressor/oppressed balance, the woman questions his judgment; her quiet scorn speaks of her rejection of this weak-willed man.

Months pass, and Lakshmi works in the paddy fields. The women are transplanting the small plants as they bend over the crop and sing a folk song. Peasant labour and crop are framed together as interconnected, in long shots. Desperate, Surya asks Lakshmi to leave the village, but she refuses to go. One day, jobless and hungry, the heavily pregnant Lakshmi approaches the landlord's wife for food. She is discovered stealing grain from the storehouse. Surya and his wife abuse her and drive her out of the house. The lush green paddy fields are a visual counterpoint to Lakshmi's hunger and deprivation.

Police officer Patel questions the landlord's decision about driving Lakshmi out of her job. The senior lord had given his mistress a plot of land and a means of sustenance. In the unwritten code between feudal lord and peasant, there is a law of protection, which the younger man refuses to honour. Rural feudal behaviour continues to exist even today. In the face of change, the landlord's responsibility to his servant, inherent in the system, is not acknowledged.

The world-weary Lakshmi wakes up one night to find her husband has returned. In a touching scene, Kishtaya shows her the money he has earned in distant villages. He is unaware that in those few months Lakshmi's world has changed. She breaks down, sobbing uncontrollably – the proud defence that she has held up against the world crumbles at this moment. The fear of detection, the guilt of betrayal, perhaps part relief at her husband's return – Shabana Azmi expresses this complexity of emotions in a staggeringly powerful articulation. The naive Kishtaya is overjoyed when he realises that his wife is pregnant. He takes her to the temple to offer thanksgiving. With newfound resolution, he decides to approach the landlord and ask him for a job. Taking his stick customarily on his shoulders, he crosses the paddy fields. Surya looks across the fields and freezes when he sees Kishtaya approaching him. In a frenzy of conflicting emotions, Surya whips the deaf mute mercilessly. From a distance, Lakshmi watches in horror, then starts running clumsily through the fields. Long shots frame the pregnant woman against the green paddy fields. The connection between the grain-filled fields, peasant and exploiter is visually underscored in the frame as the narrative races to a climax.

The climactic scene is a cleverly constructed *mise-en-scène.* Some of the villagers have gathered around the landlord as he beats and abuses Kishtaya. Lakshmi arrives on the scene aghast at this injustice and hurls a torrent of abuse at Surya and his family. 'We are not your slaves. We do not need your job,' she says, articulating the collective emotions of the villagers. She curses him, saying that he can never be happy with the sighs of the poor peasants on his soul.

The guilt-stricken man cowers at his own acts. His tortured face is a mirror to his wife's, who in that instant knows the truth between him and Lakshmi, as do the villagers. This is a potent moment of revolt. Lakshmi asserts the demand for justice and the refusal to be further exploited which her mute husband or other villagers cannot make. A single hysterical voice shatters the quiet afternoon as old power balances are shaken. The reality of caste and gender oppression rings through the climactic moment.

Lakshmi raises her injured husband and walks back to the hut. As the other villagers disperse, the little boy witnessing the scene hurls a stone at the landlord's window. As the glass shatters, the birds cry out from the trees. The boy runs off on the village path. The screen turns red. Benegal's leftist vision is unambiguously stated in this complex tale of oppression. Behind the film lies a humanist film-maker's vision of an egalitarian society, devoid of class and caste divides and gender oppression.

The realist aesthetic

Benegal used professional actors in *Ankur*, some from the Film Institute as well from the National School of Drama. He was very keen to cast Waheeda Rehman – a top actress from popular films, best known for her roles in Guru Dutt's films and in Vijay

Anand's *Guide* (1965) – as his heroine, but she turned down the role after a bad experience in a regional film in Kerala. Shabana Azmi, cast as the heroine Lakshmi, was a fresh graduate and gold medallist from the Film Institute. The style of the film was considered alien to the Hindi film industry. The actors wore no make-up and were dressed in realistic costumes. The language used is the dialect of Dakhni Urdu, commonly used around Hyderabad. The blend of Dakhni and Telegu folk songs located characters through the use of language. Both Azmi and Nag introduced a new style of naturalised acting using regional accents.

Ankur has been defined as deploying psychological realism and regional authenticity to the accepted narrative style of Indian films.[2] Yet Benegal tells a story and tells it well. The narrative baseline is one of the strongest features of his films. Here he creates a detailed microcosmic world and its characters in which the macro forces of feudal power structures and gender oppression are played out. *Ankur* is not an overtly didactic film, but in the Brechtian sense it does ask the audience to react to what is represented, rather than telling the viewer what to do.

Benegal's first trilogy – *Ankur*, *Nishant* and *Manthan* – combined the contemporary stage of peasant revolution with the consolidation of the development aesthetic (the Nehruvian vision of socialist and egalitarian society, which included five-year plans as development models). The three films comprise a trilogy in the sense that they deal with contemporary or neo-contemporary situations in India. They deal with the changes that are taking place very slowly as India moves from the feudal systems that prevailed and continue to prevail. The change has much to do with ownership and power. *Ankur* and *Nishant* – based on real-life incidents in Hyderabad – and *Manthan* – about the development of the milk colony in Gujarat – are rural stories about change. They were immediately hailed as a trilogy, even though Benegal had not set out to make this consciously.

By using regional dialect, the new cinema was able to 'forge a new aesthetic of statist realism'.[3] *Ankur* became 'a symbol of new cinema'.[4] Benegal himself attributed the success of the new cinema to the existence of a demand. 'Political cinema will only emerge when there is a need for it,' he observed.[5] *Ankur* has also been termed a 'politically inflected melodrama'.[6] Benegal himself has commented that political films are made when the need for them arises. The Indian Constitution set up in 1950 was a social contract on paper, but this did not immediately bring to an end the prevalent feudal order. In the early 1970s, the audience of new cinema was well aware of the post-independence peasant struggles against feudalism, especially the rise of the Naxalite movement, a peasant uprising which turned to armed insurrection in the Naxalbari district of Bengal and spread to Andhra Pradesh (see pp. 21–22, 151). *Ankur* is set in 1945 in a feudal state, but the background of 1970s peasant insurrection gave it a contemporary edge. Prasad argues that the spectator gains access to the fascination and power of spectacle of feudal oppression and rebellion without being reminded of its proximity in date and time.[7] Contrary to this, the film was made and seen in the context of contemporary peasant movements so that the immediacy of the narrative has its own power. Maithili Rao criticises Prasad's argument 'as a rigidly Marxist analysis [which] is blind to Benegal's extraordinary generosity to his actors – even in a tightly written script which has its own social, sexual and political points to make'.[8]

Ankur's ending was immediately read as a powerful statement of the awakened consciousness of the oppressed peasants. The film was received as an example of political cinema, incisive psychological character studies and compelling performances. The absence of closure and the act of defiance by a silent witness (in this case, the young boy) effectively point to future developments and subversions of the power equation. A brief glimpse of revolt opens up the possibilities of stronger protest and movement outside the text. The zamindar's urbanised son makes a reluctant journey into the unfamiliar world of rural feudalism. It is through him that the viewer gathers information about the feudal world order – his interaction with the village priest as well as with the village policeman. The viewer is made to follow Surya as he explores his land, but this is not a process of identifying with him. When he stops the water supply to his stepbrother's land, the viewer is forced to distance himself from the character. In this way, the viewer's knowledge of the feudal subject is objectified and sympathy for the oppressed (the peasant and his wife) and the undefined (the illegitimate son) is ensured.

Surya's gaze focused on Lakshmi establishes the woman as a sexual object. The scene in which Surya sits on the balcony watching Lakshmi grinding spice in the courtyard serves to heighten her sensuality. Lakshmi makes use of her whole body in the physical act of grinding the spice in a stone bowl with a wooden pole. She stops frequently to wipe away perspiration. Surya is overwhelmed by her sexuality and comes up to her. She is surprised both by his question and his proximity. Lakshmi, the woman of the soil, has an earthy sensuality and vigour against which the city-bred wife's pallor and frailty are underlined.

In the scene in which Surya seduces Lakshmi, then asks her to tell him about herself, the viewer gains more information about the poor peasant's life through the mediation of the zamindar. Lakshmi speaks about her poverty-stricken background, but also speaks of Kishtaya's past stability as a potter and the gradual loss of trade which has turned him into an alcoholic wreck. Again Lakshmi's fierce protection of her husband is hinted at – she will not allow her lover to speak ill of him.

The strength of the film lies in the detailed exploration of characters and their motivations, the contradictory impulses they are governed by, the stray glances and gestures, landscape details, marvellous use of folk music and natural sound. Benegal comments on the open ending in *Ankur*:

> It would be ridiculously dogmatic and simplistic to think in terms of simple solutions. There are no simple solutions to complex problems. Besides the solutions would have to be in the outside world. But it is interesting to explore the problems in Indian society, so that at least one can become aware of the forces that are at work in it and the way those forces combine and interact. The point is to clarify the directions one must take if these problems have to be sorted out.

When asked whether he considered himself part of the new wave, Benegal predictably replied:

> I am not sure if there is such a thing as a new wave. Let me put it this way, some people now attempt to make films of their own choice, different from the industry's mould. When the industry has a certain kind of mould, everything gets cast in that mould, films come out of that fantastic sausage machine. Now there is a wide range of people, from one end of the scale to the other, who want to make their own kind of films. So I certainly would think of myself as part of this group.[9]

Collaboration and repertory

Unlike Satyajit Ray, with whom he has been much compared, Benegal is not an auteur. Ray worked on his own scripts, direction, music and costume. Benegal has from the beginning worked closely with theatre practitioners in his script and dialogue and cast. In 1970s Bombay, Shyam's home and Satyadev Dubey's theatre group were the meccas of culture, where talented groups of young people were constantly brainstorming. Girish Karnad and Vinod Doshi met here; they were to collaborate on *Kalyug* later. Vijay Tendulkar wrote the scripts for *Nishant* and *Manthan*; dialogues were provided by Satyadev Dubey and Kaifi Azmi, respectively. Karnad recalls the free collaborative style of working when, during *Manthan*, he reworked and rewrote many scenes on location. Later, for *Bhumika*, Benegal collaborated with Girish Karnad and Satyadev Dubey.

Benegal remarks that the best example of writer–director collaboration is that of De Sica and Zavattini:

> The contribution of a writer is an important contribution, I do not see why I should reject this contribution. There are certain subjects where I know I will not have the same insights that a writer might have. In any case when a script is written it gets transformed through the sensibility of the director.[10]

Benegal cast first-time actors such as Shabana Azmi and Anant Nag, both of whom were used repeatedly in his later productions. This was to be the beginning of what was to become Benegal's almost repertory casting pattern. Later discoveries were Smita Patil, Naseeruddin Shah, Amrish Puri and Om Puri. These actors became the stars of parallel cinema. Some such as Amrish Puri and Naseeruddin were flooded with offers from the mainstream industry after their first appearances in Benegal films. Satyajit Ray noticed Shabana Azmi in *Ankur* and later cast the actress in his *Shatranj Ke Khiladi* (*The Chess Players*, 1977). He described her as the greatest dramatic actress in Indian cinema.[11] He also cast Smita Patil and Om Puri in the French television film *Sadgati* (1981). Both Shabana Azmi and Om Puri are recognised as international actors today. Both actors worked in *City of Joy* (1992) by Roland Joffé. Shabana appeared in John Schlesinger's *Madame Sousatzka* (1988) and Deepa Mehta's *Fire* (1996), and Om Puri was seen in *Brothers in Trouble* (1996) by Udayan Prasad, *East is East* (1999) directed by Damien O'Donnell, *The Parole Officer* (2001) directed by John Duigan and *White Teeth* (2002).

Benegal's producers were the enterprising proprietors of Blaze, Mohan Bijlani and Freni Varavia. Both journalists had started an English-language magazine in 1947. In 1950, they stepped into the field of film publicity, doing advertising for Hindi films. In 1974, Blaze was exhibiting films and slides in 4,500 cinemas every week. Blaze has done pioneering work in distributing advertising films and was among the first to start taking slides and film media into the rural sector with its fleet of mobile vans. Blaze was also distributing films in some cities.

Benegal's production team showcased the best of Indian talent. In fact, his unit is one of the best training units for younger people in the industry. Girish Karnad recalls how Benegal's unit was talented and educated 'with people conversing in English and in between shots discussing Brecht and Badal Sircar [a ground-breaking playwright from 1970s Calcutta]. We loved being together and with Shyam, and the popular industry people referred to us as snobs – which we were!' Commenting on Benegal's casting, Girish Karnad says:

> Shyam has a great casting eye, a terrific feel for the role and the actor. Once he accepted you in the team – he kept the team going, we were tied by a feeling of loyalty to him. Shyam had this great father feeling for his unit – he would be the father confessor, talk to all the unit members about their lives. One of the reasons why Shabana and Smita never got along was that both of them were in love with him – I mean as a father figure, not as a lover figure.

Govind Nihalani, who worked as Benegal's cinematographer for 11 films, later turned to direction in 1980 with *Aakrosh*. Other cinematographers who worked with Shyam include the highly regarded Piyush Shah and Rajan Kothari. Having worked with the best art directors, Bansi Chandragupta and Nitish Roy, Benegal later used Nitin Desai and Sameer Chanda, who have gone on to become big names in mainstream productions. His long-term collaborators have been Hitendra Ghosh (sound engineer), Bhanu Divkar (editing) and Vanraj Bhatia (music). It was only with the recent film *Zubeidaa* that Shyam turned to a different music director, the whizz kid A. R. Rahman.

The economics of film production

The focus on rural themes in parallel cinema was as much to do with authentication of Indian reality as the economics of

The landlord's mistress (Shabana Azmi) is ousted by his wife (Priya Tendulkar) in Ankur.

film production. It proved far more economical to take a film unit into a village and shoot for four to six weeks than reproduce this setting in a studio. Turning away from the studio environment also meant shooting in available light using synch-sound. In Bombay films, actors regularly dub their dialogue in post-production. Benegal insists on direct sound recording because he believes that the emotion of the moment is impossible for the actor to re-create later. Insistence on the natural look for actors meant they could travel without the paraphernalia of make-up artists, costume designers and hairdressers.

Shabana Azmi, fresh from the Film Institute in Pune, made her debut as Lakshmi in *Ankur*. Her finely nuanced performance fetched her the National Award in 1974 and great recognition abroad. She talks about her performance in *Ankur* (now more than 25 years old) with a great sense of immediacy:

> We went through a rigorous training process at the Film and Television Institute. Its value was in exposure to excellence and broadening the

parameters of the basis on which we were working in the Indian film industry. We found excellence by itself was an achievable goal. At the Institute itself some actors were identified as 'art film types' and others (who were tall/fair/beautiful) were expected to be absorbed more easily in the mainstream industry.

One of Shyam's assistants, Deepak Parashar, suggested I meet Shyam as he was casting for *Ankur.* I went to see him wearing a saree – which was a strange thing for me to do – my usual clothes were jeans and salwar kameez. I remember wearing an orange organdy saree with a red bindi. Shyam asked me if I was good at Dakhni dialect. I was familiar with the dialect as it is spoken in Hyderabad where my mother's family live and I visit often. After the meeting, he offered me two films: *Ankur* and *Nishant.*

I had heard from other film-makers that Shyam was a great technician, and I should not pass this opportunity. The shoot was a complete joy. Shyam has this amazing capacity of turning his unit into a family. He doesn't have to put in any extra effort because he is interested in everybody, in human beings basically, and a keen observer. He manages to create an atmosphere where everybody is comfortable. He will make sure there are clean plates, food on time, set up badminton and football courts so people would get physical exercise.

We shot at a village called Yellareddiguda, 25 kilometres from Hyderabad. The pattern was the same. In the morning, Benegal would first read the newspapers, and then we would discuss the scenes. In the evening, he would be interfering and counselling all the members of his unit about their love lives, their family problems – he knew everything about them.

With a completely urbanised background, I was totally unfamiliar with village life. I travelled to the location with Shyam three days ahead of the unit. The time we spent before the shoot was very valuable for me. While we looked at the locations, Shyam would speak to me a lot about the characters in the film. This helped me get under the skin of my character. I held onto everything that he said because later during the shoot even he would not remember all that he was saying then. This helped in bringing out the complexities of the character – what he calls the residual elements.

I was the only woman with an all-male crew. We stayed in a little hotel called Dwarka. I reached there a couple of days before shooting and wore village-stitched clothes – I had to stay in them. I learnt to pound chillies in the traditional way.

We worked with sketchy scripts. Actors were allowed to improvise, work with each other and find their space. Then Shyam would fix his camera angles. I was playing a village girl. The scenes required me to sit on my haunches, which I was not able to do. During meals while the rest of the crew sat at tables, I was made to sit by the door and my meal was served on the floor for me. He said, 'Let her sit there, she'll learn!' He is a believer in hard work and discipline. I also got into costume immediately, everything according to Shyam's instructions. I wore the hasuli and earrings (which my mother said even the poorest peasant women would wear) which gave a certain sensuality to the character. I had pencil-thin eyebrows (a very urban look) which looked out of place, and so I worked on them. I was a new actor and still experimenting with my looks. Otherwise we wore no base make-up, sometimes I cheated with a bit of lipstick.

I remember writing to my mother that this film looks like a Satyajit Ray film – with a realist aesthetic. For the last outburst scene, I would go out in the fields and scream out my lines from a play which I had done in Bombay. I was trying to find out if it still made sense. If you let go of your emotions and feel in your screaming that you are morally right, then the scene gets raised to a certain level.

The director has to make me come to him on a clean slate, with a degree of preparedness, to give what the scene demands – uncluttered by my own world. If the director gives you the input, it will happen to a certain degree of competence. But if the actor uses his or her mind [in analysis and preparation], then something extraordinary will happen.[12]

Recognition

Ankur won three National Awards in 1974 and 45 prizes in total in India and abroad. It was the official entry at the Berlin Film Festival, the London Film Festival and the Stratford Film Festival in 1974. It was also the Indian entry for Best Foreign Film at the Oscars the same year. Benegal reflects on the film reception:

> It was a very successful film, both critically and in terms of audience reception. It was liked everywhere, it had an overwhelming response everywhere in the country. Even today I meet people who talk to me about *Ankur*. They don't mention many other films, but they mention *Ankur*. It seemed a kind of pioneering film – at least the media saw it as a pioneering film. It travelled to every major international festival, but it did not get any award. It was very popular at the Berlin festival and the audiences noticed Shabana. Her photograph was published on the front page of the main newspaper in Berlin. International actors including Ingrid Bergman came up to Shabana and told her that it was one of the finest performances they had seen.

Nigel Andrew wrote in the *Financial Times Review*:

> The faces of the cast – particularly the ravishing Shabana Azmi as the peasant girl – are a landscape in themselves. The progress of the girl's infatuation with her master is evoked not with words but with subtle language of movement, gesture, facial expression.[13]

The *Guardian* carried Derek Malcolm's verdict:

> The film is angry but not a tract, since it observes its characters too well. If … it hasn't the depth of Ray, it has a directness and a frankness that is just as appealing. And the performances, like those in Ray films, are uniformly good.[14]

Contemporary Films distributed *Ankur* in the United Kingdom. The same company distributed later films from Blaze productions. *Ankur* also received continental distribution through a Swiss distributor which covered the hinterland and northern Europe, including Germany. Blaze distributed advertisement films in the largest network of Indian cinemas. They were able to ensure that *Ankur* was shown in remote corners of the country, and the film made substantial money for the producers. For a paltry investment of 5 lakh rupees ($10,000) Blaze earned a staggering 1 crore rupees ($206,000).

Residual characters

Benegal resists depicting characters in black-and-white terms. When Lakshmi steals the rice, she is not morally condemned, as we have seen in close proximity her world and her deprivation. Surya is also not an out-and-out villain, but rather a product and a victim of circumscribed life within patriarchal structures. As Benegal says:

> From the very beginning, we follow our own predilections and our prejudices. Certain characters you may not like as much as others. I don't make judgments on people in terms of right or wrong, good or bad. You allow characters their play as they inevitably take the story to a certain kind of resolution. You see many more facets of them, not just the one you want to show in your story. I like to see characters in their many shades of grey. Audience psychology is looked at rather then the characters in the story.
>
> Surya's 'educated' liberalism disintegrates in the face of old feudal pressures and attitude of possessions. In a cowardly manner, he drives her out of the house. The feudal father was aware of his responsibilities to the woman. It was indicative of the kind of change that was taking place in the countryside – the process is still on even to this day.
>
> Lakshmi's relation with Surya means a certain rise in status for her, considering her social position. But the rejection is so brutal and nasty, which makes her suddenly realise the power game altogether. She is no longer in the feudal situation which provided the father's mistress with a piece of land. Here the story is about change.

Benegal comments on the significance of the young boy's stone throwing: 'The younger generation can see with clarity that there is something wrong in the system. The young boy's view is unconditioned which affords a certain clarity and there is direct response, where you can clearly see between the wrong and right.'

Nishant (*Night's End*, 1975)

Based on Vijay Tendulkar's story which has its source in a real incident, *Nishant* continues with the theme of rural oppression in Andhra Pradesh. A schoolmaster (Girish Karnad) arrives in a village with his wife (Shabana Azmi) and son. The zamindar (landlord) and his four brothers abduct and rape the schoolmaster's wife. The teacher is unable to free his wife, and she continues to live in the mansion as the brothers' mistress. With the help of a village priest, the teacher mobilises the villagers against the oppressors. The armed villagers enter the mansion and slaughter the brothers. The youngest brother escapes with the woman he loves. His wife is also killed in the house. The injured schoolmaster frantically searches for his wife. Meanwhile, the villagers have cornered the couple on a hillock; the teacher is too far away to prevent the inevitable.

Nishant opens with a scene in which the village priest discovers that the temple jewels have been stolen. He finds a gold chain left behind by the thieves. Cut to a couple in bed; the man (Naseeruddin Shah) has lost his gold chain. This is Visham, the youngest brother of the zamindar. It turns out that the three brothers have stolen the temple jewels and sold them in the city. When the landlord asks for the chain, the priest is compelled to return it, even though he knows the truth about the theft. One of the villagers is falsely accused, beaten and sent to jail. The two men who represent individual authority, the priest and the constable, meekly submit to the hierarchy of the landlord.

The villagers are in the clutches of the zamindar and his brothers. Anna (Amrish Puri), the landlord, grabs land from the starving peasants, while the middle brothers ravish village women. Peasant women are treated like the property of the feudal lords, who are imbued with the arrogance of ownership. In a brief scene, the brothers see a peasant woman in the field. They call her husband and ask him to send her to the manor that night. The peasant has no option but to consent. At night, we see the woman silently leave the eldest brother's room. She is then sent to the next two brothers who are drinking in the courtyard. She is instructed to go into their room as the brothers equate her and other women to milking cows. The woman's silent submission speaks volumes of the sexual exploitation which is part of her lived reality.

The consciousness of injustice and the agency of change has to be an external one. Into this village arrive a schoolmaster and his family. The committed teacher represents values of reform and change quite alien to the feudal order and values of the village. The teacher's wife, Susheela, is curious about life and is astounded by the despotic nature of the landlord's brothers. Susheela also has material desires – she would like a large mirror and a new saree. The teacher would have her stay indoors, but she peers out of the window when he is greeting Anna and his brothers. He gestures to her to withdraw, but she does not seem to understand. Susheela's unwitting transgression creates a moment of epic conflict which leads to the peasant uprising. Her unconscious sexuality and free mobility in the village set her up as different and immediately draw the attention of the youngest brother, Visham. On another occasion, she peers over a wall to witness the eviction of a peasant by the brothers. Visham is standing there and stares at her again. Visham is attracted to Susheela, and his brothers offer to bring her to the manor. For them it is a routine task – they do this with every other woman in the village.

That night there is a knock on the schoolmaster's door, and the brothers abduct Susheela. The teacher is overpowered in the scuffle, while the villagers are silent witnesses. They turn away when asked to testify to the village constable. The desperate teacher travels to a nearby town, where the magistrates and lawyers refuse his case. The teacher who is part of an ordered world tries the avenues of justice and law, but does not think of any options outside this. The realist narrative is cleverly channelled into an epic dimension: the abduction of Sita by the demon in the Ramayana is an obvious parallel. Conflicting moral worlds are set up, as are the forces of struggle and resistance. The teacher hammers on the high doors of the manor crying out to the landlord, but there is no answer.

The school master (Girish Karnad) and his wife Susheela (Shabana Azmi) who is kidnapped by the landlords in Nishant.

Referring to the reworking of the epic in *Nishant*, Kishore Valicha writes:

> He condenses a past – the woman's history – into a metaphor and succeeds in making a subtle and an almost illicit comment within the Ramayana forms. It is the exorcism of Sita that is the burden of the Ramayana and it is the exorcism of the Ramayana that is performed in *Nishant*. The Ramayana is seen as contemporary because it deals with the plight of Sita whose suffering can now be viewed within a definite socio-cultural framework.[15]

The brothers rape Susheela in the spare room of the mansion. She is hurt, humiliated and terrified. The maid who brings her food tells her that she cannot possibly return to her husband and child after this. Rukmini (Smita Patil), who chafes against the brutality of her brothers-in-law, extends a hand of sympathy to Susheela. This brief empathy rapidly turns into hostility when she sees her husband Visham drawn towards Susheela. Susheela settles down in her role as mistress to the four brothers. She asks for her own kitchen in which she will cook for herself and for Visham. Rukmini asks for her rights; Visham brushes her off impatiently. One day, Susheela meets her husband in the temple and rebukes him for not saving her from the mansion. She tells him he should have burnt the house down, cut the oppressors into pieces. As he watches, she gets into Visham's car and drives back to the mansion.

A discussion follows between the priest and the teacher, which embodies the core debate of the film. The priest holds a fatalistic view of life and believes in resignation to one's destiny. The teacher says that as human beings they need not bear injustice silently. The conflicting views of tradition and modernity, of resignation and rebellion, are played out in this exchange. He convinces the priest, that as spiritual leader, if he admits the truth, the whole village will awaken. Goaded by his own words, the teacher begins to mobilise the villagers. Brief scenes follow in which the teacher and priest talk to small gatherings – the peasants are asked to fight for their rights, for the sake of their children. Loud music drowns out most of the conversation, except key phrases relevant to the contemporary context of change. The message of change, of revolt, spreads quickly around the village. In these brief scenes where little is said, a peasant declares that they will do as the teacher and the priest bid them.

The indication that things are changing quietly is first seen when the villagers hold a buffalo fight without inviting the zamindar. We have seen earlier that every ceremony or ritual required the sanction of the landlord. For the first time, the feudal lord is excluded from a village festival. The morning of the harvest festival arrives. None of the peasants has come to work that morning. Rukmini and Susheela exchange a few words in the kitchen; the older woman seems more in control now. The equation has reversed very quickly. Rukmini is now beginning to accept the other woman in her space. From across the river, a long procession winds itself towards the mansion. Anna and his brothers prepare quickly. An undefined sense of foreboding works against the visible joyousness of the festival. As Anna joins the proceedings, the schoolmaster and the villagers attack him. A long shot captures the peasants beating the man on the ground.

The militant peasants storm the mansion, lynching the second and third brothers. Visham prepares to escape, but Rukmini remains frozen on the balcony, witnessing the killing in the courtyard. Visham escapes with Susheela. They run out into the open countryside and hide behind a large boulder. Visham is distraught and dependent; the dazed Susheela holds and comforts him. She seems completely cut off from the present moment. Her thoughts are entirely about her child whom she will never see again.

Quick cuts show the armed peasants rapidly moving in on the couple. The injured teacher has been searching the mansion for his wife; by the time he runs towards the hills shouting for

Shabana Azmi and Naseeruddin Shah are both victims of the peasant revolt in Nishant.

the peasants to stop, it is too late to prevent the inevitable killings. Belonging to the mansion household, Susheela is seen as part of that world which must be destroyed. The teacher is unable to retrieve his wife from the violence which he has unleashed. In effect, the leader is left behind as the peasants climb up the hill and begin to attack Visham and Susheela. The long shot of the armed peasants effectively distances the viewer from the action, but powerfully suggests the level of anarchy in the absence of leadership. Benegal continues to work on his dialectic world view as in *Ankur*. He denies the viewer the triumph of the epic, which would entail a reunion of the teacher and his wife.

Susheela's child moves around the large mansion now strewn with corpses. The priest rises to his feet and covers the dead Rukmini. In the last scene, as chaos reigns over the village and age-old structures collapse, the children are seen huddled in the temple. This seems to be the only refuge, the only certitude. The night ends – it is a new beginning to a new age.

As in *Ankur*, the narrative follows a structure of exposition and conflict. The reassurance of a resolution is denied in the absence of closure. *Nishant* has a larger narrative frame than *Ankur* and explores complex nuances in characters and relationships. The dominant feudal power controls the lives of all the peasants, the patriarch and his brothers comprise this power grid, as much as the mansion into which the villager's produce (grain) and property (women) are sucked.

The rebellion is also on a mass scale as a result. When the peasants rise in arms, the entire feudal household is obliterated. The agent (in this case, the teacher) is unable to control – indeed, he is overtaken by the violence that he initiated. His personal agenda is lost in the larger class war that is waged. *Nishant* leaves us with a vision of a terrifying, uncontrollable mass revolt. Like the epic battle of the Mahabharata, the moral war will spare no individual. Benegal denies us the triumph of the restoration of the epic couple. *Nishant* leaves us with the spectacle of destruction, that which is inevitable before the new order is built.

Madhava Prasad writes in this context, '*Nishant* offers the spectator a considerably less secure position of contemplation

Rukmini – the powerless wife of the manor – in Nishant.

than *Ankur*.'[16] According to Prasad, the film is unable to resolve its inherent contradictions between narrative and spectacle. In *Nishant*, the rebellion is staged as spectacle in 'the absence of mediation, that is, in the absence of a purposive, goal-oriented programme'.[17] His critique of this kind of political cinema is defined as a vicarious experience of the political ferment in India's villages.

The rebellion is not based on an organised mobilisation programme of resistance and change. Benegal, as with most other new wave film-makers, is not questioning the nature of the democratic state. He is looking for changes within the system, not the replacement of the entire secular structure. This is the essential difference between Indian new wave cinema and the third cinema of Latin America, where cinema was used as an instrument to overthrow an existing government. Benegal offers an insight into the deeply entrenched feudal order which exists in many areas of rural India even today. *Nishant* emphasises the emergent need for change in a postcolonial nation-state that had proclaimed itself a democracy. In 1975, *Nishant* pointed to the pitfalls in the state (like the pit in the village which is never filled), to the breakdown of the consensual framework of national politics. Benegal comments:

> *Nishant* has a very similar basis [to *Ankur*]. The relation with the government itself and the manner in which the collusion of the privileged classes with the government occurs. The bureaucrat [the collector] is unable to deal with the situation when the schoolmaster's wife is abducted.
>
> *Nishant* is more dramatic and leads to general revolt as against *Ankur*. In *Nishant*, the woman is brutalised and victimised in a way that nothing could be worse than the inability of the husband to help her. She takes her decision on her own, that is, her empowerment. She does not need to depend on her husband who had let her die according to her.
>
> The Rukmini character is the real victim of the situation. In her case she has mutely accepted everything that has gone on. Setting up the two female characters as rivals is intentional.

About the historical truth of the peasant struggles in Telengana, Benegal states, 'It started as an anti-feudal uprising. Eventually the leadership was taken over by the communists. There was a larger uprising against the Nizams; meanwhile India became independent and the communists refused to accept that was true independence.' This evokes the paradigm of peasant movement as subaltern mobilisation that Ranajit Guha describes in his manifesto (see p. 25). The interesting thing about the Telengana movement was that it did bring a great deal of awareness about basic human rights as far as the people of Telengana district were concerned, as it affected all the districts of Telengana. The peasants grabbed the land and succeeded in pockets to create their own soviets. The land had been eventually taken back from them by the early 1950s, when Acharya Vinoba Bhave started the Bhudan movement which was supposed to change the confrontationalist pattern to one in which people voluntarily gave them land.

Manthan (*The Churning*, 1976)

Manthan is a microcosmic picture of transformative politics. The film evokes powerfully the winds of developmental change and resultant clashes in village life in postcolonial India. It is the same clash of tradition and modernity which arises as the benevolent state intervenes in the lives of the poor peasants. Benegal offers a brilliant social critique of a situation in which government bureaucrats enter a village and try to change the social and economic perceptions of its inhabitants. *Manthan* captures a dynamic picture of a nation in transition. The seeds of change were sown in *Ankur* and *Nishant* – *Manthan* shows a village in rapid transformation. It is the full articulation of the development aesthetic, particularly in relation to cooperatives.[18]

Commenting on cooperative structures, Benegal says:

> I always felt, even in Bengal, that the land reform movement would only be complete if some kind of cooperative system was set up. But the

communists do not believe in this, even though my film *Aarohan* [1982] clearly suggests that. The communist government in the early 1980s did not agree. They felt it was a kind of reformist notion. The success of the milk cooperatives in this country in the Anand pattern in Gujarat has been a milestone.[19] See, the cooperative movements started off as consumer movements and later on, to some extent, they became producers' cooperatives . In Anand, the farmers owned the co-ops and therefore the employees of the co-ops were the employees of the farmers. They have in the milk co-op of Gujarat employed technocrats of very high quality as the farmer's employees, in order to maximise production, but also to market their product. So in that sense nothing that the communists ever managed was as good. Whether this model would work with other areas of agricultural production, one really does not know. It could work with oil to some extent, but then again oil seeds come against very big monopolistic interests because there are about 20 families that control the entire edible oil of the country.

I was making Amul ad films [butter and baby food] when I was in ASP and, during that time, in 1965 when Lal Bahadur Shastri became prime minister, he was very impressed with what the Gujarat milk cooperatives were doing, and he wanted the pattern to be created all over the country. He asked Dr Kurien, who said it was possible. The Dairy Development Board was created under the auspices of the government of India. Dr Verghese Kurien was made chairman of the cooperative. He agreed to accept only under one condition, that the head office would not move from Gujarat to Delhi – he did not want any bureaucratisation of the process. He began what was known as Operation Flood. It was a movement to create milk cooperatives in all the milkshed areas in the country. I made a documentary on the movement, and a great deal of research was done and collected.

Benegal suggested to Dr Kurien that he make a fiction film beyond the documentary. He had budgeted for about 10 lakh rupees ($20,000). It was Dr Kurien's idea that the film should be funded by the farmers, which was an easy thing to arrange. The farmers would bring milk in the morning and evening to the

Manthan *publicity poster.*

collection centres. They were told that they would have to part with two rupees each. There were about half a million farmers in the Gujarat Cooperative Milk Marketing Federation, and their contribution was put into a kitty for the film's production.

Prasad reads the text of *Manthan* as symbolic of the mobilised state apparatus during the Emergency. Indira Gandhi was aided by a mobilised bureaucracy which implemented the socialist programme. The biggest challenge was the existing feudal structures in India. In 1973, bonded labour was abolished, and the princely states lost their special privileges. 'The actual achievements of this programme were of course limited and were cancelled out by the atrocities committed during the Emergency by the new ruling group and its implementation machinery. But the mobilization effect was very strong and produced a sense of radical transformative possibilities,' writes Prasad.[20]

The protagonist of *Manthan*, Manohar Rao (Girish Karnad), is a veterinary doctor and government official who is sent with his team to a village in Gujarat to establish a dairy cooperative. The urban-educated bureaucrat is a committed worker in a reformist socialist programme. The cooperative is a metaphor for a new structure which challenges existing hierarchies and power equations. The contemporary political context is established through emergency slogans on the radio. Rao faces challenge from three directions. There is the owner of a private dairy, Mishra (Amrish Puri), who has been underpaying the farmers and whose income will be threatened by the cooperative. Mishra makes a dig at the youthful idealism and says that this idealism does not last long. Rao tells him that the environment demands change and new methods have to be implemented. Rao makes his rounds in the village collecting milk samples, facing the hostility of the villagers towards outsiders. Rao tells Mishra, who represents the old order, that the change is one of technology as well as the transfer of power – now the peasants must receive their proper returns.

Rao explains the concept of a cooperative at a public meeting and encounters another challenge. The sarpanch (village head), played by Kulbhushan Kharbanda, needs the villagers on his side to retain power. His authority, which is based on caste divisions and traditional power structures, will be undermined if the villagers are given a voice in elections. Finally, there is Bhola (Naseeruddin Shah), the illegitimate son of a city engineer – volatile and deeply distrustful of city people, he represents the lower caste farmers who comprise the bulk of the populace. The poor Dalits will support the cooperative only if they can secure loans.

Rao's associate Deshmukh expresses a more conservative approach to reform and development. Rao believes in radical intervention. When a villager's child falls ill, Rao decides to treat the child in the absence of a doctor. The risk he takes pays off when the child is cured. Rao continues his strident intervention by persuading the Dalits to participate actively in the programme. Stone throwing disrupts the screening of a documentary for the villagers. Bhola is arrested, but Rao bails him out and gradually breaks his resistance. A Dalit woman, Bindu, sides with Rao and speaks up for him to the villagers. The Dalits file a nomination and, after the votes end in a tie, the Dalit candidate, Moti, is elected through a draw of lots.

When the group of vets, the outsiders, seems to have made some headway, the powers rear their head. Rao is accused of having raped Bindu (Smita Patil), and he is summoned back to headquarters. The Dalits' huts are set on fire, after which Misra offers them aid. Meanwhile, Bhola has taken up the cause of the Dalits, convincing them that the cooperative is theirs. The bureaucrats are transferred from the village, the external agents of change return to the city and the seeds of change must now come from within the most exploited group of village folk.

Bhola is liberated; he emerges as a potential leader for the Dalit farmers in his village. Putting his personal shame and anger behind him, he takes on a leadership role in this developmental strategy. The intervention by the bureaucrats has produced a development model and an 'organic leadership'.[21] Bindu is made a pawn in the power game by her husband. A subtle and unspoken attraction is shared between Rao and Bindu. Smita Patil's Bindu exudes a raw sensuality. Repeated strains of a folk song, 'Mhara gaon Kathiwada', express her emotions for the city dweller:

> My village is Kathiawad
> A river of milk runs there
> The cuckoo sings there
> Don't forget my home and my threshold.

The song is first played when Rao, the outsider, enters the village.

Smita Patil plays Bindu, an untouchable village woman, in Manthan.

Sexual frisson between Girish Karnad's Dr Rao and Bindu in Manthan.

It is heard again at the end as Rao drives away and Bindu watches from in front of her hut.

In one scene, Bindu washes herself in the canal water running through the fields and talks to Rao. Rao's suppressed attraction towards her and their physical proximity make the scene erotically charged. The near palpable sexual frisson between the two is left unexplored and is thus more intriguing. Bindu runs her household independently while her husband is away. When he returns, however, she loses her functional freedom – certainly her decision-making powers are curbed. There are larger forces in her life which compel her to accuse the doctor of sexual molestation. She is not able to explain her betrayal to Rao, and this relationship remains unresolved. On the other hand, Rao's associate Chandravarkar impregnates a village girl who is subsequently dishonoured. The city man's attitude towards village girls as sexual objects is also the downside of such an urban–rural interface.

Bindu is contrasted to Rao's wife, who joins him from the city and is disinterested in his work and his idealism. Soon the wife contracts typhoid and wants to be taken back to the city. Rao leaves his sick wife and rushes out to the village on the night of the fire. She is Rao's private handicap, while Bindu emerges as an ally in his project. Life is far more complex and, in this churning of the ocean (a reference to the churning by gods and demons in Hindu mythology), nectar and poison both emerge.

The dairy farmers were very happy not only to be producers of the film, but also to see the finished product. As a result, the film's costs were recovered. The film performed exceedingly well everywhere in India – Kurien managed to have it distributed across the country by making deals in favour of the distributors. It was a very successful film, and it had other spin-offs as well. Spearhead teams were created by the National Dairy Development Board (NDDB) – consisting of milk biologists and vets – and these people began to take *Manthan* into the villages and showed the film as a means of getting people involved. This helped in creating more milk cooperatives throughout India. Later on it was viewed by United Nations Development Programme (UNDP), as well as in countries outside India such as Africa, Latin America and the Soviet Union. More prints were made of this film than any other film made in India, on 35mm, 16mm, 8mm, Super 8 and, later, video cassette. Even today, Benegal's office receives orders for *Manthan* on video cassette. Morarji Desai presented a copy to the Soviet Union and China, where the film was widely shown. *Manthan* was also used in a UN-sponsored seminar in Seattle, Washington.

The frightening violence and anarchy displayed at the end of *Nishant* is also contained in *Manthan*. The viewer is reassured that this change involves organised structures and leadership. The desire for change has now filtered to the lowest layer of society, and the new leader has learnt from a role model. Benegal's vision is one of reform within the existing structure, instead of radical challenge to the state/system itself. *Manthan* combines a cinematic feel for village interactions and energised dynamics of change. Churning of the rural society (caste/class and gender) in a tide of change becomes a larger metaphor for the Indian consciousness caught in the politics of change. The trilogy then depicts different aspects and stages of class struggle. *Manthan* stands as the best cinematic example of rapidly changing structures in a developmental society and the resistance to change. Perhaps the energy of the documentaries Benegal made before this, the actual involvement of the farmers in the cooperative and the ability of the film-maker to work in an involved manner with real people charged the film with an unmatched energy.

Karnad, who played the lead role, remembers working on the script on location. As the writer Vijay Tendulkar had not accompanied the unit, Girish offered to rewrite the script, which was not working well:

> We were on location in the village, and there was no script. I offered to do the

> rewrites. That was how the real collaboration started. We got the actors together and made them improvise the scene. I would make suggestions and the actors would work on the scenes again. When a scene worked, Shama Zaidi would write it down. Large chunks of the film were written by me – the election scenes, Rao's confrontation with the dairy owner, Naseer's character of the bastard son. The National Awards of course went to Vijay Tendulkar for the story and Kaifi Azmi for dialogues. I was not credited as a writer, but we took this in good spirit and didn't seem to mind. We had gone for four weeks of shooting, this extended till seven weeks – and the reason for this will explain why Shyam became such a milestone. Apart from the popular cinema, there was nothing else in the industry. Those were the days of the multistars. *Sholay* [1975] had just been released, Amitabh Bachchan as a star controlled 60 per cent of the films being made, the situation for new actors was almost hopeless. Shyam said 'Buzz off' to the star system and took the new actors – he created his own star system and his technical crew. They had tremendous loyalty to him and were not losing work if they stayed in the villages – improvising, relating to real people – which is a great way to work. With TV and soap operas, the whole ambience that had made Shyam Benegal possible changed altogether ...

Manthan is infused with the modernising ideology for which the milk cooperatives stood. The story was inspired by Dr. V. Kurien, the architect of the 'white revolution', as the milk cooperative movement was called:

> The same sort of distribution should have happened with *Susman* [see chapter 6], but it didn't happen because of the bureaucratic interference. With *Manthan*, Dr. Kurien was free of government red tape. The district cooperatives would buy their own prints in Andhra and Tamil Nadu. The farmers who watched the film then were persuaded to make their own cooperatives. *Manthan* definitely helped the process.

After *Manthan*, Benegal made another documentary *Operation Flood 2*. By 1976, the NDDB had done two operations. By the year 1999, India became the largest milk producer in the world.

Dr Verghese Kurien's strength came from the fact that he did not take his salary from the government.

> He is one of the few people for whom I have the greatest admiration. Also Dr Swaminathan, the man who created the agricultural food revolution to make the country self-sufficient. They were the two great heroes of independent India. These success stories unquestionably confirmed my belief in the cooperative structure of development. I always felt in West Bengal, after the land reforms, they should have a lot of thrust on creation of cooperatives, in other areas of agricultural production, not only milk. The Left Front could have done a great deal in the 30-odd years of being in power. They could have definitely made a lot of difference.

Realism

Benegal insisted that the characters wear their costumes throughout the shoot and not change them, so that they looked worn in the village. While a set was being changed on a Sunday, people came from Rajkot (40 kilometres away from the village where they were shooting) – at that time there were not so many films being shot in that particular region. They came to get a glimpse of the stars, and asked for the hero and heroines – no one looked glamorous enough. Some young kids exchanged opinions. One pointed to Smita and said she was just a Dalit (low-caste woman) of the village. The crew and cast had frequent experiences like this. Naseeruddin Shah famously lived in his cotton shirt throughout the entire seven-week shoot, refusing to change it.

Manthan as third cinema

Solanas defines third cinema films as political weapons waging an ideological warfare and giving a voice to the exploited and oppressed. These films clearly and lucidly 'unveil the safe and comfortable bourgeois image of reality' and replace it with 'real images of living beings'.[22] Theorists such as Solanas and Gettino, Willemen and Gabriel define third cinema as cinema of the marginalised who edit, produce, distribute, act in and watch their own films. *Manthan* actually fits very well within these parameters. It was produced by the farmers in the Anand cooperative, who both acted in and watched their film.

Third cinema questions the relationships between politics, cultural traditions and sociohistorical situations. In Willemen's opinion, this cinema recognises the many-layered nature of culture, shaped by internal as well as intranational forces, inhabiting a space that is neither myopically nationalist nor evasively cosmopolitan.[23] These low-cost films condemn shoddy emotionalism and promote a critical understanding of society.

Willemen states that cultural activists outside the white Euro-American sphere 'have continued their own work … formulating both in practice and theory – in so far as these can be separated – a sophisticated approach to questions of domination/subordination, centre/periphery and, above all, resistance/hegemony'. Benegal's work can be read in this context of new cinema practice which is 'grounded in an understanding of the dialectical relationship between social existence and cultural practice'.[24]

Teshome H. Gabriel talks about the relation between activism, aesthetics and critical spectatorship which operate as much in the after-effects of the film as in the creative process itself. This Third Aesthetic forms the basis for a film like *Manthan*, in which the film-maker offers a certain perspective on the relation between cultural and social. In keeping with neo-realism, Benegal's characters are placed in a specific psychological and social environment, which is seen as a dynamic determinant of human behaviour. Gabriel mentions 'important Third World movies such as *Manthan* (*The Churning*), the Senegalese film *Xala* (*Spell of Impotence*, 1974), the Bolivian film *Chuquiago* (Indian name for La Paz, 1977), the Ecuadorean film *My Aunt Nora* (1953), the Brazilian film *They Don't Wear Black Tie* (1981) and the Tunisian film *Shadow of the Earth* (1982)', which attest the multi-faceted nature of Third World Cinema.[25]

It must be emphasised that, in India, third cinema was used as a means of social critique and to empower the subaltern. Benegal's films can be read as third cinema in their deployment of an egalitarian agenda. At no time, however, is this cinema used as a weapon to overthrow the government. Social change is sought very much within the democratic structure of the nation. In a way, Benegal's film pointed to the unrealised vision that was stated in the constitution of India.

According to writer Anil Dharkar, 'Shyam is a social historian who looks at the mass experiences of history through his films. That he is an accomplished film-maker who tells a good story rather well is a bonus we have enjoyed for a quarter century. Now for the next twenty-five years.'[26]

Kondura/Anugraham (*The Boon/The Sage of the Sea*, 1977)

Benegal next made a bilingual film titled *Kondura* (in Hindi) and *Anugraham* (in Telegu) based on a novel by the Marathi writer G. T. Khanolkar. Set in the startling visual coastline of Andhra Pradesh (Benegal's own state) the film is a complex treatment of religious superstition, human ambition and repressed sexuality. The legend of Kondura, the sage of the sea, is narrated over sweeping visuals of the rugged coastline and the sand dunes. A young Brahmin, Parashuram (Anant Nag) is visited by the sage, who gives him a boon, but its power will grow only if Parashuram leads a celibate life. Parasu turns away from his wife Anusuya (popular Telegu actor Vanishree) but is almost immediately attracted by the beautiful Parvathi (Smita Patil) the landlord's daughter-in-law. Parasu hears temple bells, which draw him to the temple every night. He has strange visitations and sees the mother goddess in the form of his wife, who demands that the derelict temple be restored. The local landlord agrees to finance the temple but Parasu discovers the feudal mansion is a place of sin and patriarchal oppression. The landlord abuses his childless wife and takes village women to his bed. Parasu sees his own wife as a goddess but is sexually attracted to the beautiful Parvathi. Parasu's reputation as a godman spreads fast, but even as he sits in the temple he has visions of Parvathi beckoning him. When he mistakenly uses his boon, he forces himself on his wife who is so guilt stricken that she kills herself. Mad with grief, Parasu runs into the fields desperately calling for Kondura to take back his boon.

A little-known film, *Kondura* is surprisingly rich cinema. The theme of superstition and heavenly oracles sets the conflict in human life. It has a fable-like quality to it – a divine boon can turn into a curse. Parasu is constantly framed against the vast seascape, the towering cliffs and the lashing waves are larger elemental forces that control human lives. The rugged terrain can also serve as a metaphor for the human mind, which in this case creates its own illusory trap. As he walks through the lush green paddy fields, Parasu's dilemma is set against the normal rhythm of everyday life. Farmers water the fields, drive their cattle home, children play games, the minstrel sings songs. The landlord's exploitation is evident around the village. Parasu sees the woman in his bed, hears the story of his sins from the villagers and finally sees the young labourer's wife lured by the estate manager. Parasu remains blind to these signs and believes that by killing Parvathi's unborn child he will cleanse the mansion of its sins. The fable-like quality still revolves around real-life issues – the landlord's cruelty and exploitation; the school teacher who offers a voice of reason; and Parasu's own suppressed sexuality. *Kondura* is one of Benegal's few overtly tragic films: Anusuya is once again the victim – rejected and then raped by her husband. Benegal links sexual repression with guilty desire in this strange tale of passion and fear. The conflict here is not the product of an outside agent, as in the trilogy, but comes wholly from inside.

Kondura predates *Bhumika* as an early example of Benegal's exploration of narrative style. Govind Nihalani's lyrical camerawork, outstanding art direction and costumes by Neera (Benegal's wife) and Smita Patil's fine central performance, lend the film excellent production values. The temple scenes in which Parasu has his divine visitations, the decadent opulence of the feudal manor and the sensuous beauty of the two women create a visually rich palette, externalising the latent conflicts of Parasu's story. The last scene showing Parasu disappearing into the hills heightens the mythical element of the story. Benegal demonstrates great skill in the design, look and atmosphere of the film. Reality slips into fantasy – very different from Benegal's realist, politically inflected films. The surreal atmosphere and the central theme of superstition evoke Satyajit Ray's *Devi* (1960) in which a zamindar's belief that his son's wife is the goddess triggers a series of events which lead to the young girl's fatal belief in her own divinity.

Kondura points the way to themes that Benegal was later to explore in *Bhumika* (the female protagonist's sexual choice), *Trikaal* and *Suraj Ka Satwan Ghoda*. His central concern remains that of social change and conflict in human life. The two trajectories are realist (sometimes even polemical) and expressionist (verging in *Kondura* and *Trikaal* on surrealist). The filmmaker's creative conflicts are evident in this early film, which some critics have considered as constituting the first quatrology of rural films. However, *Kondura* probably stands best on its own – its language of cinematic expression continuing to surprise the viewer.

4

The Woman's Voice: *Bhumika* and *Mandi*

Bhumika (*The Role*, 1977)

Benegal turned to an actress's autobiography for the narrative of his next film, *Bhumika*. *Bhumika* was a departure from his first trilogy, *Ankur*, *Nishant* and *Manthan*. Those films had entailed documentary research; however, with *Bhumika*, historical reconstruction was required for a period film. Benegal recalls:

> The first trilogy had used up my creative enthusiasm for that area, and I wanted to move to something else. The autobiography of Hansa Wadkar, *Sangtye Aika* [1970] was read out to me, as we were travelling together, by Mr Govind Ghanekar, my partner in Shyam Benegal Sahyadri Films.[1] He was a veteran of Prabhat Films, the executive producer there and also director for old regional films including those in which Hansa Wadkar had acted. Kamat Ghanekar was my cameraman and my partner as well. R. S. Mani was the fourth partner. He would read out interesting things in Marathi. I was enthralled by the autobiography and felt it was a great subject for a film. It was a difficult script to write. It had contributions from Girish Karnad, Satyadev Dubey and myself, and we shared the National Award for best screenplay. These were collaborations, the best drafts were put together to form the final script.

The Narrative

Starting her film career at 11, the talented Hansa Wadkar went on to become one of the most sought after and colourful of Maharashtrian film actresses. She was pulled out of school to become the sole earner in a poor family. By the time she was married at 14, she had already acted in ten films. Her autobiography *Sangtye Aika* (*Listen I Am Telling You*) was narrated to the writer Arun Sandhu and serialised before being published as a book by a Pune-based publishing house. Her story created much controversy, as several well-known men had been involved with her, although their names had been changed before publication.

In her life story, she comes across as a brave, rebellious woman relentlessly striving to get what she wanted. Alcoholic and broken in health, she died at the age of 50 in 1972. Her husband, Bandarkar, dominating and suspicious, turned out to be as exploitative as her own family. She left home several times and had affairs to spite her husband. At the peak of her career, Hansa left home for three years during which she lived as the third wife of a rich landlord. One of her best-known roles is that of the tamasha dancer Baya in *Lokshahir Ramjoshi*

Bhumika *publicity poster.*

(1947), thus creating an enduring screen image culminating in the classic tamasha film *Sangtye Aika* (1959).[2] The opening sequences of *Bhumika* refer back to the film *Sangtye Aika*.

Benegal turns to the urban world of Bombay for the first time. *Bhumika* is the story of Usha (Smita Patil), whose screen name is Urvashi, a famous film star and singer of 1930s and 1940s Marathi cinema. Flashbacks of her childhood indicate the psychological cause of her increasing waywardness. As a child, Usha (Ruksana) lives a fettered existence with her mother, grandmother (a traditional courtesan) and alcoholic father. She belongs to a family of performing women. Her mother, Shanta (Sulabha Deshpande), is the first woman in the family to marry. The neighbour's son Keshav Dalvi (Amol Palekar) is a family benefactor who starts taking more interest in the adolescent Usha. Usha's only escape is flight to the woods, as we see in the opening scene in which her pet hen is killed and served to the *ustad*, or music teacher, who visits their humble home. Her miserable childhood is transformed during those moments when she receives music lessons from her kindly grandmother, a noted singer who has even made records. When Usha's father dies, Keshav steps into the household. He brings Usha to Bombay, hoping that her talent as a singer will give her a break in Bombay films. She receives work with her first audition. Poverty and inconsiderate family demands push Usha into the world of films at a very young age, where she eventually becomes a famous film star.

The period setting gave Benegal the scope to show glimpses of the world of movie making, the popular genres, the people behind the scenes and, in general, the social attitudes towards women in films. Usha's rise in the film world is meteoric, but her search for emotional security leads her to her co-star, the popular actor Rajan (Anant Nag). This handsome, egocentric man is not ready to commit himself to relationships. In defiance and also to spite her mother, Usha marries Keshav, who steadily loses money in his business and forces Usha to continue her work in films. She would have liked to settle into domesticity, especially after her daughter is born. This cannot happen, as she is the sole breadwinner in the house. The family here is seen as parasitic, depending entirely on her earnings, but unconcerned about her happiness. Usha is a strong-willed woman who is in search of happiness. She lives a false life of glamour and romanticism in the film studios. When she enters her home, she feels isolated, distanced from her exploitative husband and grudging mother. Frustrated in her undefined emotional needs, she leaves her home to join Rajan, but he refuses to be part of her complicated world. Usha enters another illusory relationship with the pretentious director Sunil Verma (Naseeruddin Shah). When Usha becomes pregnant, her suspicious husband forces her to have an abortion. Sunil and Usha enter into a suicide pact which fails because both have duped each other.

Usha cuts herself off from her husband and moves into a hotel. She meets a middle-aged man, Kale (Amrish Puri), who is staying in the same hotel. Kale is a wealthy feudal lord and a patriarch in every sense. Usha is taken to his feudal estate and given the authority to run the household. She earns his son's affection and respect from his paralysed wife. Soon, however, Usha realises that she is virtually a prisoner in the tradition-bound household. She is not allowed to step outside the mansion. She secretly writes to her husband, who arrives with the police to rescue her.

Usha returns to the hotel in Bombay. Her daughter offers her a home, having settled and married. Usha turns down her offer. She also refuses her husband's request to return home. Rajan keeps ringing her, but she does not answer the phone. She has to deal with her loneliness and face her future alone. Fame and independence come at the cost of terrible isolation – Usha looks out with a calm dignity that has replaced her previous anger and hysteria.

In the 1978 London Film Festival Programme notes, Derek

Malcolm writes about Hansa Wadkar, the actress whose life is depicted in the film:

> In a way she was the Joan Crawford of the Marathi scene, getting through men by the dozen and bottles by the thousand ... what Benegal has done is to paint a magnificent visual recreation of those extraordinary days, and one that is also sensitive to the agonies and predicament of a talented woman whose need for security was only matched by her insistence on freedom.[3]

The central character, Usha, is trying to break with the conventions of stereotypes represented in the film roles she has to perform. The film censorship directives during the Emergency prevented Benegal from showing Usha's addiction to drink. Nor did he research her life story by interviewing her family and acquaintances. The actor Rajan Javle, who lived with Hansa until her death, was in Bombay; however, the scriptwriters did not approach him, preferring to say that the film was not based on, but inspired by, Wadkar's autobiography.

Recreating the sets for a 1950s musical: Benegal instructs the actors in Bhumika.

The flashback reconstruction of old Indian cinema had a certain nostalgic implication with regards to its development and its various genres. It dealt with the way in which Indian women had been treated in Indian cinema. Each clip defines the Indian woman in cinema as a self-sacrificing martyr; the central character has to play all these parts in films and, of course, in real life as well.

Reconstruction of the city in the 1930s, 1940s and 1950s was not so difficult, largely because Benegal's office was on the premises of Jyoti Studios on Nana Chowk, which was the oldest studio in Bombay. It used to be known as the Imperial Studios. Ardeshir Irani had started the studio, and the first talkie, *Alam Ara* (1931), was made there. It was also the first studio Prithviraj Kapoor worked in.[4]

Benegal speaks nostalgically about the studio and his office (which was moved to its current site in Everest Building in the busy area of Tardeo in 1978):

> There was so much material there from the thirties. Nothing had changed, it was marvellous. It was like living in a time warp. Living in the world of silent cinema and early talkies. So reconstructing that part was much fun. Much of the shooting was done in that area – set in the thirties and forties. Some of the houses there, some of the greatest classical singers of Bombay actually live in that area around Nana Chowk. All the great singers of Gwalior, Kirana, Jaipur *gharana* [styles or schools of Hindustani classical music] – Maharana Rao Vyas, Vinayak Patwardhan, Mogubai, her daughter Kishori Amonkar – all lived in that area. It was a great sense of being there, of living in that period in that area. It was a very alive neighbourhood, and then Jinnah House was also located there. Also some of the red light districts there, where *mujras* [song-and-dance performances] were held by performing women. It was fascinating. Much of the film was shot on location in actual places in that area. Reconstructing the fifties was easy because that was an era largely familiar to me through the films of Guru Dutt and others. We also used some of the costumes from Dutt's *Kaagaz Ke Phool* (1959) to get the cut of the suits right. These were stored in Nataraj Studios.

> Two things happened when I planned to make *Bhumika*. I had planned to shoot the film entirely in colour. There was a tremendous shortage of colour stock in India; it was severely rationed. As a result, I changed the entire pattern of the look of the film. I shot 1930s in black and white, and then coloured them, gave them an amber and blue tone as they used to colour monochrome in those days. This was to get a sense of the periods, as well as how films were actually done at that time. They would give them different colour tones. The first monopack colour system to come to India was Gevacolour and Orwo [an East German colour system] in the fifties. After that came Eastmancolour. I brought raw stock according to availability. I bought black and white, Gevacolour, Orwo and Eastmancolour. I used the stock to represent different periods of the Indian cinema itself and the evolution of this cinema. This was out of sheer necessity, but creatively it added a different dimension to the film. This was not part of my original plans, but we made a virtue out of necessity.

Benegal's partners, Prabhat veterans, had witnessed during their careers the transition from black and white to colour. He planned his scenes in close consultation with them regarding the look of the different decades.

The women's movement in India

In 1980s India, as part of postcolonial historiography and women's studies, there was an energetic reclaiming of women's voices silenced in the annals of male-dominated history – through oral histories and the lives of older writers and artists. In addition to valuable research done in regional states, the milestone *Women Writing in India* edited by Susie Tharu and K. Lalita was published in India in 1991. An extract from Wadkar's autobiography was translated into English to be published in the second volume of the anthology.[5]

Bhumika was the first Indian film based on a woman's autobiography. Benegal's continued concern with the female perspective, and in this case the private and public worlds inhabited by his protagonist were worked out with great

Smita Patil's Urvashi performs a folk dance in a recreated 1940s film set.

sensitivity. In every film, Benegal was deconstructing the stereotype of a glamorised heroine, working against the accepted models of devoted wives and idealised mothers found in Bombay films. From *Ankur* to *Bhumika*, women are at the heart of Benegal's narratives, with the first trilogy clearly pointing to the manner in which gender is implicated in caste and institutionalised power struggles. In this realist aesthetic, the viewer looked at real-life women located in specific cultures and histories. Here we had deep psychological studies of characters grounded in reality, with their own conflicts and compulsions.

The title *Bhumika* (*The Role*) serves as a metaphor for the predominant themes of the film: the public and private world of the protagonist, the various roles she plays in her career and the socially sanctioned roles offered which she both desires and transgresses. Or is it the role of history as embodied in cinema through three decades? In Benegal's words, *Bhumika* is a homage to Bombay cinema, recreating the studio atmosphere of the 1930s, 1940s and 1950s. The opening sequence shows Usha performing a vigorous, sexually charged song and dance in the regional folk tradition of tamasha. The camera dwells on her made-up face and her desirable body. The song goes 'Mera Chithila Balam Na Aya' ('My passionate lover has not come, I am dressed and waiting for him'). The glamorised female figure seems to offer a visceral desire no different from the Bombay film.

Recreating the stunt film set in Bhumika: *Benegal directs Smita Patil and Anant Nag for a fencing sequence.*

Soon, however, the camera pulls back to reveal that the action is part of a film set. When one of the dancers slips and hurts her foot, the shoot is called off. Usha is seen standing in the studio waiting for her car, tense and irritable. Her public role as an actress gives way to her private life. This is cinematically established by her habit of changing her saree every time she returns home. Standing in front of the mirror, partly undressed in her blouse and petticoat, she is captured at that moment when she transforms from the glamorous heroine to the unhappy wife and mother in her tension-ridden household. Keshav is suspicious of Usha's relationship with her co-actor. Her disgust for her parasitic husband is barely concealed as she spits out, 'You need my earnings, don't you?' At the end of an argument, she leaves the house; Keshav's reaction suggests that this has happened many times in the past.

Bhumika is not only a powerful exploration of a public woman's psyche, but also a documentation of the changing times through the history of the Bombay films – the world of which Usha is a part. Through the highly creative deployment of the film-within-film technique, Usha (or Urvashi, the star) is seen playing different roles in the prevailing genres of the time. When Usha visits the sets of Surya Films for the first time, she witnesses the shoot of a mythological story, in which a king tries to seduce a virtuous woman. The dialogue is declamatory and theatrical; the special fire effects are crude but typical of the 1930s. In the 1940s, Usha and Rajan are seen in a stunt film in masked costumes fencing with each other. This is evocative of the *Hunterwali* films of Nadia, the stunt queen of Wadia films in the 1930s and 1940s.[6]

Soon after follows a montage of billboards, posters and film clips featuring Urvashi. She plays Savitri in a mythological film, the true Hindu wife who wishes to follow her husband to death. Savitri, like Sita, is a definitive role model for Hindu women in India. They must show unquestioning devotion to their husbands. A poster shows Urvashi clinging to an infant, the title

'Mera Munna' ('My Child') points to the role of the sacrificing, glorified mother which is another great cultural stereotype for Indian women. In another brief scene, she plays a virtuous married woman who refuses to prostitute herself. The scene switches to colour with the reconstruction of a 1950s clip – a woman in white saree testifies in a courtroom.[7] In an ironic and visually stimulating sequence incorporating mythological, social and romance films, the three cultural roles are presented: the devoted wife, the suffering mother and the virtuous married woman. In her own life, Usha both desires and transgresses these ideal roles. Benegal himself comments on the treatment:

> This was my first film to be inspired from an existing literary source. There is a tendency towards literariness which I have tried to curb with an increasing use of montage. The book may be egocentric, but it fascinated me because it deals with a woman who is trying to find her individual place in the society of that time.

Shanta (Sulabha Deshpande) forces her daughter Usha (Smita Patil) to take an oath in front of the gods in Bhumika.

The narrative is complex and non-linear. There are five long sequences given in flashback which reconstruct Usha's childhood, adolescence and her involvement with other men – Rajan the actor, Sushil, the pretentious film-maker and Kale, the feudal patriarch. Ultimately, Usha rejects the world of men and overcomes her insecurities. She can retain her autonomy only if she lives alone. Usha's story is a metaphor for the rapidly changing postcolonial nation. News relayed on the radio constantly places the historical time of the narrative – references to Nehru's secular speech, to the Bhakra Nangal dam as a symbol of progress, to the Sino-Indian war. The modern nation on the move and Usha's struggle for freedom and control over her life are constantly counterpoised. Politics may move fast – the film seems to say – but cultural and social mores take far longer to change. The woman's struggle for autonomy, the seemingly irreconcilable spaces of the home and the world, the vigorous questioning of familial and social roles – all these set *Bhumika* at the heart of the 1980s debate over the role of women in India.

Bhumika's Usha is the victim of a dysfunctional family. She grows up with the desire for independence and a secure family life, both of which seem impossible. The scenes depicting Usha's early life are dramatically taut and economic. Usha's mother, Shanta, has a young lover, Keshav, who also takes care of the family. Her alcoholic husband despises this situation, but is unable to do anything about it. The young Usha resents the relationship between her mother and Keshav. One day when she is rude to him, her mother beats and abuses her. Usha's father intervenes and turns on his wife, beating her mercilessly until he collapses from the exertion. Usha is a witness to this domestic violence and later subjected to similar treatment herself. When Shanta realises that Usha is involved with Keshav, she forces her daughter to take an oath. The middle-aged Shanta is losing her man to her daughter. Hostility between the two is powerfully conveyed through looks. The ideal mother–child relationship is disturbingly shaken in this

Victim of domestic violence: Usha (Smita Patil) and Shanta (Amol Palekar) in Bhumika.

power struggle that becomes a role reversal. Usha is now the money earner in the family, while her mother and grandmother are dependants. The authority of the mother slips as she exposes her jealousy and insecurity to widen the rift between her child and herself. Usha marries Keshav to spite her mother and soon realises that she is in a bad marriage. Shanta is reduced to a silent dependant in her daughter's household, shielding her granddaughter from the scenes of violence and rage enacted between Usha and Keshav. The film offers deep insights into intergenerational relationships and cultural roles that have their own continuity. Usha's daughter is as close to her grandmother as Usha was to hers.

Disillusioned with the film world, she wishes to settle down in her domestic life. Her extortionist husband, however, forces her back to her career. Restless, she enters into futile relationships, and, when she does leave her husband's home, she must leave her child as well. After spending years in a feudal estate where she is virtually a prisoner, Usha returns to the city. Refusing to go back to her husband or her daughter's home, she finally finds independence, but at the cost of immense loneliness. By breaking family and social codes, Usha's transgression cannot be contained within any sanctioned relationships. In her quest for happiness, Usha can only find betrayal and sorrow. She faces the future from the periphery of normalised society. As a performing woman and actor, the split between Usha's public and private world is effectively delineated. She gains success as a film star, but her personal life is in ruins. In the 1940s and 1950s, there were several legendary female stars whose tragic personal lives were the stuff of popular imagination. *Bhumika* draws heavily on this frame of reference and demystifies it. Public ambition and success come at a cost for a woman.

Benegal's films burst onto the screen at a time when the first waves of the women's movement were being felt in India. *Bhumika* specifically raises fundamental questions about female selfhood and family structures, about autonomy, power structures and conflict. The interdisciplinary nature of women's studies allowed *Bhumika* to be examined as a multilayered text. It was a study of women in the film industry of the 1930s, 1940s and 1950s. It was a study of the devadasi (performing women) tradition, as well as of the folk theatre from which many film stars originated. It was also a historical journey through dominant film genres and modes of production. *Bhumika* raised questions about women's sexuality and accepted moral norms. Most importantly, it constructed a female hero whose specific world and psyche are explored in the tradition of psycho-realism.

Bhumika in effect privileged the woman's voice (Hansa Wadkar's autobiography) and her story, her subjectivity (Smita Patil's powerful depiction of Usha). *Bhumika* almost instantly became a film text to be discussed and written about in the mainstream press, as well as in feminist circles. The possibilities for reading the text as an extension of Satyajit Ray's *Charulata* have always been interesting. Charu, confined in her upper-class house and neglected by a workaholic husband, falls in love with her dashing and dynamic brother-in-law. Her literary ambitions are curbed and stifled until the younger poet inspires her to write. Charu's inner world is explored through close-ups, music and writing. Eventually the home becomes a sacrosanct space. Charu and Bhupati reach out to each other tentatively – they can perhaps build their world again.

Thirteen years on and the home is unable to contain Usha's sexuality. The home itself is a structure of exploitation. She transgresses and enters other worlds, but none can give her what she seeks. Ironically, when she seeks domesticity, her husband and manager pushes her into the public world. The director documents the creation of middle-class society (upwardly mobile migrant families which settled in Bombay). The world cannot fulfil Usha's search for love. She retreats into the familiar but neutral space of a small suburban hotel. Her grandmother's song plays on the soundtrack.

Benegal remarks, 'The song in raag Shudh Kalyan is a recurrent theme and associated with the grandmother in the story. The raag recovers that moment in time in terms of vivid recollections of childhood. In films, music is a sure way of capturing and recapturing certain times and spaces.' Benegal used classical singers Saraswati Rani and Feroze Dastur to create the music for Usha's childhood. The song she learns from her grandmother recurs periodically and at strategic moments in Usha's life, depicting her search for something elusive, but also for the security which her grandmother offered. The subtext of classical music being overtaken by film and popular music is a statement on the rapid changes in the entertainment market and the depreciation of traditional arts.

Gender studies analyst Jasodhara Bagchi comments:

> This society is not able to give Usha her due status, nor is her work in the film industry duly rewarded. Whether she donned modern or traditional roles each relationship has tied her with fresh bonds. Only the undulating branches of the tree outside the hotel window bring a hint of freedom in Usha's life.[8]

Benegal is always interested in human stories, in exploring complexities, but not in providing judgments or answers. Usha's narrative remains open-ended, but she has moved from the position of a victim to that of someone who is in control of her own life. This comes at a cost of frightening urban isolation, a denouement which raises further questions about the patriarchal institutions within which women operate.

Sumita Chakravarty locates *Bhumika* close to the courtesan film genre through the analogy of sexuality as labour. 'Actresses and courtesans both live by their bodies: they are driven by a sexual economy ... the immoral traffic of the body, even if entered into consciously and not for money, as in the case of Usha, must be transcended in order to attain self-fulfilment.'[9] Benegal was to return to the story of the performing woman in *Mandi* – the kotha singer; *Sardari Begum* – a thumri singer; and *Zubeidaa* – an aspiring actress.

Bhumika also generated controversy, with some critics expressing their disappointment with the film adaptation of Hansa Wadkar's life. Some scathing reviews accused Benegal of being far removed from the reality of Hansa Wadkar. Dnyaneshwar Nadkarni wrote in the *Times of India*:

> The screen heroine Usha, played by Smita Patil, emerges as a mechanical doll when compared to her unconventional and vivacious real-life counterpart ... While Benegal is largely successful in creating a period feeling in some of the sequences and while his satire of the film industry

The woman's story: Smita Patil gained iconic status after her performance in Bhumika.

> before the war is quite to the point, he has thoroughly missed the essence of Hansa Wadkar's life story.[10]

Smita Patil's powerful performance received due recognition in India and abroad, fetching her the National Award for Best Actress. Shyam recalls working with Smita, fondly admitting that he misses her in his films:

> Smita came on board very early, from the time of the script. I would feed her with details of her character. We were in Cannes for *Nishant*. I remember I would walk up and down the boulevard in front of the Palais and talk to her about *Bhumika*. She was very much involved from the beginning. Smita had to learn horse riding, fencing and dancing. I used to be like a schoolmaster, calling every morning to wake her and make sure she left for her classes. In the beginning, I had to direct her, but not so much later. She projected tremendous transparency in her personality. Yes, and you could see that quality on screen, she was never artful on screen.
>
> Smita was very instinctive. What we saw of her talent was just the tip of the iceberg. If she had lived longer, she would have developed her craft.

> After all she was so young when she died – she was only 30. If she had lived and continued to act, she, too, would have developed her craft because instinct can only take you to a certain point.

In an interview for *Filmworld* in 1977, Smita Patil talked about her nervousness over the role in *Bhumika* and how Benegal had assured her that she was the right choice:

> Shyam reassured me – he said, 'I know you can do it, and that is why I have taken you. Now stop worrying and start living.' It was his confidence in me – the responsibility that he took for my performance – that helped me to essay the part to his satisfaction. Somehow, when someone is ready to take the burden from your shoulders, you are relieved, and this relief can do wonders. We started our schedule with some of the most important scenes – with Amol Palekar – and this did nothing to get me over my nervousness. Then Shyam told me something that once and for all lifted the clouds from my mind. He said, 'No man is his own judge. You are not entitled to judge your own work. You are only entitled to do your work, and any work which is done sincerely and honestly is never bad.'[11]

The budget for *Bhumika* was 13 to 14 lakh rupees ($29,000). The film collapsed within the first week when it opened the first time. It was a complete failure in its first release, something attributed to the A (adult) certificate it was given by the censors. The censors had a rationale for applying this rating: adultery was an adult subject. Their decision had disastrous effects on the film's market. In those days, an adult certificate would split the family audience, meaning the automatic loss of 30 per cent of potential viewers. Even women would not go to see an A-rated film. Some people would go expecting to see a sex film and end up disappointed when they were confronted with a film such as *Bhumika*. Benegal explains how the film was more successful when it was re-released:

> When it was released a second time, it did reasonably well. In pre-television

days, a film could be released two or three times. When Blaze released the film the third time, word of mouth for the film was so good that it became a success. Now it is not possible, of course. Now if a film collapses in the first week it goes into oblivion. There is no opportunity to revive it again, not even a memory is left of it. Of course, in those days we did not spend so much money on marketing and promotion. These days we have to package films, create events around it, create hype for the music. Music companies spend a lot of money publicising the film. It is much more difficult when talking in terms of recovery. In those days we could rely on good old word of mouth to take the film to its successful conclusion.

The music of *Bhumika* and *Manthan* would sell quite well. In those days, the music rights fetched nothing. Music companies thought they were doing us a favour by releasing cassettes. Of course, now people cover three-quarters of their costs with music sales. Particularly film-makers like Subhas Ghai and others of his market stature. It happened to *Zubeidaa* to a certain extent. But for *Zubeidaa* we had to pay 50 per cent of sales to the music director.

Mandi (*Market Place*, 1983)

Benegal returned to an ensemble film with *Mandi*, placing the drama in a small-town brothel. Partly inspired by *The Best Little Whorehouse in Texas* (Colin Higgins, 1982), this is a burlesque on politics and middle-class morals through the motif of prostitution. The grand utopian vision of the golden-hearted prostitute had been explored in Indian literature and cinema – from *Devdas* (1930, 1950, 2002) to its later reinventions such as *Amar Prem* (1972) and *Muqaddar Ka Sikandar* (1978). The courtesan or prostitute was almost always the tragic lover and often loser to her foil, the socially integrated woman whom the hero will love. *Mandi* treats in full the themes of female sexuality as commerce and its 'othering' by bourgeois society. Benegal enters a forbidden space to explore it from the inside, with incisive irony and rare humour. Having crossed the border of bourgeois respectability, the film takes us into a chaotic and hilarious world in which female sexuality spills over. It is a bawdy comedy in a whorehouse, as engaging as the drama of Jonson, Sheridan or Molière. The burlesque tone, however, does not shield the director's compassionate eye for his characters. Benegal says of the film:

> The story was told to me many years ago. It is only a four-page story, but worked as a wonderful springboard. I thought it would be unmakeable for a long time, but then Shama Zaidi and I started tossing ideas and things emerged as in the script. I was very interested in creating a whole microsystem of Indian life, the survival instinct that is evident in the Shabana character, middle-class hypocrisy, the manipulation that goes on constantly, the young pecking the old – each one on his or her level of power is constantly pecking another who is less capable.

Rukmini Bai (Shabana Azmi) runs a kotha, or brothel where prostitutes sing and dance, which had its heyday in the eighteenth and nineteenth centuries, but now faces decline. The

Rukmini, the proprietess (Shabana Azmi, centre), and her girls (Smita Patil, right and Soni Razdan, left) in the menagerie of Mandi.

performing women have lost their old patronage and are dependent on middle-class clientele. This world is stripped of the glamorous, romanticised lens of courtesan films such as Kamal Amrohi's *Pakeezah* (*The Pure One*, 1971), *Utsav* (*Festival*, 1984) and *Umrao Jaan* (1981). Nor does it evoke a nostalgic past or a romantic hero. *Mandi* is contemporary: the characters are flesh-and-blood characters. Rukmini is like a loving matriarch to her girls and cares especially about Zeenat (Smita Patil), who is reserved for special up-market clients. The courtesans in training provide enough scope for song-and-dance sequences. The other girls are set up in quick deft strokes, their differing natures underlined.

In an interview with writer Shobha Kilachand, Benegal discusses his treatment of *Mandi*:

> I was using a lot of kids, but, no, it wasn't meant to be camp. I was attempting to do essentially two things: I was attempting on one level to define survival and on another level to define freedom. Those were the twin themes basically. I was also very interested in not simply telling a plotted story ... I was more interested in looking at the different facets of people without making any value judgments that come automatically when anything is filtered. I am not stating any moral – if there is a moral then the audience must arrive at it.[12]

The house is a site of unbridled female sexuality. Tundlus (Naseeruddin Shah) is an impotent (perhaps castrated) male in this all-female habitat. The local police constable (Harish Patel) finds gratification with the inmates of the *kotha*. Om Puri plays a pornographer who steals into the household to photograph girls in the nude. Chakravarty describes this whorehouse as 'a menagerie of temperamental creatures'.[13] The uncontrollable wildness (underlying the apparent control of Rukmini) of this house is made explicit in a sequence featuring a monkey. A performing monkey escapes from its trainer and enters Zeenat's room on the terrace. This small incident throws the household

Lesbian undertones in the relations between women in the brothel, Rukmini Bai (Shabana Azmi, left) and her favourite girl Zeenat (Smita Patil, right).

into complete pandemonium as the girls run in all directions and the manservant Tundlus tries to grab the monkey. Rukmini is very concerned about Zeenat's safety, while she, it appears, is greatly entertained by this sudden intrusion. It is a comic foreboding of things to come when Zeenat falls in love with an aristocrat's son, and he scales the walls to enter her room late at night.

The film also lampoons the pretentious middle class who feel that the brothel is contaminating society. The rational world order of the bourgeois is embodied by the social worker Shanti Devi (Gita Siddharth), who becomes the spokesperson of the 'decent', moral society that deposits its excesses in the brothel. Shanti Devi runs a women's centre, but has little sympathy for the female residents in Rukmini's household. Distinguished businessmen and the cream of society such as Major Agarwal (Saeed Jaffrey) harbour dark secrets in this kotha.

The comic tone gives way to something more sinister when a mute girl is brought to the brothel by a pimp. Phoolmani (Srila

Mazumdar) has been tricked into a false marriage and is now taught the tricks of the trade by the other prostitutes. The parrot in the cage is used as a visual metaphor for all the girls trapped in this sexual economy when the mute girl falls into a coma after being raped by a client. The grim social reality of poor girls who are coerced into prostitution creeps into the narrative. The girls are all jailed for a few days.

Meanwhile, Agarwal is planning to have his young son married to the daughter of another businessman, Mr Gupta (Kulbhushan Kharbanda). The latter owns the building in which Rukmini and her girls live. The arranged marriage is purely a commercial transaction between two respectable members of society. At the engagement ceremony, Zeenat is invited to perform a mujra, a song and dance in courtesan style. Agarwal's son Sushil (Aditya Bhattacharya) is smitten by the beautiful courtesan and soon wants to elope with her. The theme of incest darkens the tone as Rukmini reveals that Zeenat is in fact Agarwal's illegitimate daughter, Sushil's half-sister.

This repository of secrets and crimes is caught between larger social forces – the businessman and the social workers succeed in closing down the brothel so that the women are relocated to the margins of the city in a rocky, sterile area. By now the viewer's sympathy is directed towards these women, as the moral duplicity of the town residents is relentlessly exposed. Although initially drawn in broad strokes of caricature, Rukmini is real enough to evoke an emotional response from the viewer. Overweight, gregarious, religious, with a suggestion of sexually transmitted disease, this middle-aged prostitute past her prime is convincingly brought to life by Shabana Azmi in one of her career-best performances.

Rukmini chances on the shrine of the fakir (holy man) to whom she has been praying on the instructions of the local shaman. As it happens, the men from the town start to frequent her new brothel. Whether it is chance or urban economics, business picks up and the place becomes a site of bustling activity. One of the prostitutes has a baby, and a promise of new life and hope is fulfilled.

Zeenat and Sushil still pine for each other. The two elope, and a long chase scene parodies similar sequences in most Hindi films. Like the bird that flies out of the cage, Zeenat also breaks away from a life which holds no future for her. She disappears, probably to another town. Meanwhile, the other girls begin to question Rukmini's authority, and there is a minor rebellion. Shocked and hurt, Rukmini prepares to leave for a pilgrimage with her manservant, Tundlus. But she hears a magical voice in the wilderness asking her to pray to her saint. In the distance, she sees Phoolmani running towards her. Rukmini knows she and her trade will survive once again.

Mandi is considered by many to be Benegal's most masterful film, a brilliantly ironic examination of middle-class notions of respectability and values, and a sympathetic inquiry into brothel life. True to his sensibilities and commitment to human stories, Benegal treats the sex workers as individuals and reconfigures the representations of courtesans and their space. It is worth noting that two spectacular courtesan films before *Mandi*, *Pakeezah* and *Umrao Jaan*, were hugely successful and went on to become cult films. Replete with song and dance, glamorous costumes and beautiful women, they evoked a nostalgia for a romanticised past. The courtesan cannot be part of normative society, so she remains defined as a loner, unrequited in her love. Of the novel *Umrao Jaan* (the courtesan's autobiography by Mirza Mohammed Rusva), Aijaz Ahmed notes, 'The scandal of Rusva's text is its proposition that since such a woman depends upon no one man, and because many depend on her, she is the only relatively free woman in our society … Rusva was a very traditional man and he was simply tired of certain kinds of moral posturing.'[14] Discussing the figure of the prostitute in Hindi films, Chakravarty writes: 'As an image of female oppression, of class oppression, and of psychic and moral ambivalence, the haunting figure of the prostitute can be a searing indictment of social hypocrisy and exploitation.'[15]

Film critic Iqbal Masud commented that Benegal's attitude towards the kotha is ambivalent. According to the critic, 'the director has successfully used it as an instrument of satire … but also sees it as a repository of high and popular culture. Excellent music, sumptuous interiors and colourful photography are allied to vibrant performances from Benegal's regulars.'[16]

Actor Om Puri, who played a key role in the ensemble film, comments on Benegal's method of work:

> One of Benegal's greatest contributions has been in introducing new talent. After graduating from the Institute of Film and Television in Pune, Benegal was the only director I met. I was then called for a small role in *Bhumika*. Even today aspiring actors and freshly trained technicians can approach him at his office. He advises them and gets in touch with them when he plans his next production.
>
> He would offer his actors detailed scripts and shot division. In the 1970s only Shyam and Govind Nihalani would do this at that time. Dialogues would be polished and detailed during rehearsals. He allows an organic approach to actors, they are allowed to move around and find their space. He also allows a fair amount of improvisation during rehearsals, before he places his camera.
>
> Benegal formed this wonderful repertory cast. I remember during *Mandi*, we were a fabulous cast of 15 actors. Each one of them later made their mark on national and international cinema.
>
> The team spirit was very uplifting. All actors had to go to the location every day, even if they had no scenes that particular day. In the morning all of us boarded a bus that took us to the village of Bhongi, 40 kilometres from Hyderabad. The actors would play volleyball till each one was called for his or her shot. There was a great spirit of camaraderie. Great sense of democracy in the unit – all unit members would eat together. Actors never felt they were stressed out, there was always time for a joke or two. In fact, Benegal was probably a bit casual. Sometimes actors felt they could better a scene, but the director was happy. Shyam is extremely disciplined. He

> would never shoot beyond eight or nine hours, so there was never any scope for upset schedules.[17]

The media had for some time been playing up the professional rivalry between Shabana Azmi and Smita Patil. Both extremely talented actors in effect needed each other to hone their standards. At the time of shooting for *Mandi*, the tension between the two female leads was near palpable. Both had recently been cast in Mahesh Bhatt's *Arth* as rivals – Shabana as the hero's wife, Smita as his mistress. Benegal was often pushed by the press to comment on his preference between two of his favourite protégées. In an interview, he finally voiced his opinion that Smita had a wider range:

> Smita could play anything. She could play glamorous roles and dance. These were things she was instinctively capable of. Shabana is essentially a dramatic actress – the best of her kind. Her concentration as an actress has been on that line. Those are the parts she looks for. She may have done the running around trees – I can't imagine her doing it. But she is so confident

Shabana Azmi cast against the grain as Rukmini Bai in Mandi.

> of her position. Who is there to challenge her as a dramatic actress? She transcends all competition in that area.[18]

The director went on to say that Karishma Kapoor's work in *Zubeidaa* was on par with Shabana or Smita performance.

Benegal's heroines

In 2000, Benegal made *Zubeidaa* (discussed at greater length in Chapter 7), a big-budget film with the leading actress of mainstream Hindi cinema, Karishma Kapoor. Benegal returned in this film to the same theme he had examined in *Bhumika*, that of the public and private faces of a woman protagonist. The protagonist's story unfolds through the pages of her diary as her son reconstructs her life from fragments. Zubeidaa's name has been obliterated from the official pages of history. She is re-created through her private voice. The idiom of this film is one of a much broader canvas with big stars and a popular soundtrack, and it is a far cry from *Ankur* with its low-caste heroine or *Mandi* with its ensemble structure and ironic tone. But even though *Zubeidaa* was developed with a much grander marketing strategy in mind, there are frequent echoes of Benegal's previous heroines: Usha in *Bhumika*, Sardari in *Sardari Begum* and Zeenat in *Mandi*. All of them are women who loved life and were spirited and strong-willed. Each of them has her individual destiny crossed by larger political forces. Collectively, they serve to remind the viewer that in so many of Benegal's films a female point of view shapes the response of the audience. In this he emerges as a remarkable figure not only in India cinema, but also in the entirety of what we call world cinema today.

5

Histories and Epics

Junoon (*Possessed*, 1978)

In the 1970s, Shashi Kapoor, a major Bollywood star, wanted to work with Benegal. Kapoor set up his company Film-Valas initially to distribute the Merchant-Ivory production *Bombay Talkie* (1970). He then branched into production in 1978 with *Junoon*, followed by *Kalyug*, Aparna Sen's *36 Chowringhee Lane* (1981) and Girish Karnad's *Utsav*. Benegal had just finished reading 'A Flight of Pigeons', a short story by Ruskin Bond about an Anglo-Indian woman abducted by a Pathan during the 1857 Sepoy Mutiny against the British. The revolt had started in the area called the Doab, a region between the rivers Ganga and Jamuna, and the story was set in Shahjahanpur. The slim and charming story needed to be fleshed out, so Benegal set out on a long period of research in Lucknow to locate the family and explore its history. He met old Anglo-Indian families and saw the church in which the British had been massacred and where the Labadoor family, the Anglo-Indian family in the story, was buried. The gazettes of the time provided a great amount of information on the events in 1857. Research also involved searching for the history of the Pathans in that area. The historical character Javed Khan (played by Shashi Kapoor) belonged to this community. Benegal found himself facing a project much larger than anything that he had handled before. Shashi Kapoor was a generous producer, and the action scenes (including cavalry charges and battles scenes) raised the budget to 55 lakh rupees ($113,000) in 1978 (almost 9 crores [$1.85 million] in today's terms).

With this film, Benegal secured something of a casting coup

with big stars such as Shabana Azmi and Shashi Kapoor, Naseeruddin Shah and Jennifer Kapoor (née Kendal). Jennifer Kapoor was Shashi's wife, who was persuaded to return to films after her work in Merchant-Ivory productions. Nafisa Ali, the national swimming champion, and the Urdu feminist writer Ismat Chugtai were also among the cast. What Benegal enjoyed most was the recreation of a nineteenth-century ambience, as well as the multi-layered conflicts relating to racial identity.

The film opens with a Muslim shaman chanting deliriously, 'Everything will turn red.' This is a prophetic pointer to the revolutionary violence to follow in which social barriers between the ruler and ruled collapse and an Anglo-Indian family finds itself in a Muslim household. Benegal explains that one of the myths of that time was about a mullah who travelled from mosque to mosque making oracular statements about the fall of the British. 'I intentionally bring in a dimension of the myth, a lot of people in the revolution needed that sort of divine

The passionate Pathan soldier (Shashi Kapoor) faces the Anglo-Indian mother (Jennifer Kapoor) in Junoon.

*Shabana Azmi in her debut role as Lakshmi, a low caste village woman who is seduced by the landlord (*Ankur*).*

The mute peasant Kishtaya (Sadhu Meher) and his pregnant wife Lakshmi (Shabana Azmi) in Ankur.

After the collapse of the feudal manor: Shabana Azmi and Naseeruddin Shah in Nishant.

Rukmini (Smita Patil, right) shares a quiet bonding with her husband's mistress Susheela (Shabana Azmi) in Nishant.

Smita Patil plays the 1940s actress Urvashi in Bhumika.

Usha (Smita Patil) seeks feudal respectability with Kale (Amrish Puri) in Bumika.

Smita Patil as filmstar Urvashi performs the tamasha dance in Bhumika.

A dance performance in the whorehouse of Mandi. *Om Puri, Shabana Azmi and Neena Gupta.*

Dona Maria (Leela Naidu) and her hysterical daughter (Anita Kanwar) in Trikaal.

Shabana Azmi and village children in Antarnaad.

Benegal and Amrish Puri on the set of Suraj Ka Satwan Ghoda.

Raghuvir Yadav (left), plays a low caste peasant and Rajit Kapur (centre) as the city-bred director shooting in a village in Samar.

Shabana Azmi and other actors rehearse on the set of Hari Bhari *while Benegal looks on.*

Karishma's Zubeidaa enters the royal household of her prince (Manoj Bajpai) in Zubeidaa.

Zubeidaa (Karishma Kapoor) rejects the royal codes represented by the first queen Mandira (Rekha).

Zubeidaa sings to her prince, of her desire for a new life.

Shyam Benegal.

The soldiers revolt and massacre the British in a church. Naseeruddin Shah as the rebel sepoy in Junoon.

oracle to participate in the violence. The British had very cleverly created a myth of their own invincibility, so these countermyths were floating about.'

Against the turbulent background of the Mutiny, *Junoon* tells the story of a Pathan's obsession with an adolescent half-English girl. Javed Khan (Kapoor) lives in a small town with his childless wife, Firdaus (Azmi). In the cantonment lives Ruth (Nafeesa Ali) with her Anglo-Indian mother (Jennifer Kapoor) and father, a British civil servant. Javed has often seen Ruth from a distance and dreams of her. She represents the unattainable for him and is the repository of his fantasies. Javed Khan's brother Sarfaraz (Naseeruddin Shah) leads a band of rebels against the British. They massacre the congregation at church on a Sunday morning. Ruth, her mother and her grandmother are the only survivors. A Hindu moneylender shelters the women, but Javed hunts for them and takes them to his home, much against the wishes of his wife. Javed announces that he wishes to take the firangi (white girl) as his second wife, defying the will of his family. To Javed's wife, Ruth and her mother are the political enemies against which the country has arisen. On a personal level, Ruth is also her rival for her husband's love. Ruth's mother opposes the marriage and strikes a bargain with him. Javed can only marry Ruth if the sepoys (Indian soldiers) overthrow the British in Delhi.

Meanwhile, the battle rages, and Sarfaraz returns home with the devastating news that Delhi is lost. Javed is horrified, but bound by his word of honour. Ruth finds herself strangely attracted to this man, but Javed leaves her alone. He joins the battle after his young cousin is killed in action. Sarfaraz dies in a major battle, and the sepoys are routed. The British soldiers resort to brutal action in the towns, and people are forced to flee their homes. Javed follows the exodus, desperately searching for Ruth and her mother. They have stayed in the town waiting for the British forces. In a state of obsession, and unheeding of his wife and aunt's warnings, Javed rides back to the town church. Ruth's mother refuses to allow him to see her girl. Again his sense of honour pulls him back, and he turns away to leave. Ruth runs out of the church and calls his name. Her ambivalent feelings seem now to be resolved in his favour. But for Javed this is a moment of defeat, both personal and political. He rides away with a last look at her. A caption on the frozen image tells us that Javed died in battle soon after. Ruth Labadoor died in England 55 years later, still unwed.

Junoon shows the frenzied violence unleashed by revolt in dialectic opposition to the Pathan's passionate obsession with the British girl. A significant chapter of Indian history is brought to life as a political force that affects the lives of the characters in the story. The relationship between the coloniser and the colonised is complex and contradictory. Ruth's grandmother, a Muslim woman married to a British colonist, is a reminder of the cultural assimilation that was possible in Anglo-Indian families. This is also reflected by Ruth's mother's bilingual facility – she speaks both Urdu and English. The rupture of the

Jennifer Kapoor shields her daughter Ruth (Nafisa Ali) in Junoon.

family (the father's death) and the subsequent displacement of the women underline the threat to the ruling class. What looks like abduction is actually Javed's strategy to protect Ruth and her family in his house. On the other hand, he is not allowed to marry this half-caste girl in the middle of a revolt against the Raj. In the silence of the night, Javed walks through the corridor to the quarters where Ruth and her mother are asleep. He looks at her with naked passion on his face. Ruth's mother shields her daughter from his gaze. From the terrace above, Javed's wife watches her husband slowly slip away from her grasp. Javed's sexual obsession for Ruth works as a metaphor for the fascination of the colonised mind for the coloniser.

Junoon explores the complex attitudes and relationships between people from three different communities: Hindu, Muslim and Christian. It has often been compared to Satyajit Ray's film *Shatranj Ke Khiladi* (*The Chess Players*). Both films deal with chapters of nineteenth-century colonial history and the confrontation between the Muslims and the British. Whereas *Shatranj Ke Khiladi* (based on Premchand's well-known short story) explores the psyche of the aristocrats so immersed in their world, Benegal characteristically throws his characters into the centre of a crisis that is both political and moral. The complex motives of characters and their actions always offer the viewer an added insight into life. Why is Javed's code of honour stronger than his love? What is it that begins to attract Ruth to this stranger? Benegal's psycho-realism is well grounded in a cultural understanding of his characters.

It was claimed that *Junoon* was the first authentic portrayal of the Mutiny. The camera and art department helped to recreate the nineteenth-century milieu – lyrical episodes such as the lazy afternoons in the garden or the decorous, limpid interiors where women chat. It does appear, however, that Benegal exceeded his limits in the battle and action scenes, which look awkward and embarrassing. Such scenes not only escalated the budget, but also look completely out of character for the film-maker. Yet *Junoon* still works forcefully today at the level of characterisation and drama. The film never really comes to fruition as an epic, and the tragic end deprives the audience of a pay-off. Some of the film's limitations have been interpreted as Benegal's submission to the commercial expectations of his Bombay film producer (Kapoor). *Junoon* has also been criticised as a colonial sexual fantasy and because it 'sidesteps any engagement with the issues underpinning what is described as the first Indian war of independence'.[1] But a film-maker is entitled to test and extend his range. Even so, *Junoon* did not fare well with the audience. Perhaps it was a rejection of the mixed-race relationships or the reminder of the failure of the Mutiny that made the audience turn their backs on the film. The huge sum invested by the producer could not be recovered, and the film did only average business.

The unprecedented media attention surrounding *Junoon* raised expectations, but also invited strong criticism. While the press praised the film for its recreation of a century-old milieu, there was also strong criticism: 'Meticulous attention is paid to dialects, period costumes and atmospheric details. The framework is ornate but the canvas is almost empty. The people are shadowy caricatures going through a series of turbulent events.'[2] In defence of his film, Benegal says:

> The kind of storytelling I involve myself in – or the kind of characters that I create – are not the kind that will make a huge box-office success. Film entertainment in India automatically assumes some dimensions – people expect simple characterisations and simple narratives. If you have complexities, they find it difficult to accept, they want a resolution at the end. *Junoon* did not have a neat ending …

Kalyug (*The Machine Age*, 1980)

Benegal continued his search for an epic idiom and form in *Kalyug*, which was also produced by Shashi Kapoor. This time the film was an allegory. The interiorised nature of the narrative works in a closed, claustrophobic environment. Benegal was trying to fashion a contemporary story from the Indian epic the Mahabharata, playing with the idea of archetypes. Discussing archetypes, the film-maker says:

> The Indian mind creates stereotypes from essential archetypes. We see the nature of people in archetypal terms. The Mahabharata is said to contain all of India, characters like Yudhisthira [the honest one], Arjuna [the warrior], Karan [the illegitimate son] – you see them in real life, they are essential archetypes. The parallels are those of essence rather than of specific incidents. The idea is not to take specific characters from the ancient epic, but to present certain archetypes contained in the original story which display universal characteristics.

According to the Mahabharata, there are four epochs through which humanity will pass before apocalypse and the start of a new cycle. The last age is Kalyug (the dark age of sin, violence and corruption), after which the world will cleanse itself. 'Kalyug' also translates as the mechanical or industrial age – an apt reference to contemporary times. Benegal uses the ambiguity of the title in this dark tale of family feuds, betrayal and incest.

Set in 1980s Bombay, *Kalyug* works as a perfect metaphor for contemporary urban experience. The epic resonance provides a structure for a tale of greed and ruthless power-seeking among the elite business families of India. Two branches of a giant industrial family, the Puranchands and the Khubchands, are locked in a feud over a 57-crore deal with the government. Khubchand's sons Dhanraj (Victor Bannerjee) and Sandeepraj (Akash Khurana) compete ruthlessly with their cousins Dharamraj (Raj Babbar), Balraj (Kulbhushan Kharbanda) and Bharat (Anant Nag), the sons of the deceased Puranchand. Drawing from the familiar frame of epic reference, Khubchand (Vinod Doshi), the token patriarch, is crippled (based on the blind Dhritarashtra). The sons are aided by the crafty Karan (Shashi Kapoor), an orphan who has been raised by Bhisham (A. K. Hangal). In the other family, the widowed matriarch, Savitri (Sushma Seth), watches with consternation the growing antagonism between the two houses. In social gatherings, an apparent cordiality must be maintained, as we see at the party and wedding. Under the surface of domestic harmony in Savitri's joint household, there are darker secrets. Dharamraj's wife, Supriya (Rekha), on the surface the dutiful daughter-in-law, is secretly in love with her brother-in-law Bharat (in the epic Mahabharata, Draupadi is married to all five brothers, but she loves only one of them, Arjuna). When Bharat is married to her niece, she tries to object, but the men in the household silence her voice.

The Khubchand brothers try all means possible to foil their cousins' business deals. Forced factory lock-outs by union leaders on the management's payroll, police raids and income-tax inquiries, blackmail – every method is used to sabotage the others' schemes. Meanwhile, the excitable Bharat finds out that his office manager has been siphoning information to Karan. Dhanraj plans to kill Bharat to avenge the accidental death of his brother. Savitri reveals a secret she has guarded for many years,

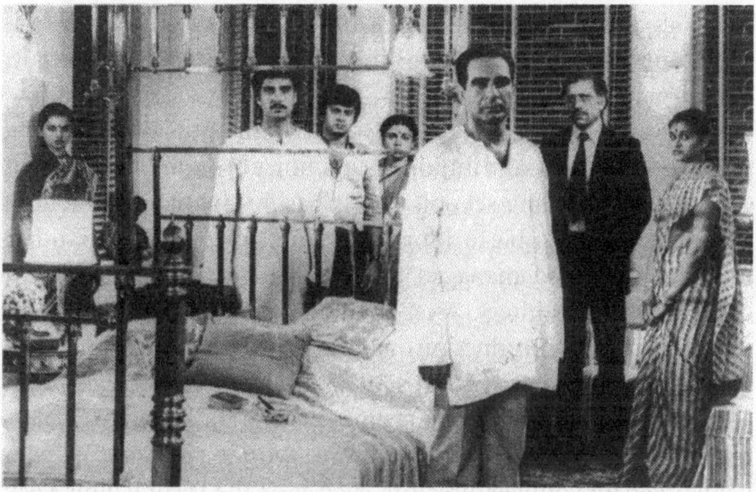

Family feud in Kalyug. *(l to r) Rekha, Raj Babbar, Anant Nag, Reema Lagoo, Kulbhushan Kharbanda, Amrish Puri and Supriya Pathak.*

the truth about her children. Married to an infertile man, she was forced to bear the sons of a swami (god man) who lived with the family. Karan is shattered when she tells him that he is her eldest child, son of the same swami who impregnated her before marriage. He tries to prevent Bharat's killing, but instead Balraj's son is killed.

Violence is unleashed – as we saw in *Nishant* – with cruel inevitability.[3] Karan is killed by Bharat, who later realises he is guilty of fratricide. His snobbery regarding lineage is shattered when he learns that he is not his father's son. The other family comes to ruin when the eldest brother commits suicide. The senior members decide to leave on a pilgrimage. Bharat remains a survivor, his name evoking the nation (Bharatvarsh, or India) and standing for the industrial capitalists who control a major part of the country's wealth. At the end, Supriya takes over Bharat's life as she cradles him in her lap in a protective and erotic gesture. She assumes the role of mother and lover – an ambiguous departure from the epical Draupadi.

Critic Iqbal Masud's review states, 'as epic it is faithful to the origin in all the major characters and incidents to the point of – sometimes strained ingenuity. And yet the majesty, the splendour, the spirit of the original is lost.'[4]

With this film, Benegal explores the world of the Bombay rich, their large mansions and imported cars, horse breeding and children groomed at boarding school. With Shashi Kapoor's production, Benegal was finally able to afford an art director. Prior to this, other unit members had managed this department, with the help of carpenters and painters. After Benegal brought Nitish Roy over from Calcutta, the production qualities improved vastly. Nitish Roy was the best art director in 1970s/1980s Bombay – his protégés Nitin Desai and Sameer Chanda are prominent in art direction today. His daughter Sharmishtha Roy is an award-winning art director who has worked for younger directors, such as on the Yashraj films *Kuch Kuch Hota Hai* (1998), *Mohabbatein* (2000) and *Kabhi Khushi Kabhie Gham*.

When asked about the choice of rival business dynasties as his epic subject, Benegal said, 'I tried placing them in contemporary situations of a family-run business – which is the tradition in India – and the breakdown of family enterprises, the moral dilemmas involved. But I was never satisfied with the way it turned out, there were script problems which did not get untied till the end.' This was perhaps Benegal's first experience of facing compromise and being unable to do solely what he had intended. Characters are hurtling along in the sweeping tide of events, so that the film-maker was unable to explore their inner worlds. Benegal's teaming up with Shashi Kapoor as producer/ hero as well as the inclusion of commercial stars such as Rekha and Raj Babbar was widely perceived as a step towards popular cinema. This marked the end of close collaborations with playwrights (script and dialogue), as some of the old partners began to feel alienated by the larger Kapoor clan and the other popular stars.

Both Shyam Benegal's *Kalyug* and Kumar Shahani's *Tarang* (1984) attempt to reclaim the ancient epic for contemporary interpretation. *Tarang* was a more experimental work deploying the epic themes in a Marxist critique of industrialism. In *Kalyug*, both capital and labour are seen as corrupt. Family structures collapse, and incest and fratricide challenge the moral order. *Kalyug* is a plot-driven, fast-paced narrative which in the event fails to evoke the philosophical aspects of the epic and larger questions about the human predicament. The state-owned television channel Doordarshan commissioned two mega-serials around this time based on two Indian epics, the Mahabharata and the Ramayana. B. R. Chopra's *Mahabharata* (300 episodes) and Ramanand Sagar's *Ramayana* were made in the convention of traditional mythologicals. Both achieved overwhelming family viewership: it was said that the streets would be deserted on Sunday mornings when these series were televised at prime time. The right-wing ideology reflected in these series was much debated and considered to be a crucial factor in the cultural construction of neo-Hinduism in the 1980s.[5]

Both *Kalyug* and *Tarang*, by contrast, represent resistance to reclaiming the grand epic from its purely religious connotations and are instead an attempt to find contemporary meaning in it. Chakravorty considers both films 'as efforts to reclaim for the cinema, India's ancient epic and dramatic traditions, to wrest them away from the domain of the "mythological film," these films are self-consciously "academic."'[6]

Kalyug did not fare well at the box office. Not surprisingly, though, the film has been very influential on younger film-makers. Benegal's depiction of the cityscape, the long sequences offering glimpses of south Bombay as characters drive in their cars, the religious processions on the streets – all work powerfully to site characters in the urban milieu. Karan's social isolation is established in the scenes where he silently contemplates the city from his high-rise apartment. At a climactic moment, Karan is caught in a traffic jam as the street throngs with people joining the Ganapati (Hindu elephant god) immersion ceremony on the beach. The moment of claustrophobia potently conveys the sense of an individual caught in the web of larger forces. Immersions of the clay images of Ganapati and of the mother goddess Durga signify that the gods have turned away from Karan, momentarily recreating a high moment of Greek tragedy. This also intensifies Karan's sense of betrayal by his mother.

More than 20 years after it was made, *Kalyug* is still powerfully relevant. Today, the subtext of corrupt Indian politics is the primary text in several Bombay films exploring the city politics–crime nexus. Contemporary film-maker Ram Gopal Varma, best known for realistic Bombay gangster films *Satya* and *Company* (2002), considers *Kalyug* Benegal's best work. Benegal's stylistic influence is evident in *Satya*, particularly in the scene in which vast multitudes gather on the beach for the Ganapati immersion ceremony and the protagonist Satya stabs the mafia don in the middle of the crowd. Benegal in turn cites Varma's work as the best example of how the realist aesthetic has been coopted into mainstream cinema, which he feels is an inevitable process.

Trikaal (*Past, Present and Future*, 1985)

The opening image of *Trikaal* sets up the contradictions explored in the rest of the film. Bare-bodied Goanese peasants walk through green paddy fields carrying a coffin. For Benegal, this was a haunting image, signifying a symbiosis which he worked into the narrative relationships. *Trikaal* marks a fresh, inspired energy in Benegal's work and a radical departure in cinematic treatment. It was made at a time when he was growing increasingly restless with linear storytelling and absorbed with the possibilities of fragmented narration and magical realism. Benegal says:

> *Trikaal* was inspired by a feeling of the past in the present. Everything that has gone before often has a way of repeating itself in the present. I feel that

> every individual is the sum total of his past. I found this theory fascinating. And once when I was visiting my friend Mario Miranda, at his big old house in Goa, I suddenly found this theory getting fleshed out with ideas.... There is a cultural formation in Goa which is very fascinating and interesting; at the same time, it is not very exposed. Goa has a certain distinctive quality of life with a culture that is 500 years old. While the rest of India was ruled first by the Moghuls, then the British, Goa on the other hand was developing a different cultural configuration under the Portuguese. The place has a different atmosphere, yet it is very much a part of India.

The year is 1985. Ruiz Pereira (Naseeruddin Shah), a man in his forties, returns to the village in Goa where he spent part of his youth, where memories have still not lost their colour. As he passes through the countryside, he remembers the times when he would visit Goa during his holidays from Bombay. Things have changed now. Gulf money has brought prosperity, and ugly concrete houses break the landscape of paddy fields. Ruiz travels to the Soares mansion, empty and lifeless, its gardens in wilderness. As he steps in through the door into the hallway, Ruiz is transported to the past.

It is 1961, a few months before the liberation of Goa from Portuguese rule. At the centre of the Soares household is the grand figure of old Maria Soares (Leela Naidu). Her husband lies dead in the main bedchamber. Black-clad figures whisper around the corpse. Ruiz introduces the main characters in the family. Young Ruiz (Nikhil Bhagat), a handsome young man of 19, hovers near Anna (Sushama Prakash), Soares's granddaughter with whom he is in love. Anna's parents are there, too – Sylvia (Anita Kanwar) and Lucio (K. K. Raina), along with Senhor Renato and Amalia who have come all the way from Portugal to marry their son Erasmo to Anna. Everyone is there except Dona Maria, the old man's widow, who sits silently in her rocking chair in her room absently listening to a Portuguese song on the hand-wound gramophone. When it ends, she gestures to her maid Milagrenia (Neena Gupta) to put

Leela Naidu plays the matriarch Dona Maria in Trikaal.

it on again. Ruiz's voice-over tells us that the latter is an illegitimate child of Soares raised by Maria.

A long sequence explores the funeral ceremony of Ernesto Soares. Dressed in black, the family walk through the village to the cemetery, accompanied by the village band. At the dinner after the funeral, a discussion follows about the blockade in Goa and the imminent arrival of the Indian troops. Dr Pereira (Ruiz's uncle) argues that Goa is a part of India and the Portuguese must leave soon. Dona Maria's inability to accept her husband's death is symbolic of the community's non-acceptance of the imminent death of the Portuguese regime. Benegal talks of his fascination with the subject: 'I did not simply want to tell a story. I wanted to film the life of a people. The dramatic life of a feudal Catholic family in Goa, then a Portuguese colony, was my main concern.'[7]

The title *Trikaal* suggests the film-maker's concern with a moment in historical time that conflates the past, present and future. Benegal further explains, 'the film is about these people, their lives, attitudes, their values, their background, their culture and the kind of events that overtake them. This is a time of upheaval, change, and my story deals with how these changes affect this particular family living in this particular village in Goa.'[8]

As Dona Maria pines for her dead husband, it is a lament for a lost way of aristocratic life in Portuguese Goa. Refusing to face reality, she retreats into a world of séances and hallucinations. Invoking her husband's spirit, she instead recalls the spirit of the dead Rane, who was killed by her ancestors in the freedom struggle against Portuguese rule in the nineteenth century. Yet another séance session recalls the second Rane who was killed by Maria's grandfather, as the spirit forces her to recall the oppression by the Portuguese and the subjugation of several revolutionaries. The spirits return to question her about the misdeeds of her ancestors who had willingly accepted their foreign masters and their religion. Maria has traumatic images of how her family was involved in the worst things that the Portuguese had done – during the Inquisition, the Pinto revolt, the Rane revolt. Goa's historical past is evoked through these surreal sequences. Strongly influenced by Gabriel García Márquez's magical realism, Benegal conjures suppressed history through a stylised departure from realism.

Dona Maria's acute nostalgia is balanced by an uncanny understanding of people around her and the present situation. Although she talks of holding on to old values and customs, Maria is the first to respond to the change around her. Her family members comically imitate the Portuguese while servants and simple village folk surround them. The evocation of the period is meticulously detailed – every object touched and gesture made by the enigmatic matriarch Maria and her faithful maid Milagrenia. The contradictions and metaphors (life/death, feudal/rural, norms/free will) are developed with a self-assured ease and great visual charm. The house itself, with its majestic staircase and long corridors, takes on a life of its own with its mysteriously lit rooms and secrets.

Ruiz serenades Anna from the garden, while Erasmo, the fiancé from Portugal, follows her with doglike devotion. Times are changing. The Indian government is ready to take over the little Portuguese colony, the upper-class members of Goan society want to flee to Portugal, Erasmo's parents who have settled in Portugal worry that they will never be able to get back. Meanwhile, Maria's nephew Leon (Dalip Tahil), a freedom fighter, arrives secretly, asking for protection. Anna, who is in love with Leon, finds out he has been hidden in the cellar. While the household is searching for some missing jewellery, Anna makes love with Leon, and Ruiz with Milagrenia. When the police search the house for Leon, Maria hides him, but asks him to leave soon after. She also agrees to Anna's engagement to Erasmo. The engagement ceremony is presented in unhurried detail – the gathering at church and the party in the house. Music and dance flow, as does the wine and food. At this moment, it is discovered that Anna and Milagrenia are both pregnant. Ruiz confesses he has sinned, but with the maid. In a heightened state of tension, Erasmo's family leaves in a huff, Anna runs off with her lover Leon, and Ruiz is packed off to Bombay. Anna's parents angrily leave Maria's house where they have lived all these years.

Goa is liberated, and a new order replaces the old. The house is now empty except for Maria and Milagrenia, pregnant with Ruiz's child. Maria has strange visions: a Chinese opera dancer holds up flags symbolising the elements. Maria is now able to accept the winds of change and her imminent mortality. With her, the last remnants of a cultural heritage recede to the past. The grand old ruin of the Soares mansion stands as a witness to the past. Ruiz, who may have come in search of his child, continues on his journey.

According to the *Guardian* critic Derek Malcolm, 'The film paints an extraordinary portrait of a little known society totally different from its Anglo-Indian equivalent. *Trikaal* could almost be some Eastern version of Chekhov and is certainly Benegal's most subtle attempt to illuminate the present by looking at the past.'[9]

Eminent critic Chidananda Dasgupta has termed *Trikaal* Benegal's master work:

> *Trikaal* has everything – a grand design, memorable characters, irony, humour, historical and social signification, a complex texture.... It is the first time that a self-enclosed foreign way of life lived by Indians in this country has been portrayed. It has an engaging autonomy and fine integrity of organisation despite its distance from mainstream India or perhaps because of it.[10]

Maithili Rao, who has written extensively on Benegal's films, also talks of the Chinese lacquer box quality of the film.[11] In the introduction, the narrator evokes a fragile, old-world feel when he says that his Ming vase is the Soares mansion.

Benegal's exposure to Goan history took place in the very

Spectacular top-lit ambience in Trikaal. *Raj Zutsi's police officer interrogates Leela Naidu's Dona Maria and Neena Gupta's Milagrenia.*

manor in which *Trikaal* was shot. The house belongs to the artist Mario Miranda, who related many stories about Portuguese Goa to Benegal. Benegal wrote the script himself, but he has acknowledged the contributions of Miranda and Mario Cabral de Sa, who helped with historical facts about Portuguese Goa and the Goan and Portuguese dialogue. The evocative mood of a past world and a mansion with period decor are largely the effect of the art direction and camera. Nitish Roy, who had previously worked on Benegal's *Mandi*, handled production design and art direction. Ashok Mehta's brilliant light and camera scheme re-created a certain kind of top light typical of these mansions in which most of the available light filtered through skylights. The night interiors were shot in candlelight, leading many critics to remark on the Bergmanesque quality of *Trikaal*. The goldwash, toplit quality of the light invests a magical visual charm, evoking the lost past which is recreated

Recreating a lost Portuguese culture in Trikaal. *Dona Maria (Leela Naidu) with her daughter (Anita Kanwar), son-in-law (K. K. Raina) and maid (Neena Gupta).*

through memory. *Trikaal* is an experience intensely lived as long as it lasts. Benegal's masterful stamp is everywhere – an accomplished narrative economy, a haunting visual quality, intricate period detailing, innovative cinematic devices (the séance, the Chinese opera dancer). The departure from realism in effect constructs a wider reality that encompasses life and death, past and present, sexuality and repression, and a philosophy of acceptance.

Benegal's first producers, Blaze Films, were back to support this exploratory, adventurous work. Led by Leela Naidu as Dona Maria, the cast deliver strong performances, in particular that of Neena Gupta as the sensuous servant girl Milagrenia and Anita Kanwar as the hysterical and tearful Sylvia. The story demanded a fresh cast for the roles of younger generation characters. Once again, Benegal's unerring eye introduced new talent in Sushama Prakash and Maksoud Ali (now known as the pop star Lucky Ali). The film also marked the introduction of pop singers Remo Fernandez and Alisha Chinai for the song-and-dance sequences – both of them subsequently went on to become very successful artists. Leela Naidu refers to *Trikaal* as one of the most joyous experiences in her life:

> One thing about Shyam is that he may have his own opinions and appraisals, but, on the sets, he does not function on ego. Neither do I. He's got everything on his fingertips, yet if he feels there is a valid suggestion from somebody he will accept it. He has no big-boss attitude, and he is never an autocrat. Basically a gentleman, he is uniformly polite to everyone on the sets and there is no hierarchical nonsense. Actually, Shyam Benegal is the way a director should be. He's interested in literature, in music of all kinds, in politics, in good food. I hate the word 'intellectual', but I can say that he is an intelligent man, there is an all-roundedness about him, and it is a joy to work with him. I had also worked with him way back in 1966 for three ad films for Finlays Fabrics.[12]

Trikaal goes beyond being a period film according to Benegal:

> It's much larger and goes into planes of human experiences where I find myself groping. There is an extended sense of reality we all live with. Your history is part of you. Different aspects of your past have a role to play in your present and future. That is what I feel about India. People's concerns are constantly limited about the new situation, when in fact the new situation is nothing but an extension of your past and your hopes for the future.

The tourist image of Goa as a fun place for drunken revelry has been used often in mainstream cinema. In fact, musical romances set in Goa – such as Raj Kapoor's *Bobby* (1973) and Ramesh Sippy's *Sagar* (1985) – made full use of its folk music and dance traditions. Reacting to the clichéd representation of Goans in Hindi films as drinking revellers, Benegal remarks:

> Goa is not just people drinking feni and dancing. They do dance like in *Trikaal*. They have a lot of music. Dance is part of their lives. But this does not mean every Goan is a drunken loafer. And that is the normal image of a Goan. Goans have to be accepted by the majority. It is not for the minorities to accept the majorities. The majority has the choice, and they have to exercise it. This is far more profound to me than anything else. Particularly in India today, there are so many people here trying to create their own empires and not looking at the totality of it.[13]

Trikaal addresses the past from the present to look towards the future. The story of Dona Maria deals with history through her guilt about her past. It is also guilt that brings back Ruiz Pereira after 24 years to search for Milagrenia and his child. When he reaches the sleepy village of Loutlim in Goa and finds no one there, he asks how long can one hold on to guilt. When guilt retreats to the past, what remains are bittersweet memories. Benegal deals with multiple levels of thinking in *Trikaal*: 'This is the kind of film which I am most attracted to, I can express myself better as to how I feel and think about things. Also there is total freedom, no set ideologies. So you can really examine all of them.' Benegal's use of the Chinese warrior queen and the

Eastern symbolism of the elements adds a rich philosophical layer to the film. The film-maker explains:

> There were so many aspects of life, living, about right and wrong and oppression and guilt. It just came together. In 1984, when I was writing *Trikaal*, I was in China watching a lot of Chinese opera. I was very involved in it. The warrior queen in the film holds four flags each representing the elements – earth, water, wind and fire. The visual representation in Chinese opera is similar to the Kathakali.

There had been a swamping of the Raj nostalgia in films during this time, including the popular television series *Jewel in the Crown* (1984), Merchant-Ivory's *Heat and Dust* (1982), David Lean's *A Passage to India* (1984) and Richard Attenborough's *Gandhi* (1982). Benegal has consistently insisted that his films *Junoon* and *Trikaal* do not fall into this category and that, in fact, these films, like *The Making of the Mahatma* (1995), approach history from a new perspective. In an interview with writer Anil Dharkar in 1986, Benegal stated:

> I'll tell you what I really enjoyed in *Junoon* or in *Bhumika*. It was placing yourself into a time in our history and getting that history to become tangible; tangible enough to be part of one's environment – including all the trivia of history which are important but which we never get to see in history books … aspects of lives hardly ever referred to in most histories. And when you flush them out, they become an extended reality for yourself. That's why *Junoon* was so satisfying. And *Bhumika* and *Trikaal* … it was not just an evoking of a certain period … but finding your bridges into the present from there.[14]

Derek Malcolm, who has been instrumental in promoting new Indian cinema in the West, observes that it was with *Trikaal* that changing international market conditions were made evident. The enthusiasm for Indian new wave cinema was beginning to wane. A European producer who was considering buying the film dropped it at the last moment. After that, Benegal's films – as well as those of other art-house film-makers from India – have not found many buyers abroad.

The Making of the Mahatma (1995)

Benegal turned to the early life of Mahatma Gandhi for his double-version biopic in English and Hindi. South African writer Fatima Meer's biography *An Apprenticeship of the Mahatma* provided the source material for the script on which the writer collaborated with Benegal and Shama Zaidi. The film focuses on Gandhi's early years in South Africa, where he was closely involved with the Asian migrant community and their civic demands. These early years were crucial in shaping Gandhi's mindset of non-violent resistance to the establishment, a strategy that he used during the nationalist movement in India, where he returned at the age of 40. Benegal met Fatima Meer, member of the African National Congress, soon after Nelson Mandela was freed. Benegal did not know much about Gandhi's early history in South Africa before he came upon Meer's biography, which was banned during the apartheid era in South Africa. Benegal says:

> I read much about Gandhi after this, his *Experiments with Truth* and the journal *Harijan* opened up an area of Gandhi's life which was unknown to me. What made Gandhi the person he became? After he returned to India in 1914 till his assassination, Gandhi had never changed. South Africa was crucial to his development. This is where he developed his political weaponry. Very few Indians know about Gandhi's early years before 1914. This is the chapter before the life depicted in Richard Attenborough's *Gandhi*. I went to Cape Town, Johannesburg, Durban to trace Gandhi's travels in South Africa, where he finally set up Phoenix Farm and Tolstoy Farm.

Produced by the National Film Development Corporation (NFDC) in partnership with the South African Broadcasting

The Making of the Mahatma. *Rajit Kapur as the young Gandhi*

Corporation, this was the first international collaboration for Benegal. With cast and crew from India and South Africa, the project was ambitious in its scope and scale. The linear narrative starts in Rajkot in 1893, where Gandhi sets up his law practice soon after returning from London. He receives a letter from the Indian community in South Africa requesting him to go to that country to represent them in court. Tiring of the corruption in Indian courts, Gandhi (Rajit Kapur) decides to leave for South Africa to settle a legal family dispute between prominent Indian Muslim traders. The scene shifts to Durban, where Gandhi arrives in May 1893. The nineteenth-century colonial period is recreated through meticulous art direction and excellent camerawork by Ashok Mehta. The young Gandhi arrives in European clothes and is received by local Asian leaders, the Muslim trader Dada Abdullah and the Parsi businessman Rustomji Seth. An early indication of his short temper is evidenced in a scene in the Durban court in which the British judge asks him to take off his turban. Gandhi leaves the court in anger, taking exception to what he sees as an insult to his tradition. Soon after, Gandhi travels to

Pretoria on a first-class ticket. During the journey, the conductor hurls him out of the first-class compartment which is reserved for Europeans only. (This first direct encounter with racism is recorded in detail in his autobiography.) An overhead camera looks down at the prone figure of Gandhi, thrown onto the platform with his luggage as the conductor asks him to join the other natives in the luggage van. Bewildered, Gandhi watches as the train leaves the platform. He sits on the platform and begins to read the Qur'an and almost coincidentally reads a passage about the need to fight for those who are ill treated and oppressed.

When Gandhi has to take a coach to Pretoria, he faces discrimination and abuse once again. Coloured people are not allowed to sit inside the horse carriage, so Gandhi is forced to travel on the coachman's seat. He observes the humiliation to which black natives are subjected. Once in Pretoria, he finds no hotel ready to take him in; only a poor widow in need of money agrees to offer him lodgings. In Pretoria, the police beat him when he mistakenly walks on the pavement meant only for Europeans. Despite this, Gandhi refuses to charge the policeman as he was only obeying orders. At this stage, Gandhi acknowledges his unfamiliarity with the Hindu religion and his keenness to study all religions as he attends Sunday mass in a local church. The need to discuss the problems of local Indians appears an urgent issue to him. He discovers that the municipality does not clean the Indian quarters. A succession of incidents in two days underlines the strong racial discrimination in the country.

The New Indian Franchise Bill is passed which restricts the Indians' right to vote. Gandhi warns the Indians that they will subsequently lose their right to trade, property and, finally, the right to live in South Africa as British citizens. Dada Abdullah and other community leaders urge Gandhi to stay on and oppose the Bill. Gandhi applies to register as a barrister. On 27 August 1894, the Natal Indian Congress is formed in answer to Gandhi's call for an organised voice for the community and better understanding for people of colour. Gandhi takes on cases of indentured labour, making a motion to the court to repatriate slaves who worked for their white masters under inhuman conditions.

The scene shifts to 1896, when Gandhi returns to South Africa with his family. The ship, containing several Indian immigrants, is held midstream for several days as the anti-Indian committee refuses to allow it to dock. Gandhi and the community leaders force a landing, soon after which Gandhi is physically assaulted by anti-Indians. Most of these scenes are worked out as docudrama – the plot-related events play out historical detail, rather than offer deeper insights into the main character. The crowded canvas of the public scenes are in stark contrast to the private scenes in Gandhi's home. It is within the domestic sphere that the personal conflicts between Gandhi and his wife and sons are enacted. Gandhi enters into direct conflict with his wife Kasturba (Pallavi Joshi) over his principle of self-help. He threatens to drive her out of the house following an argument over cleaning a guest's chamber pot. This is a serious caste issue for Kasturba, who ultimately relents to her husband's wishes. She also resents the fact that Gandhi refuses to send his young sons to the local schools. The scene in which Gandhi turns the pregnant Kasturba out of his house and she accuses him of being unreasonable is dramatically executed with a spirited performance by Joshi. Despite his quick temper, Gandhi also displays deep compassion, as in the scene in which he delivers Kasturba's child in the middle of the night. The paradoxes in his nature and the danger brought by his strong principles are displayed in tight, well-executed scenes allowing the human dimensions of the man to come forth. (Most of these experiences are recorded in Gandhi's memoirs.) Just before leaving South Africa, Gandhi forces Kasturba to return all the expensive jewellery she has received as gifts. He impresses on his family the importance of renouncing material desire; Kasturba reluctantly agrees. As a more practical person, she worries about the future security of her sons as Gandhi uses all of his savings in service to the community.

Intimate domestic scenes alternate with panoramic historical sweeps, as in the reconstruction of the Boer War in which Gandhi and his compatriots help the British army by tending to wounded soldiers. In return, Gandhi hopes that the government will deal with Indian grievances. Archival material is put to judicious use in the sequence showing Gandhi starting the first Indian newspaper, *The Indian Opinion.* Atrocities against the Indians continue, as labourers are driven out of their homes and cholera breaks out in the coolie colonies. At this point, the writings of social reformer John Ruskin give Gandhi direction. He decides to start a farm and lead a simple life. His eldest son, Hari, is drawn into conflict with his father when he decides to stay on in Bombay and marry the girl chosen for him. Kasturba returns to South Africa with the younger sons. Having studied the scriptures, Gandhi now decides to lead a life of celibacy, 'free of all attachments – wealth, family and wife'. He asks Kasturba to support his ideals. Gandhi's principles regarding equality and justice for the people grow firmer as he sees increasing injustice around him. Supporting the British against Zulu uprisings, he finds soon that it is a racist war. In the Zulu camps, he finds the natives tortured inhumanly. His compassion for the oppressed grows.

In Johannesburg, 1906, Gandhi calls for satyagraha (passive, or non-violent, resistance) against a new Bill that demands compulsory registration of all Indians. Several times Gandhi trusts the British, only to have them betray their promises. Consequently, he alienates people in his community and is assaulted by Muslim leaders. As Gandhi mobilises people in large numbers to demand their civic rights, he finds himself in another domestic crisis. His eldest son, Hari, demands to be sent to England for further education. Accusing his father of egotism, he questions Gandhi's decision to work for the larger community and deny his own family a decent life and education. Gandhi is seen as almost inhuman when he refuses to visit the critically ill Kasturba while being held in jail. The personal goals and ideals he sets for himself are in direct conflict with his families' interests. It is only natural that his son challenges his judgment. When Hari leaves for India, his father is devastated, but does not allow personal problems to distract from the larger cause.

The next sequence spans a series of events, including Gandhi's setting up of Tolstoy Farm and the revival of satyagraha against racial discrimination. This time Kasturba helps in mobilising women to join the protest movement, and they invoke the famous bhajan (devotional song) associated with the Mahatma, 'Raghupati Raghava Raja Ram'. They incite the miners to strike, and the people raise slogans in the name of Gandhi Baba. Quick edits accelerate the film's pace, as mobilisation grows and thousands of people start on the long march across villages and townships. It is at such moments that the film rises to epic heights – extensive long shots and broad pans capture the growing number of people swelling the processions in a sea of humanity. The satyagrahis surge on, marching to the patriotic tune of 'Bande Maataram' on the soundtrack. Gandhi emerges as leader of a people's movement as his followers sing another bhajan, 'Vaishnava Janato' ('God's true saint is he who holds others' woes to be his own'). Large crowd scenes rebuild the people's movement started by the single-handed effort of one true visionary. As violence erupts at the Transvaal border and Gandhi is arrested several times, he reminds people of the message of non-violence. The same political tool was to be employed strategically in the nationalist movement some years later in India. The British finally submit to the Indian demands. They recognise Indian marriages and permit the entry of domicile Indians into the Orange Free State. Gandhi shaves his head and wears cotton clothes as a sign of mourning for those who were killed in defence of satyagraha. The visual transformation of the anglicised lawyer into a saint-like figure is now complete. As Gandhi walks towards the sea, a voice-over informs the audience that he lived in South Africa for 21 years, where he realised his vocation and the truth that humanity is one and should live in peace and equality.

An eventful two decades are captured in the span of this film – the transformation of Gandhi and his crucial role in the struggle for Indians in South Africa. Benegal once again turns to the periphery, a little-known chapter in the life of a public hero, the crucial formulation of thoughts and values which made Gandhi the man he was. These early years encapsulate the conflicts and changes in the young Gandhi, a subject which interests the film-maker more than the public figure after his return to India in 1914. Even though the broad brush strokes of a chronological narrative are always apparent, the talented lead cast, Rajit Kapur and Pallavi Joshi, both rise to the demands of the script, and the camera and art direction teams deliver impressively. Benegal had hoped that *The Making of the Mahatma* would become a true crossover film for an international audience. The fact that it did not indicated once again the failure of the NFDC to promote or market its own productions. Benegal says with some bitterness that there was no atmosphere created for a film of this scale or any adequate publicity built up for it. The film was televised in both language versions, English and Hindi. In South Africa, there was an enthusiastic response both to the making and the reception of the film. Nelson Mandela, a long-standing admirer of Gandhi, saw the film and went on national television to promote it.

6

Subaltern voices

One of Benegal's principal concerns has been the problem of caste and community. A recurrent theme, right from his first film, *Ankur*, has been the conflict between the peasant and the feudal lord. An equally powerful and tenacious concern has been the paradox of development, the dialectics of modernisation. At various phases in his career, he has returned to the life of the oppressed subaltern and explored various structures of power and powerlessness.

Susman (*The Essence*, 1986)

A film financed by the Association of Co-operatives and Apex Societies of Handloom (ACASH), *Susman* is the story of Ramalu, a weaver from the village of Pochampally in Andhra Pradesh, famous for its handwoven sarees. A docudrama style recreates the hardships of the threatened handloom weavers, who have neither control over their products nor any recognition of their craft. Benegal focuses on the predicament of the ten million handloom weavers for whom the cooperative movement has come to mean nothing. Middlemen buy products from the village weavers and sell them at high prices to city clients.

The film starts with stunning images of handwoven sarees being collected for an exhibition in the city. Mandira Rai (Neena Gupta), a city-based designer, commissions sarees from village weavers through her agent, the master weaver Narasimha (Kulbhushan Kharbanda). Mandira wants the best of ikkat weave, a tie-dye fabric for which Pochampally is famous, for a forthcoming exhibition in Paris. Narasimha takes her to the village, where she meets the widely respected weaver Ramalu. The village of Pochampally is introduced through a religious procession in which weavers take their spindles to the temple to be blessed. Local village women carry earthen pots on their heads and sing to the deity, directly evoking the opening sequence of *Ankur*.

The villagers have set up their own cooperative to protect their interests, but its existence is threatened by corrupt systems and dishonest officials. The president of the society looks on askance while his subordinates sell raw material illegally to the agents. Once again, Benegal reveals an economy in crisis because of the short-sighted and uncommitted nature of state support. The power looms in the cities draw the poor weavers away, as handloom weaving fast becomes a dying craft. This development is placed in the larger context of the government marketing India abroad. In the 1970s and 1980s, there were numerous international festivals and exhibitions held in the West celebrating Indian art and craft, music and dance.

The protagonist Ramalu (Om Puri) is a poor but much respected weaver who lives with his wife, Gouramma (Shabana Azmi), and daughter Chinna (Pallavi Joshi). He also supports his no-good brother and sister-in-law. Domestic wrangles are rife in the household. There is not enough money for basic needs, and frustration often turns to anger. Ramalu's brother physically abuses his wife, while Gouramma desperately seeks the finances to have her daughter married. Ramalu feels trapped by his situation, but stoically performs his duties. The relationship between the weaver and his loom is lyrically, almost mystically, elevated by the medieval saint Kabir's song on the soundtrack. Weaving is a metaphor for life itself: 'I pray as I weave the cloth of life,' Kabir writes; the camera pans over loom and thread as the weaver moves in perfect rhythm.

The state-supported culture brokers come from the city to patronise the weavers. Mandira, the city designer, orders an exclusive design for a saree; the weaver's wife secretly puts aside some silk yarn to weave a similar saree for her daughter's wedding. Gouramma argues it is their labour, their loom and their time; Ramalu says that it is theft. When Mandira and Narasimha discover the clandestinely woven saree, they humiliate the weaver. The self-respecting Ramalu rejects the loom and withdraws from his family. Gouramma spins tirelessly with other helpers to complete the order, as she has already received a prepayment for it. In a memorable scene, Gouramma comes up and sits quietly beside her husband. She begs forgiveness and asks him to return to the loom. Ramalu continues to drink in silence. Gouramma is driven to a rage, and, in a state of drunkenness, Ramalu sets fire to his loom. His wife puts out the fire, and both break down in utter hopelessness. There are strong performances here from both actors. Puri's Ramalu stands tall as the reticent, honest and dignified weaver.

Nearly all the weavers are desperate to leave their craft and the dismal conditions of the handloom work. Some educate their sons; others, like Ramalu's brother, turn into marketing agents. Ramalu's daughter is married to Nageswar, a villager who has migrated to the industrial town of Bhiwandi. He contracts labour for the power looms, and, after years of exploitation by traders and middlemen, the poor weavers are lured to the city. Benegal offers a glimpse of the mill workers and the union agitations that led to the closure of several big mills in the 1980s. The newly married village girl finds herself in urban slums where the mill workers live in appalling conditions. Feeling completely alienated, she hastily returns to her village.

The handloom crisis is referred to in an angry exchange between Mandira and her boyfriend, Seth. It is Seth who articulates Benegal's critique of artificial state support when he says that government loans and exhibitions cannot support a dying cottage industry. Mandira retorts. 'It is a living art, and you have to be sensitive to it.' She glorifies repeatedly the handmade products, yet she does nothing to improve the living conditions of the poor weavers.

Meanwhile, Ramalu returns to his loom, and the exhibition

orders are completed. He is voted president of the cooperative as it starts afresh with the weavers in control of resources and products. Finally, the weaver is invited to Paris for the garment exhibition. A French journalist asks the craftsman if he will continue with his art in the face of rapid industrialisation. The weaver replies that there is nothing more satisfying than working with one's hands. Mandira carries on, 'We must create a constant and growing market for craftsmen who work with their hands.' Ironically, it is her vision that converts a living art into exhibition and museum pieces.

Lately, multiple reports of suicides in Pochampally village throw sharp light onto the economic depression suffered by the weavers that was focused on so many years ago in *Susman*. As one of the society workers suggests in the film, this dying art could only be revived if the weavers had control over resources and marketing of their goods. The film does not, however, adequately suggest the potential of the cooperative movement, apart from a few speeches. *Susman* remains an important though structurally flawed film, examining the position of the craftsman in an industrial society. Documentary film-maker Bikram Singh writes about the docudrama form:

> An inherent and to some extent insurmountable problem with docudrama is that it is documentary disguised as dramatic fiction and so the inner pressure to 'present' the matter and deliver the message tends to show. Individual lives and problems are taken up bravely, but you can see the docudrama's real concern is the totality and the collective.[1]

With *Susman*, Benegal was in his element, exploring a microcosmic world responding and succumbing to larger forces of economic change. The docudrama breathes reality. Among the excellent cast, Om Puri and Shabana Azmi demonstrate that they are the best method actors of their time. Neena Gupta is very credible as Mandira, the urban sophisticate who in her own way exploits the weavers. The enduring image of the weaver at his loom and the lingering shots as he rhythmically weaves his cloth move away from the grim realism of the film. As the world goes by, Ramalu sits at his loom; Pandit Jasraj sings the medieval saint Kabir's song 'I am a weaver, I repeat your name, Oh God'. The vulnerability of the craftsman and his immediate history is transcended by the song, a reminder of the timeless relationship of the artist with his tools and a tragic indicator of the craftsman's plight when faced with the machine.

The actor Om Puri was required to learn the art of weaving on the handloom. He recalls, 'I spent several days learning to work on the loom. Eventually I wove 40 metres of cloth, made scarves for Shyam and Govind, Shabana and Nira. This was not just a role, it was a material reality I had to get close to.'[2] One review of *Susman* concludes, 'The film conveys, in its striking, sombre way, the precarious reality of an Indian artisan's life and craft. And marks a return to form of one of the most accomplished directors of Indian cinema.'[3] The film was seen by the weavers' community through the cooperative association that produced it, but it was a flop in the cities. Film historian and ex-director of the National Film Archives P. K. Nair makes a critical observation that the film-maker was losing touch with his middle-class audience:

> Shyam was making films very quickly, with no time to check the markets or distribution networks for his films. His earlier producers, Blaze, already had an established network. But with the cooperative or ministry films, there was no distribution system. The ministry's budget would be spent off on production and no initiative taken about marketing. The films did badly because of no marketing support. Shyam's films have a much larger audience than Adoor Gopalakrishnan, whose regional films have an audience only in Kerala. Yet Adoor takes two or three years between each film and ensures every new work reaches his audience and recovers costs from screenings. Adoor also has a say in the distribution of his films.

Nair maintains that it is the film-maker's responsibility to ensure that a film is shown and that it is used as an agent for debate and change.[4] Benegal in turn blames bureaucracy and red tape for the distribution failure of *Susman*. In marked contrast, *Manthan*, produced by another cooperative, made inroads into the remotest corners of India because of the initiative taken by the director of the milk cooperative concerned.[5]

Aarohan (*The Ascent*, 1982)

In the early 1970s, a small report about a Bengali sharecropper, Indra Lohar, was published in the leftist journal *Frontier*. The economist Ashok Mitra, a minister in the West Bengal cabinet, had written the report. It interested Benegal, who was always in search of human stories and at this point was keen to return to rural subjects after his big films *Junoon* and *Kalyug*. The peasant's story represented the same experience of oppression, struggle and tragic ends seen in his earlier films *Ankur*, *Nishant* and *Manthan*. In 1980, the West Bengal government agreed to fund the project with a sum of 50 lakh rupees ($1000,000). The universality of Indra Lohar's story appealed to the State Minister of Information, Buddhadev Bhattacharya (now the Chief Minister of West Bengal).

Benegal decided to make a film on the effects and impact of land reform. After independence, the Zamindari Abolishment Bill was passed. Through Operation Barga, landless farmers in Bengal were given ownership of land, or bargas. *Aarohan* offers a critical overview of state politics and documents the turbulent era from 1967 and the United Front until the Left Front came to power in 1977. This proved a watershed for the deprived millions in rural Bengal. After two spells of presidential rule, followed by a short-lived coalition, a Congress ministry finally brought the Left Front back to power. The resultant effect of these political changes forms the broad canvas for *Aarohan*.

Benegal had previously handled the subject of peasant revolt in his native state of Andhra Pradesh in *Ankur* and *Nishant*. Now he faced the challenge of traversing unknown terrain. Field trips to the countryside of the Birbhum district included long discussions with sharecroppers, political leaders and panchayat members. In addition to long discussions with Mitra, he also spoke at great length to Debabrata Bandopadhyay, the land reform commissioner in West Bengal. Both Mitra and Bandopadhyay from the National Labour Institute are credited with the story of *Aarohan.*

With this film, Benegal returns to his root concerns, exploring a changing map of human destinies as agrarian reform takes place. Structurally, *Aarohan* demonstrated a new approach by the film-maker, now more interested in establishing a relationship between himself and the audience. This purpose is stated at the outset of the film. Both the audience and the director should interact with each other. The film is set in Giripur village in the district of Birbhum. Sitting in the open fields, actor Om Puri talks to camera about the Barga movement and its history. Operation Barga was a state initiative by which the landlord had to distribute land to peasants as their rightful share. In 1955, when the initiative was launched, the peasant was to own 60 per cent of the land; in 1972, this share was increased to 75 per cent and made hereditary. What appears an ideal policy for equitable land distribution turned out to be far more difficult to implement in the face of outmoded legal systems, political crises and changing governments. The narrator reminds the audience that the history of the peasant's struggle dates back to the nineteenth century. In 1967, the Bengal peasants rose in armed conflict against their oppressors – this was the Naxalite movement. The agitation rapidly spread to the cities, where urban youth took to violent protest against poor education and unemployment.[6] The actor (Puri) then introduces the rest of the cast and his own persona as Hari Mondal, the sharecropper whose struggle for his land was documented as a case study and whose tragic life inspired the film. The film displays its own artifice (Brechtian style), with the actor addressing the viewer directly before he enters his role. The

Om Puri as Hari Mondal in Aarohan, *a film about peasant revolt in Bengal.*

brief introduction to the unit creates another dimension to the film-within-film device. Benegal was to return to this structure much later in *Samar*. Meanwhile, Mrinal Sen had already made powerful use of this cinematic structure in *Akaler Sandhaney* (1980).

The first section of the narrative set in 1967 establishes the context of armed peasant conflict in the Naxalite movement. In the dead of night, a group of armed peasants pull a landlord out of his house and kill him. The charges against him are peasant oppression and murder. A political procession through the village signals the victory of the First United Front in Bengal. The schoolteacher, a party worker, asks the peasants to register their land, reminding them of legislation and rights. Later, he tells the farmers to ask for receipts for the grain with which they repay past loans to the landlord.

The political changes have not yet touched Hari's life. When he approaches the landlord to ask for a loan to pay for his sister's dowry, the latter agrees on condition that Hari will not register his barga. He also demands all the crops from the land to repay

Hari's past loans. Hari and his brother Bolai soon find that they have been reduced to labourers on their own land. Hari's mud hut (a superbly realistic set by art director Bansi Chandragupta) houses Hari's wife, two boys and his brother Bolai. A distant aunt and her daughter Panchi live in the smaller adjacent hut as Hari's dependants. Panchi is secretly in love with Bolai and hopes to marry him in future. The bitter relationship between Hari's wife and the destitute aunt recalls Sarbojaya and Indir Thakuran in a very similar situation in Satyajit Ray's *Pather Panchali*.

The hot-headed Bolai is driven off his land. He leaves the village and joins the dockland workers. Soon driven out of that work, he joins a group of antisocial miscreants in the city. The plot branches out to tell the story of the displaced peasants who find no place in the urban world. During presidential rule, Bolai joins a band of notorious party workers and is arrested for murder. Hari's aunt Kalidasi leaves for the big city to work as domestic help with a family. She must earn money so that her daughter can be married. Soon Kalidasi's daughter Panchi is also lured to Calcutta by a pimp and is forced to live as the mistress of a middle-aged businessman.

It is 1969, and another victory procession marks the second United Front government. Hari loses ownership of his land. To preserve his rights as a sharecropper Hari gets embroiled in a legal battle that will last for years. A lawyer from the local town – a Marxist comrade – advises him to hold on to his grain. A land reform officer makes a spot enquiry and finds that Hari has not registered his land during the settlement operation.

Abrupt scenes and a deliberate distancing from characters give the impression of a semi-documentary. It is 1972, and another political procession hails the Congress (R) government to power. New laws lead to an injunction on Hari's land, and the landlord's henchmen assault him, then set his house on fire. Hari is persuaded by the local party leaders to file a case against his landlord. The illiterate peasant thus becomes caught in a chain of events beyond his comprehension and control. Hari is hurtled from district courts to High Court. Hari's total alienation and incomprehension is underlined by the irrelevance of English-language court sessions. In a district court scene, after the judgment is read out in English, the baffled farmer asks in confusion, 'What about my land?' In that one moving moment, the subaltern voice resounds in the labyrinthine corridors of justice. In another scene in the village, the postman reads out a court summons in English to Hari's uncomprehending wife, Batashi.

The plot hurtles towards relentless tragedy. In the city, Panchi loses her mind after being forced to abort her child. Her mother finds her wandering in the city streets chased by pavement children. Kalidasi dies of shock, and Panchi disappears in the urban multitude. A rapid series of events is followed by that wonderfully lyrical sequence in which Hari walks back home through the fields against a stormy sky. Peasants drive their cattle home as Hari limps over the land which has been snatched from him. The giant banyan tree and darkened horizons appear to be elemental forces against which man must continually struggle. The folk ballad of 'Hari Mandal', sung by Purnadas Baul, plays on the soundtrack. Briefly, Hari joins the armed peasants, but he withdraws swiftly after witnessing the meaningless death of the villagers when they are shot down in a police confrontation.

In 1977, the Left Front government comes to power. Hari is asked to file his nomination for the panchayat elections. When floods sweep the village, he takes on a leader's role. At a panchayat meeting, Hari calls for the farmers to unite and work on their own, instead of waiting for government support. A call for organised mobilisation has rung through many films – *Manthan*, *Susman*, and *Antarnaad*. Finally, after 12 years of struggle, Hari gets back his land. He leaves for Calcutta again to search for his brother, aunt and cousin. A memorable sequence follows in which Hari is seen limping across the street, dwarfed by the giant Howrah Bridge and magnificent colonial buildings.

The camera pans over the city, before zooming in on the character walking with the multitudes. Almost lost in the crowd and traffic, the man still retains his human dignity. Over a black screen, the titles inform us that Hari failed to find his family members, who were tragically lost in the city. Years of bitter suffering took their toll, and Hari died in May 1980.

The script sacrifices the subtleties of characterisation for the portrayal of an historical class struggle. The need to tell a political story in effect pushes the human stories to the background. A busy script is unable to contain the multiple narratives it churns out. Panchi and Kalidasi recede from the viewer, as well as from the plot. Bolai serves as an agent to tell the story of city violence. Hari is Everyman, embroiled in the legal system – the film-maker does not attempt to get closer to him. Characters serve symbolic purposes, some of the complex weave of former scripts with earlier writer-collaborators such as Karnad and Dubey is missing. (Although Karnad is credited with the additional story, the script does not register his contribution, if any.)

Govind Nihalani's camera is the real hero of the film. What remains with the viewer are the visually rich images of the tranquil village and pond, the processions passing by the baffled Hari, the dark clouds looming over peasants as they return from work, the wide pans across the city of Calcutta and the narrow city streets with their political hoardings and graffiti. Only an actor as intensely involved as Om Puri could draw on the flawed script to create a memorable persona. An outstanding method actor, he spent days tanning himself under the hot sun and training to walk as with a broken leg.

As with his earlier films, Benegal flavours the dialogue with regional dialect. The language relies heavily on Bengali words; the rural characters engage in very culture-specific activities. Benegal once more restores this regional space to Hindi films. Despite its obvious flaws, *Aarohan* remains a valuable documentation of the history of political upheaval and change during 12 crucial years in Bengal. Ironically, the film, which was commissioned by the West Bengal government, was not even given a cinematic run. It remains one of the best films produced by the communist government to portray their programmes. *Aarohan* strongly deserves to be rediscovered and seen, particularly by those interested in the political history of the state. As Benegal explains:

> The Bengal Government operated the barga system which has contributed largely to the Left being in power for six terms. The reforms settled the countryside in some equitable manner. Apart from Kerala and Karnataka, such sweeping land reforms have not taken place in most parts of the country – certainly not in Northern India. *Aarohan* is an earnest analysis of the decade of the 1970s which left in its wake not only corpses, but also a collapse of values.

Antarnaad (*Inner Voice*, 1991)

Intrigued by the rapidly spreading Swadhyaya movement, Benegal, along with his writer Shama Zaidi, spent many months around the villages on the Gujarat coastline.

Benegal directs actors and local villagers in Antarnaad.

Swadhyaya is study of the self. In the late 1950s, a man of faith, Pandit Pandurang Shastri Athavale, sought to use Bhakti (devotion) as an active principle in the transformation of both individual and society. Along with friends, Shastri visited several villages while on a Bhaktipheri (devotional visit), raising the self-confidence of low-caste villagers – in particular, the fisherfolk. In due time, these villages showed profound social and economic changes. The villagers created a working concept of impersonal wealth. By the 1990s, this work had grown to become a silent revolution embracing 15,000 villages and five million people who are part of the Swadhyaya family. Always motivated by peoples' movements, Benegal found this a subject worth investigating; *Antarnaad* is made on the basis of what he saw, heard and researched.

The subject matter immediately lends itself to docudrama treatment. With a core group of repertory actors, Benegal involved real people, those who were in reality converted to Swadhyaya. This movement was neither religious nor sectarian. Rather, true to the medieval Bhakti tradition, it was a popular

Villagers join the Bhaktipheri (devotional procession) led by activists (Kulbhushan Kharbanda and K. K. Raina).

humanitarian movement in which people transformed their personal and social lives by aspiring to higher ideals. The film's plot involves the dedicated work of the principal agents, the lawyer Arvind and his wife Ragini, the neo-convert Parvin and the young idealist Ajit. The process involves social uplift and development through which the villagers are able to improve their lives. The action takes place over a year in two villages, Neemda and Kanakvada.

Arvind (Kulbhushan Kharbanda) makes regular visits to neighbouring villages with his friends. The childless Ragini (Shabana Azmi) is regularly harassed by her mother-in-law. She spends a lot of time with women's groups in the village. Arvind tells her of his plans to visit the notorious village of Neemda, which is ruled by bandits. The scene shifts to Neemda to offer us a glimpse of this world. Notorious bandits Ranchod and Tilu loot a family wedding. When Tilu is killed, his widow, Hansa, vows to make her sons avenge their father's death. Arvind and his friends are robbed and driven out of Neemda by the suspicious bandits.

Shyam Benegal on location with the fisherfolk in coastal Gujarat for Antarnaad.

In Kanakvada village, the process of conversion to Swadhyaya has already begun among the fisherfolk. The two principal obstacles are the wealthy smuggler and fish merchant, Arjun (Om Puri in a brilliant performance), and his drunken stooge, Shiva (Kishore Kadam). Amid a congregation of Swadhyayis, Arvind urges the people to become self-reliant. The villagers agree to save a part of their weekly earnings to buy a communal boat, just as many other villages have taken done. The low-caste Shiva is persuaded to give up alcohol.

Arjun tries to win the volunteers over by bribing them. He is unrepentant about his smuggling activity – this has been part of the family business since the days of the Portuguese, he argues. He has a change of heart when the fisherfolk insist that he stand for the panchayat election as their leader.

The volunteers return to Neemda, this time accompanied by Ragini. Ragini befriends the women and children in the village. After facing initial resistance, they are able to spread the word of Swadhyaya among the villagers. The women find a voice and collectively resist the violent lives of the bandits. The widow

Shabana Azmi and Joan David in Antarnaad.

Hansa, too, conquers her thirst for revenge. Ragini and Arvind may act as agents of change, but their middle-class world is shrouded in unhappiness. Ragini has been stigmatised because of her sterility; she has still to find her sense of self-worth.

The film ends in Aurangabad where, on Human Dignity Day (19 October 1991), five million Swadhyayis gather to celebrate their faith. Ragini speaks of how she overcame her self-conflict and Arjun, the newest convert, asks, 'If God is with me, then why the question of high and low caste or of feeling inferior?'

Antarnaad ends on a note of celebration, as the involvement of the people in the movement reaches a crescendo. The notion of a popular movement leading to mobilisation towards economic and social improvement is a subject very close to the film-maker's heart. Yet the film suffers from a sense of dry documentation, as the characters are not allowed the space to develop. Like *Aarohan*, the film borders too close to the chronicling of an historical movement. The script is too prosaic, the tone too polemical, to warrant any aesthetic structure. The characters remain largely one-dimensional, and there is little conflict which is cinematically realised. Talented actors such as Azmi and Kharbanda are unable to enliven an unimaginative script. On the plus side, however, Om Puri is once again able to explore shades of grey, this time in his characterisation of Arjun. And there are visually stunning sequences such as the colourful fishing boats on the sea and the launching of the communal boat *Matsagandha*. The wide pans around the Neemda village establish a sound sense of the geographical locale, but the characters serve simply to illustrate the purpose of the film. The energy and frisson of *Manthan* or even *Susman* are sadly missing in a script which seems written in haste.

If the intent was to inform the audience about this silent revolution, *Aarohan* serves its purpose. But it fails to touch the heart or offer a character who stays with the audience long after the lights come on. Benegal's strongest critics accuse him of being too productive (on average, a film a year), resulting in hasty scripts and polemics. Commissioned films also have an uncomfortable manner of preaching. Funded by the fishing community, the film does propagate humanitarian values, but unfortunately the Benegal signature is sadly missing.

Samar (*Conflict*, 1998)

With *Samar*, Benegal returns to his prime concern of caste conflict. Using the film-within-film structure, Benegal is able to offer an incisive look into caste prejudices, not only among the rural populace, but also among educated middle-class city dwellers. Even after 50 years of independence in India, the reality of caste politics in rural India is still a theme which Benegal chooses to examine. The award-winning *Samar* questions the notion of progress and exposes deep-seated prejudices about caste and class that Indians still harbour.

Financed by the Ministry of Social Justice and Empowerment, *Samar* is based on a true incident drawn from a series of case studies on the caste system in rural Madhya Pradesh, recorded by an IAS officer, Harsh Mandal. It is based

Raghuvir Yadav and Seema Biswas play untouchable peasants in Samar.

on the experiences of a Dalit peasant, Nathu Ahirwar, who suffered gross injustice and indignity at the hands of the village head. The story is of an upper-caste village headman of Kull village, in Bundelkhand, who humiliated the Dalit (low-caste) community in 1991. The installation of a hand pump in the Dalit settlement instead of in his own fields so enrages the headman that he lays off the low-caste peasants from his fields and sets fire to their homes. The peasants approach a sympathetic state official and police officer who succeed in restoring the Dalits' lost dignity.

Benegal rejects the linear narrative and employs the cinematic device of film-within-film. *Samar* thus marks a return to formative aesthetics as well. Seven years later, a film unit from Bombay arrives to film the incident. The Dalit villagers are not allowed to access drinking water from the village well. State officials who arrive to build a hand pump face the wrath of the landlord. Nathu's wife suffers from leprosy, but is afraid to treat herself, fearing further ostracism. Benegal's concern for women as doubly oppressed through class and gender receives a rather pragmatic treatment in this subplot. City-bred actors who enact the parts of the villagers – many of whom enter the frame during the shoot – are forced to confront their own caste prejudices. The cast as well as the audience is shaken out of smug complacency that the issue of caste is a rural problem. Trouble brews in the film unit, as the Dalit actor playing the low-caste Nathu (Kishore Kadam) is humiliated by the upper-caste actor who plays the landlord. Under the garb of liberal education and city sophistication, some of the crew harbour deep-seated animosity towards the Dalits. The conflict in the film crew offers a double-edged tool for the film-maker to explore deeply flawed attitudes in social behaviour. The poor Dalit villager whose life story is being told is in effect exploited by the unit – the director and actors intrude upon his privacy and take from his life what they want for the film. The re-enactment of the humiliation scene for the film stirs up violent sentiments between the actors. Kishore refuses to enact a scene in which the landlord urinates on his head. The real Nathu (Raghuvir Yadav) tells him, 'When I had the real thing on my head, why should you have a problem just acting it out?'

Samar relates two stories and explores the interaction between the villagers and the film unit. The film is sophisticated in its self-reflexivity. Benegal's view is tongue-in-cheek as he critiques the film-making process with ironic humour. One of the unit members says, 'Nobody will see the film anyway, except for some highbrow critics. It will win a few prizes at film festivals abroad. That's all.' The ethical questions raised by the issue of art exploiting reality are thrown up as debate in the fabric of the film itself. In her review in the *Times of India*, the critic Meenakshi Shedde writes, 'Equally, he lays bare the oppressive, vice-like connection between the caste system and patriarchy. As a Dalit woman tells Rajeshwari Sachdev (the actress playing Nathu's wife) ... caste is a male concern.' This statement is reinforced by the fact that Rajeshwari is the only unit member who overtly supports the Dalit actor, Kishore Kadam.[7]

Samar was shot in the very village where this incident took place. Benegal says:

> The Constitution accepts every human being as equal, and for the past 50 years attempts have been made to eradicate the caste system, but even today rural India has a certain attitude towards Dalits. In fact, this prejudice exists in a subtle form even in urban areas. But the real issue is not one of one caste oppressing another – it is about attitudes which resist change. The urban actors come with their own baggage of beliefs. This creates its own contradictions and gives you different kinds of insight into the nature of the problem.

The dynamics of working in the field are twice layered with the film-within-film technique. The film-maker underlines the fact that this is an oppression story, but one told in an engaging and entertaining manner:

> Because the kind of films people are watching has changed. It has become very different from what it used to be. Entertainment is the big thing today, and few people are ready to risk going beyond the conventional definitions of entertainment.

For Benegal the crusader, as he has said repeatedly, it is most important to carry on making films which reflect his sensibility. A review in *Outlook* says:

> It's easy to write off his kind of films in these profit-driven times, but the very fact that Benegal, as active as he has ever been in his career continues to project his humanist, socially informed vision on the big screen – and on his own terms at that – is cause enough for unstinted applause.[8]

Heavy polemics stall the scene in which the civil servant admits that he is a Dalit and sermonises to his son over dinner on self-esteem. It is a limiting but unavoidable device and an understandable one when you consider that the film was sponsored by the state as an instrument for social change. Yet in the face of rapidly changing ideas about audience entertainment in the Bombay film industry, it is remarkable that a film such as *Samar* got to be made as late as 1997. It went on to win the National Award for best film – a first for Benegal, whose films had won awards in different departments (direction, acting, photography, etc.), but not the Golden Lotus. The jury lauded the work 'for the innovative and human manner in which the director structures and presents a continuing social evil'. Ashok Mishra's richly layered script also fetched him a National Award.

Benegal's effort at generating debate about the caste issue remained unsuccessful as the film failed to receive distribution. A Delhi-based company picked it up after the National Awards, but subsequently let it lie unwatched in its cans. The usually polite and patient Benegal did show his impatience at this, particularly as there were other distributors in Bombay ready to market the film.

On average, Benegal has managed to produce a film every year since 1974 (barring the years spent on the television epic *Bharat Ek Khoj*). Some critics have opined that back-to-back films or the treadmill approach have proved counterproductive to his career. According to them, a film-maker needs time out to return with more energy and imagination. Also, when films are commissioned from state organisations, the message becomes more crucial than the treatment. Such films have their good moments, but lack the organic nature of a *Manthan* or *Ankur*. The audience missed the remarkable *mise-en-scène* and sensitive characterisations that marked Benegal's older work. By this time, a new crop of talented actors had taken centre stage – Rajit Kapur, Kishore Kadam, Rajeshwari Sachdev – but the screenplay works more as a series of brief sketches than as a unified form.

Hari Bhari (*Fertile*, 2000)

Benegal made an ambitious move with *Zubeidaa*, his most expensive production to date. *Zubeidaa* boasted a big star cast and was mounted on a large scale with production values that were on a par with contemporary Bollywood products. Almost at the same time, the film-maker made a smaller film in his trademark style, continuing his commitment to issue-based film-making. *Hari Bhari* is a completely different film to *Zubeidaa*: it promotes a cause. It's about women's reproductive rights and gender equality, with a fairly large canvas and multilayered issues. *Hari Bhari* was shot in less than a month in Ramoji Rao Film City in Hyderabad.

As with *Mandi* and *Samar*, Benegal brought together an amazing ensemble cast. But this was no conventional love story. Benegal states:

> The movie basically deals with human rights. But within human rights, women's rights are an important feature. In this film I deal with women's reproductive rights. If a woman has to give birth to a child and nurture

> it, it should be the right of that woman to decide how many children she should have. That right has never been recognised and often been totally denied to a woman.

Hari Bhari is the story of five women from three generations. There are vignettes of specific experiences of each one of these five women.

The Ministry of Family Welfare commissioned Benegal to make *Hari Bhari* when it was felt that the lack of success in family planning programmes was due to the lack of recognition of women's reproductive rights. Consciousness raising would take care of the problem and, in keeping with human rights, no coercion would be needed. Previously in India, there had only been coercive methods of family planning. Yet the message was not meant to be heavily didactic – Benegal was to present interesting stories in an entertaining format that the paying public would like to see.

Once again, Benegal returns to his concern for gender empowerment and a search for women's histories. Set in a village in the northern state of Uttar Pradesh, *Hari Bhari* is the story of five women from three generations of a rural Muslim family. The script is drawn from case histories. The film's subject is reproductive rights for women in India, a matter of relentless debate even in the twenty-first century as Indian women still enjoy little power over their bodies or their reproductive systems. Hasina (Surekha Sikri) is the matriarch with one married daughter, Ghazala (Shabana Azmi) and two daughters-in-law, Najma (Alka Srivastava) and Afsana (Nandita Das), Ghazala's teenage daughter, Salma, is played by Rajeshwari Sachdev. Ghazala is a victim of marital abuse until she leaves her husband's home and comes to live with her mother.

The film opens with Ghazala's story. Ghazala is walking to her mother's home along a crowded street escorted by her younger brother-in-law. Her unexpected entry into the crowded household is greeted with little surprise apparently

A film based on five women's stories in a Muslim family. Hari Bhari *is about reproductive rights for women and is based on case histories.*

her abusive husband, who blames her for not producing a male child, has turned her out of her marital home often in the past. Her brother and mother offer her emotional support, and she settles into the household much to the reluctance of a younger sister-in-law, Afsana. Ghazala's story unfolds in flashback, a woeful tale of domestic abuse and humiliation. Ghazala's teenage daughter Salma watches in horror as her father summons her mother to the bedroom. He accuses her of being cold and aloof, as she refuses to sleep with him. For Muneer (Shrivallabh Vyas), producing a male heir for his family is an urgent need, and he is impatient with his wife's poor health. Ghazala has been visiting the village clinic and has learnt that infertility could well be her husband's problem and not hers. Enraged at this suggestion, Muneer abuses his wife and turns her out of the house. He demands more money and objects such as a colour television from Ghazala's brother as preconditions to taking his wife back. 'The goods are damaged, so I am asking for more,' he says, referring to Ghazala's inability to produce a son. When Ghazala mixes some holy ash in

Muneer's drink, she drives the man into a violent frenzy. This time when Ghazala returns to her mother's home, her daughter Salma joins her as well.

In the extended household, Khaleel (Lalit Tiwari), a wealthy farmer, lives with his wife, Najma, and their children. Najma runs the household, overworked and tired in the last stages of pregnancy. Afsana, more educated than other family members, lives in the same household with her children. Her husband, Khurshid (Rajit Kapur), is a younger son who works in town and plans to settle there with his family. Hasina, the matriarch, is aged and ailing, yet it is still she who takes the decisions on money and property matters in the family.

The narrative universe is one in which people are products of social conditioning – they search for exit routes and sort out relationships. As the family sit to dine, Hasina tells her story. Betrothed to her dearly loved cousin, the young Hasina is forced to marry her brother-in-law after her sister dies in childbirth. Hasina's efforts to elope with her lover are aborted by her parents. She survives her marriage with a man 20 years older than her and bears him two children. In flashback, the young Hasina is seen leaving her marital home with the infant in her arms as her lover watches the bullock cart from his door.[9] Hasina's story testifies to the lack of autonomy faced by women in her social milieu. It also explains and establishes Khaleel's deep devotion to his stepmother and his siblings. Hasina announces that she wishes to keep some money aside for Ghazala if her husband does not take her back. 'A woman should have some money of her own,' she tells her children, having spent a lifetime totally dependent on her husband. The largely sympathetic and supportive family also opposes the notions of family honour in Hindi film melodrama where a married daughter would bring disgrace if she returned to her marital home. Here is a sensitive mother–daughter relationship, even if it is one that is not fully explored, as the narrative is more issue-driven.

Abused and unfairly accused of unfaithfulness, Ghazala tries to retain her dignity in her mother's home. 'It's better to be alone rather than be someone's slave,' she tells her sister-in-law. During an argument, the jealous Afsana accuses Ghazala of living on charity. Ghazala endeavours to make a living by sewing clothes to contribute to her mother's household. She offers to stitch clothes for neighbours at lower rates than the local tailor's. When Ghazala hesitatingly asks the maid to solicit some orders from the neighbours, her mixed emotions rise to the surface. Shabana Azmi – cast by Benegal after a gap of ten years – plays a survivor who wishes to carry on with her life and gain control over it. The quiet dignity and sensitivity that Azmi invests in the character go beyond the demands of the script. The story is one of oppression, but, more importantly, of survival, of claiming rights.

The brother's wife is pregnant, but against her wishes. In rural families, the woman has no right to refuse marital sex or make any decisions concerning children. Indian culture celebrates female fertility, but does not entail seeking the consent of women when it comes to their reproductive rights. Benegal stresses:

> It's automatically assumed that the right to have children is the right of the man, which I think is an absurdity. It is the right of the woman, she should have right over her body – it's a fundamental right. But it is not seen this way here.

The feeble Najma has been burdened with frequent pregnancies – only two of her children have survived, and her own health is failing. She begrudges Ghazala's daughter her education and expects Salma to share in the housework. Najma's predicament points to the fate of most uneducated women who bear the burden of childbirth and child rearing unquestioningly. Chronic anaemia and weakness lead to weak children who do not survive. After Najma's newborn child dies, Ghazala persuades her to have an operation, a decision which is greatly resisted by the other women, but eventually supported by Najma's husband. By deciding on the operation, Najma takes a decisive step towards controlling her life. The parallel between Najma's annual pregnancies and that of the buffalo Moti is overtly established, but here Benegal is attempting to communicate with the masses. In Indian society, the childbearing role of a woman has been traditionally underlined by comparisons to fertile animals, green fields or mud pots.

The overtly religious Afsana welcomes every new child as a divine blessing. She is a paradoxical product of education and religion. Afsana avoids mundane housework and recites the Qur'an to her mother-in-law. Her rooms on the upper floor are better equipped and reflect the superior status that she has elevated herself to in the family hierarchy. When a medical officer comes around to tell the women about contraceptive pills, Afsana drives her out of the house as contraception goes against her religious tenets. When Khurshid announces that he has had a vasectomy, Afsana becomes hysterical, threatening Khurshid with the worst consequences of defying her religion. Nandita Das's Afsana is a study of the literate woman who is still bound to religious superstition. The film-maker's quiet irony is expressed in the scene in which Afsana threatens to leave the house with her children, but her husband keeps the children behind. With a love song on the soundtrack, Khurshid goes in search of his wife, who is sulking in the cemetery. Afsana returns a more subdued woman.

Ghazala's teenage daughter Salma's story points to the future. Salma has been witness to scenes of domestic violence between her parents and has occasionally turned against her father in rage. When Ghazala is driven out of her house for the second time, Salma joins her. She wants to be like her schoolteacher, whose independence she admires and to which she aspires. Salma's story appears flawed with stilted scenes. The family plans to have Salma married, throwing Ghazala into a dilemma.

At this time, the mother falls seriously ill. The doctor suspects cervical cancer, an outcome of early pregnancies and childbearing. Ghazala finds an answer to her dilemma: she will not have her daughter marry early and face such consequences. As the morning sun shines through into the room, Ghazala wakes her daughter and sends her to school. In the last scene, the young girl is seen running across the fields with her friends, school bag on her back. She sings in regional accents, '*Panchi rey, panchi rey, uran humko dedey*'.

> O bird, give me wings to fly
> I emerge victorious
> I was mute – give me a voice – I, too, want a fistful of sky.

Benegal himself says, '*Hari Bhari* is what one would call a film that promotes a cause.' Commissioned by the Ministry of Family Welfare, it has to address the largest possible audience, risking an element of pragmatism. Making films on small budgets also does not allow any exploration beyond the essential message. Benegal explains, 'When one is working within a tight budget, one is compulsively made to think about financial resources every minute.' *Hari Bhari* is a well-acted ensemble piece, but is far too loaded with issues and the drama is often sacrificed for the message. Nevertheless, it is probably only this film-maker who would be able to secure funds from ministries for a film on reproductive rights – to Benegal, it is part of the debate on human rights. Also, it is left to Benegal to draw together a brilliant repertory of actors for this film with a cause.

Long after the genesis of the women's movement in India, Benegal's concern for women's causes continues unabated. It is a world vision that he renews with every film. Although the film is based on case studies of Muslim families, the social problem it presents is one faced by people in every community or religion. It is a universal concept. For centuries, women have been oppressed on several fronts: within caste, class or community.

Now they are much more conscious that they cannot live in an unequal situation:

> As we move towards deepening our democracy, it becomes very important for us to realise that women must have equal rights and privileges that otherwise we took for granted. As a film-maker, my primary interest has always been human rights. Whether it is a problem of caste or class, political oppression has always been of consequence to me. It so happens that this film deals with another kind of oppression. If it is a Muslim family, I am not saying that it is a Muslim problem.[10]

Concern for the rights of women is manifest in this film with a cause. The limitations of the script, as a fictional version of real-life case studies, are overcome by sensitive and memorable performances by the repertory cast: Surekha Sikri (cast in the last trilogy) and Shabana Azmi, new actors such as Nandita Das and Alka Shrivastav, Lalit Tiwari and Rajat Kapoor, who have acted in many of Benegal's films. *Hari Bhari* is a performance-based document of female narratives, moving as much as it disturbs.

The fact that Benegal made *Zubeidaa* and *Hari Bhari* almost simultaneously indicates his willingness to experiment with market factors, as well as continue to make small-budget, cause-oriented films on his own terms. Some 30 years into his career, Benegal has once again established that he is a master storyteller, as well as a social interventionist. Benegal's realist aesthetic, compassionate search for human stories and unflinching examination of characters (through use of close-ups) serve to remind the viewer of the enduring power of his vision and commitment to reform and development.

Benegal has been criticised for joining hands with the government to make films such as this. The fact remains that we see a film-maker using his craft in the larger national project of intervention and enlightenment. Women remain the focus of a society in crisis or in self-conflict. The paradoxes of change and development, of internalised cultural values and the complex levels of oppression within family structures – all this has been examined in Benegal's films before. He reminds us:

> I was always interested in women's rights from my very first film. Denying women their rights is one of the major reasons why India is not evolving as well as it should have. I look from a very human point of view and, even in terms of telling a story, I find stories which deal with women's problems very interesting.

Hari Bhari was released in 2000 in India by commercial distributors Shroff Films and has been distributed on video and DVD internationally. The film has travelled to festivals worldwide, and been used for seminars and community screenings in the United Kingdom. In India, it has also been used extensively in National Development Family Planning programmes for rural and small-town audiences.

7

The Last Trilogy: Search for Identity

Mammo (*Grandmother*, 1994)

After the demolition of the Babri Masjid in December 1992 and the ensuing Bombay riots in January 1993, there was an urgent questioning of the position of minorities and, in particular, the Muslim identity. To counter the growing right-wing Hindu ideology, in the arts there was a conscious effort to create space for the minorities and to represent the cultural space of the Indian Muslims. In big-banner Bollywood films, there appeared an uncomfortable spillover of the *Hindutva*, or saffron sensibility, in big-budget films such as *Hum Aapke Hain Koun* (Sooraj Barjatya) conflating the themes of romance, joint families and divine intervention. The forces of globalisation were in any case threatening to flatten out issues of language, and regional and communal identity. The realism offered by parallel cinema and its basic premise of cultural specificity seemed to be fast losing ground. Big-scale entertainment with its emphasis on spectacle, song and dance, and 'traditional' family values was fast taking over the space for alternative expression in Indian cinema.

It is characteristic of Shyam Benegal – both the man and the film-maker – that his concern for the oppressed would extend to the threatened minority community. Benegal recalls walking to his office in Tardeo (a crowded trading area in the heart of old Bombay) during the riots and the violence he witnessed in the crowded streets outside. The Muslim bakery directly across the road was set on fire by an angry mob. Benegal campaigned for normalcy and, as one of the chief spokespersons for the Citizen's Forum, was instrumental in convincing the police to reopen local train services. Unwilling to dramatise the recent and painful history of the Bombay riots directly (as in Mani Rathnam's *Bombay*), Benegal produced in quick succession *Mammo*, *Sardari Begum* and *Zubeidaa*, a family trilogy relating the stories and journeys of three women from Muslim families. The new cinema movement had made attempts to explore women's subjectivity and their familial and social roles. Benegal continued this concern with his narratives of marginalised females.[1]

Mammo marked a new collaboration with scriptwriter Khalid Mohamed. A well-known film critic and editor of the popular film monthly *Filmfare*, Khalid had written a small article in the *Times of India* about his great-aunt. Benegal describes how the story roused his interest:

> I came across a little personal piece in the Sunday edition of the *Times of India*. It was about a woman who had married a man from Lahore and moved there after Partition. On the premature death of her husband, unable to deal with the hostility of her husband's relatives, she decided to return to Bombay to live with her only surviving relative, an older sister. She intended to live the rest of her life in her sister's home. She managed to stay long after her visa expired. When the immigration authorities eventually found out, she was unceremoniously deported back to Lahore, where she had neither a family nor a home.... I was deeply moved by the story. It was one of the myriad human tragedies that took place in the aftermath of the Partition of India, tragic stories of families torn apart by man-made borders and barriers. It was an exquisite miniature and in a microcosm expressed the trauma that had effected the entire subcontinent. I felt that this little piece had the makings of an excellent film.[2]

Khalid Mohamed had never been sympathetic to the kind of films Benegal had been making; his reviews of *Ankur* and *Bhumika* had been harsh readings. Understandably, Benegal was unsure of Khalid's response when he approached the writer. Khalid not only welcomed the idea of a film on the subject, but also offered to write the script himself. It proved difficult, however, to raise funds for the films. Until the mid-1980s, the 'pre-television era', raising money for Benegal's films had been easier as cinemas offered screen time. There was an identifiable niche audience, consisting mostly of the middle class in the metropolitan areas who looked beyond the conventional product turned out by the film entertainment industry.

The single state-owned television channel, Doordarshan, did not pose any competition to cinema. In fact, from the 1970s a younger group of film-makers had been making individualistic films to redefine cinema entertainment and some had created a devoted audience – Benegal himself, Ketan Mehta, Govind Nihalani, Saeed and Sudhir Mishra. The National Film Development Corporation (NFDC) supported their films, and some produced independently as well. Between 1986 and 1991, Benegal had been intensely involved in his television magnum opus, *Bharat Ek Khoj*. He writes:

> When I got back, it was like waking from Rip Van Winkle's slumber. Everything had changed. The non-traditional cinema had lost its entire audience to television.... The beginning of the 1990s was a particularly difficult time. Private television channels began to mushroom. By the middle of the decade, there were more television channels than you would care to count. The film was going into a crisis mode that seemed almost terminal.[3]

To lure the audience back to the cinema, films had to boast excellent production values. Small-budget films had little technical polish and lost out entirely in the marketplace – the only outlet for such films was on television. To negotiate this altered state of affairs, the NFDC entered into a strategic collaboration with Doordarshan to produce films. The state television network retained broadcast rights, and the NFDC was in charge of cinema distribution. *Mammo* was produced within this scheme on a paltry budget; however, for Benegal, the opportunity to make the film under these conditions was better than not making it at all. Benegal had turned to the NFDC for the first time with his earlier film *Suraj Ka Satwan Ghoda*. High rentals and large cinema halls had blocked small films from the cinemas altogether. Despite recognising that the NFDC had a flawed marketing strategy, Benegal made use of the only funding sources available to him.

Mammo is a small film, but a great human document, particularly in the context of communal strife and rising fundamentalism. Much like his predecessor Satyajit Ray, Benegal turns away from the immediate history of violence to a tragic tale of an old woman trying to return to her land. The film throws up serious questions about citizenship, nation and identity. By choosing two women and a child as his principal characters, Benegal again draws the peripheral to the centre. Mammo (Farida Jalal) arrives in Bombay, where her sister Fayyazi (Surekha Sikri) lives with her orphaned grandson. Turned out from her husband's home after his death, she returns from Lahore to Bombay, hoping to live with her only kin for the rest of her life. The story unfolds from the point of view of the 12-year-old Riyaz (Amit Phalke, in an award-winning performance). Riyaz's mother, Zubeidaa, died when he was young, and he has been told his father is also dead, when he in fact has remarried. Fayyazi has raised her grandson under great hardship, but she sends him to an English-language school. We find a family forging relations to keep together, as other members have been lost through death or estrangement (Riyaz's father, Fayyazi's younger sister). Riyaz, a film buff, dreams of being a writer when he grows up. Into this small household steps Mammo, garrulous and inquisitive. Riyaz resists this intrusion into their cramped Bombay flat. The sisters spend time talking about life after Partition, about the early popularity of Hindi films and their subsequent withdrawal from Pakistan. Riyaz misses school and goes to the cinema with his friends. In an amusing sequence, Riyaz

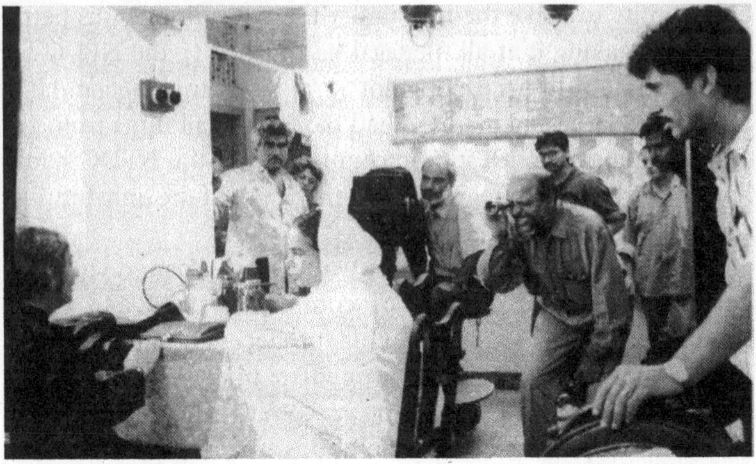

Benegal directing Surekha Sikri and Farida Jalal on the set of Mammo.

borrows his grandmother's burkha (the black coat which veils a woman's face) to disguise himself and sneak into an adult screening of Hitchcock's *Psycho* (1960).

Riyaz accompanies Mammo to the police station, where she has to register as a foreign national. The police allow her to stay for three months. As she walks through the filthy streets, she tells Riyaz that, despite the squalor, the scent of one's country is wonderful. Initially resistant, Riyaz soon warms up to Mammo. She introduces him to Urdu literature – Manto's fiction and Faiz's poetry. When Riyaz learns that his father is alive, Mammo reassures him. When Mammo walks to the slums to confront her maid's abusive husband, Riyaz accompanies her. This is a coming-of-age story as much as it is about borders and belonging. The sequence in which Riyaz walks out of his home and runs along the seaside path on Marine Drive poignantly establishes the boy's emotional turmoil.

Riyaz gains a glimpse of the neighbouring slums when Mammo takes him along to search for their maid. On the way back, Mammo tells Riyaz of her experience of Partition. A static camera focuses on Mammo's face in mid-shot, as she narrates the horrifying story of a young woman who loses both her babies while crossing the border. Without the benefit of any dramatic highs, the film-maker unobtrusively confronts the question of a land and its people torn apart by artificial borders. Later in the film, when Riyaz and his grandmother find Mammo in the mosque and walk back along the raised pathway across the sea, their passage is made difficult in the face of a rising storm. The three figures huddled together form a picture of vulnerability; in the background we see several pavement dwellers hold up their little plastic sheets against the coming rain. This metaphor for a threatened community (and family) could not have been more touching.

Mammo bribes a visa agent and a police officer to extend her stay. After her visa runs out, the police one day arrive at the door and unceremoniously haul Mammo away. She is interrogated and sent back to Pakistan on the *Frontier Express*. Riyaz rushes to the station just in time to catch a glimpse of Mammo as the train pulls out of the platform. Those fragmented images return to

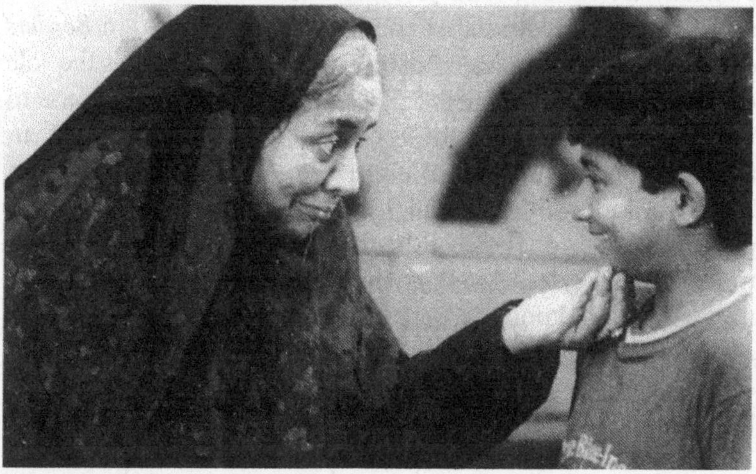

Rizoo (Amit Phalke) finally makes friends with his grandmother Mammo (Farida Jalal).

haunt the adult Riyaz in his dreams. The story has unfolded through flashback; in the present, Riyaz has grown to be a writer; Fayyazi has aged considerably. With a touch of magical realism, Mammo returns after many years. This time the feisty woman succeeds in outwitting the state system. Making use of the same corrupt bureaucratic machinery, Mammo arranges a false death certificate, thus annihilating her official existence. This time she has come to stay.

Countering the blatant stereotyping of Muslims in commercial cinema, *Mammo* shows the Pakistani and Indian women as ordinary middle-class people, the Hindu and the Muslim schoolboy as not really different from each other. Khalid Mohamed's script demystifies the Muslim family. In fact it goes against the grain to depict kinship ties through women – in this case, sisterhood. In a review article, Ruth Vanita calls this a path-breaking film: 'This representation has the advantage of highlighting those silent halves of the population who have little to say in deciding political destiny at national or local level.'[4] The two Muslim sisters, citizens from two nations, painfully try to forge and preserve a family. In fact, *Mammo*'s sense of agency is strongly underlined several times. In *Borders and Boundaries*, Ritu Menon and Kamla Bhasin discuss the role of women in India's Partition: 'The aim of the enterprise is to make women a focus of the enquiry, a subject of the story, an agent of the narrative.'[5] We are reminded several times of Fayyazi's independence and how she managed to rear her grandson under extremely difficult circumstances. Yet this is an unusual family desperately trying to hold together against the forces of law and politics. Benegal's impatience with the corrupt and inefficient bureaucracy is this time evident in his treatment of the system – corrupt officials and bullying police who humiliate this helpless widow.

Mainstream films have repeatedly idealised and romanticised Hindu–Muslim bonding, as in *Amar Akbar Anthony* (Manmohan Desai, 1977), the story of three brothers who are separated and raised as Hindu, Muslim and Christian; *Muqaddar Ka Sikandar* (Prakash Mehra), a story of friendship and misunderstanding between Muslim and Hindu; and the Hindu–Muslim marriage in Mani Ratnam's *Bombay*. *Bombay* is structured as a conventional melodrama in which a Hindu boy falls in love with a Muslim girl. Together they elope to Bombay, where they start a family. Their secular aspirations face growing threat from surrounding fundamentalist forces, in particular, the saffron-clad political party. Soon after the destruction of the mosque, the leader of the Hindu party unleashes a vicious reprisal against the Muslims in the city, accusing them of being Pakistanis. The couple lose their children in the riots, recreated with chilling realism by Mani Rathnam. After an impassioned plea for peace by the hero, people see reason and stop the riots. Much of the controversy surrounding the film was related to the issue of the film's violence being too provocative and realistic. It also offered a simplistic solution in the hero's pacifist notions.

What saddens the secular-minded Benegal is the tendency 'to define the self in terms of us and them ... the real definition of our country is us.... Mammo is a human being, and human problems are of ultimate importance.' Thus he turns to gendered narratives of displacement and dispossession. The film-maker addresses the issue of Muslim refugees in the city by tapping into the historical tragedy of Partition and consciously avoiding incidents of recent violence. True to his sensibility, he searches for women's stories and explores the kinship of sisterhood. Women are doubly oppressed and victims of communal hatred, and have been since Partition.[6] Always the humanist, Benegal makes *Mammo* a realistic document of courage and human dignity. Vanita writes more in her review:

> Still, it is in quiet efforts like *Mammo* and through the courage of ordinary people like its protagonist that hope for the future lies, not in the noisy heroics and self-conscious controversiality of films like *Bombay*.[7]

Sardari Begum (1996)

Liberalisation of the economy in the 1990s channelled new energy into the entertainment business. Corporations such as ABCL (Amitabh Bachchan Corporation Limited) and Plus Channel were starting to produce entertainment software. In 1995, Plus Channel planned to produce 12 films, mainly for television. *Sardari Begum* was one of these, as well as Sai Paranjpye's *Saaz* (1996) and Sudhir Mishra's *Is Raat Ki Subah Nahi* (1996). The market for film music by this time had grown phenomenally. In fact, the pre-sale of music and hit songs could often determine the success of a film run. *Sardari Begum* offered the possibility of good songs and music – this was the story of a thumri singer who becomes an unwitting victim of communal riots in the old quarters of the city of Delhi. It offered the possibility of using songs in the thumri style, a traditional genre of light classical music usually presented by performing women in mehfils, or small private concerts.[8]

The phenomenal growth of the music market had made film songs determining commodities. As the songs are marketed well before a film is out, popular numbers could even determine the fate of the film at the box office. The music for *Sardari Begum* was directed by Benegal's long-term collaborator Vanraj Bhatia. Javed Akhtar, whom Benegal describes as arguably the best Urdu poet among the contemporary generation of poets today, wrote the lyrics, in the style of traditional thumris.

Khalid Mohamed's second script for Benegal is a story of a middle-aged singer past her prime. Sardari (Kiron Kher) lives with her daughter Sakina (Rajeshwari) in the Muslim quarters of old Delhi. One day as she sings in her room, her riyaz (practice) is disturbed by a commotion in the streets below. A Hindu procession passing through the Muslim neighbourhood leads to the outbreak of riots. Sardari steps out onto her balcony and is hit by a stone. Her accidental death leads to further tension in the area, as local leaders turn this incident into a communal issue. A young journalist, Tehzeeb (Rajina Raj Biseria), investigates the singer's death, and Sardari's life is recreated in multiple voices through interviews by the journalist.

Tehzeeb arrives at the riot scene and speaks with the police and local political leaders. Muslim leaders appear determined to turn this incident into a political and communal issue; the police officer callously dismisses Sardari as a whore. Inside the house, Sardari's funeral procession is prepared. Tehzeeb is surprised to find her father among the mourners. She discovers that Sardari was her aunt, disowned by the family because she chose to become a professional thumri singer. Tehzeeb's father recounts those early days when the young Sardari ran away from her home after her father refused to allow her to sing in public concerts. Sardari's personal ambitions and passionate love for music are in conflict with her family's middle-class values of respectability. In desperation, she turns to her teacher, then to a wealthy patron, settling in his household as his mistress. Sardari's family give her up for dead. Many years later, when her brother is suffering financial problems, Sardari offers him money for Tehzeeb's further education.

Inspired by the story, Tehzeeb describes Sardari as a free spirit who broke out of the social roles of daughter, wife and mother. She challenges her father's conservative judgment, leading to his total estrangement from the sister he had dearly loved. Tehzeeb also faces her father's disapproval about her personal life – she is in love with her married boss, a relationship which holds no future. Tehzeeb turns down an offer to cover an international beauty contest so that she can investigate Sardari's life further. The dead singer sets the journalist on a personal quest.

The sarangi player (a sarangi is a stringed instrument which accompanies thumri music) knew Sardari since she was a young girl. He recounts his earliest memories of the girl who insisted on learning music from his previous employer, a performing woman, Iddan Bai (Surekha Sikri). In a flashback scene, Sardari interrupts when Iddan is giving a private concert for her patron, Khemchand (Amrish Puri), asking to be taught. Her magical voice enthrals the older singer, who agrees to take her on. When Sardari decides to perform herself, she faces the wrath of her father, who believes that thumri singers are women of loose morals.[9] Sardari escapes from her father's home and seeks refuge in the patron's home. Soon she becomes his mistress, as he invests money to train her as a singer. Sardari has passionately declared that, without her music, she would simply die. Debutante Smriti Mishra's young Sardari breathes fire as she rebels against family and society to sing her music. The journalist discovers a woman who defied social norms to live life on her own terms.

The wealthy patron Khemchand is now dead; an interview with his widow charts more flashback scenes. Khemchand's wife has to suffer silently through her husband's attention to the beautiful singer who is lodged in her home. A long song-and-dance scene recreates a mehfil, or concert, in which Sardari performs for Khemchand's private guests. The singer sings with bhav (expressive facial and hand gestures), then dances on the floor. One of the guests, Sadiq (Rajit Kapur), is completely besotted by the beautiful singer; he proposes to Sardari by the end of the evening. This account reveals a scheming woman who lures Khemchand away from his wife and steals the family jewels. This is the widow's point of view, herself a victim of circumstances.

Sardari's husband, Sadiq, recalls his first meeting with Sardari at the recital in Khemchand's home. When Sardari discovers that she is pregnant, Sadiq offers to marry her and give the child his name. Sardari cuts her first music record and becomes a radio artist. As the song continues, the young Sardari is replaced by her older self (Kiron Kher). The script makes a leap in time with a number of relationships unresolved. We learn that Sardari is estranged from her husband, but no reasonable explanation is offered for this.

Finally, we hear the daughter Sakina's story. The aged Sardari could barely support herself with her music. She worked as a

Smriti Mishra plays the young Sardari, a performing woman in Sardari Begum.

marriage negotiator in the neighbourhood to earn a little money. A flashback scene shows Sardari arranging a Hindu–Muslim marriage, yet, ironically, she disapproves of her daughter's relationship with a Hindu boy. Sardari wants to shape Sakina's career in music, with little thought for her emotional needs. Sakina finally confronts her mother with all her grudges – she has been denied education, estranged from her father and her lover. Sardari, always immersed in her music, had made little effort to know her daughter well; in revolt, Sakina turns away from music. The last flashback returns to the opening sequence of Sardari's accidental death. Sardari asks her daughter to sing as she dies, a poignant thumri using the metaphor of death, 'Chali Pi Ke Nagar':

> I leave for the land of my love
> My heart is restless in my mother's home
> Now I travel to my true home
> This is a false world.

Sardari's death proves the catalyst for bringing Sakina back to her music. In the last scene, Sakina sits in her mother's room and sings the same song – in a manner, this is how she resolves her relationship with her mother. The camera pans out onto the balcony and into the narrow street facing the mosque. For a moment, the song transcends the individual's voice and sweeps over the locality, a threatened genre and a threatened community, yet quietly resilient as Sakina picks up her mother's music. Benegal's chief concerns for history, tradition, community and gender come together in Sardari's story; the non-linear treatment reflects the relativity of views and values at a time of crisis. The senseless violence of which Sardari is a victim does lead, however, to more life-affirming messages in the end. Sakina returns to her music, and Tehzeeb takes control over her life by making a wise career decision. As Amod (the Hindu boy) hears Sakina's music from the street and stops below the balcony, the possibility of renewed love opens up.

Like most of Benegal's other films, *Sardari Begum* is a film with a relatively new cast and made on a fairly tight budget, approximately 76 lakh rupees ($157,000). It has a strong narrative structure, but, then, telling a story has always been Benegal's single greatest passion. The film revolves around female characters, once again Benegal's terrain as he has always excelled in exploring the female perspective. The film-maker explains:

> It is not as if I want to always present women as victims. There is something very interesting about women, particularly in India, because the social pressures on them are so much more than on men due to the way Indian society is. What I intend to show is the ability of Indian women to handle the situations they have been placed in.[10]

Dwelling on Sardari's character, Benegal says that she is a woman who makes it on her own in life, and the kind of music she sings is now on the decline. It is also about the world of the public singer and her relationships in private. She is a different person to different people, and, for the film-maker, this subjective attitude is what is interesting to explore in cinematic terms. In another context, Menon and Bhasin write about fragmented histories: 'The fragment is significant precisely because it is marginal rather than mainstream, particular rather than general, and because it presents history from below.'[11] Sardari makes her brief claim to fame and fades into obscurity, meriting only a single column in the newspapers when she is accidentally killed in the communal riot. Several unresolved relationships resurface on the event of her death: her estranged husband and brother arrive for the funeral, the music producer and her musician shoulder the bier, her grieving daughter is inconsolable.

Sardari is a spirited and passionate woman who dares to follow her dream. Sardari and her music also symbolise a community and art the existence of which is threatened. Sardari's imperilled existence and the dying art of thumri are woven together in a seamless and unforced manner. Benegal once again reminds us of the loss of a rich tradition, of a cultural and historical crisis, through the journey of a woman and her song. The sensitive and understated manner in which a daughter picks up her mother's art indicates the film-maker's humane vision and hope for the future. Two contemporary women are propelled to make choices in their lives, inspired and empowered by Sardari, who is both an agent and a victim of conflict.

Benegal seemed to have finally found the right form: multiple narratives and fragmented memories to explore the nature of truth. The film suffered from changing production plans, however, and thus failed to realise its potential. The producers had initially planned this as a telefilm, but decided on a cinematic release after Benegal had gone into pre-production. This meant a change to widescreen format, more expensive camera equipment with anamorphic lenses and sets to suit the altered scale. The production budget went out of control. *Sardari Begum* also fell short of the cinema standards of the

1990s technically. The analogue mono sound system was unacceptable in metropolitan cinemas already boasting Dolby sound systems. What was worse, there was no publicity budget to market the film at a time when promotional budgets for commercial films were astoundingly large. The producers finally decided to forego the cinema release and opted for a television premiere, hoping this screening would later draw the audience to the cinemas. Unfortunately, *Sardari Begum* had a short run in the cinemas when it was eventually released. As with its other productions, Plus Channel failed to plan cinematic distribution successfully, hindered by inadequate marketing strategies and funds.

Sardari Begum had remarkably strong performances by Smriti Mishra and Kiron Kher, who played the younger and older protagonist, respectively. Both actors received considerable critical praise. Mishra received the National Award for best supporting actress, and the film was awarded the best Urdu film of the year. Poet-lyricist Javed Akhtar received a National Award for the extraordinary thumris penned for the film. Although the film failed at the box office, its music did well, bringing in revenue for Plus Music, a subsidiary of Plus Channel. *Sardari Begum* received a special music award at the Tashkent film festival.

Zubeidaa (2000)

Zubeidaa is the third of a family trilogy which present three women's stories. Here Benegal deals with a subject that required period reconstruction. *Zubeidaa* is a love story set in 1950–52, when India was a newborn republic with 550 princely states and a large Muslim population. The country was preparing for the first general elections, and princely India was set to move towards its grand decline – a fascinating period from both political and social viewpoints.

Khalid Mohamed's third script is based on his mother's life, a 1950s starlet who married Prince Hukam Singh of Jodhpur.

Mohamed was brought up by his grandmother in Bombay and had only fragmentary knowledge of his mother Zubeidaa. It was his curiosity and determination that helped him to piece together the compelling story of his mother. For Mohamed, this autobiographical script was a process of therapy; for Benegal, it offered the trappings of a grand romance with a tragic end. This required a budget much larger than what Benegal usually raised for his films. He offered the script to Plus Channel, which tried to secure the biggest stars for the cast. Most of the leading male actors turned down the film because the central character was a woman, and plans with Plus Channel fell through. In 1999, Khalid Mohamed introduced Benegal to Farokh Ratonsey, who agreed to produce the film. The search for an actor who could play the wilful and vulnerable Zubeidaa finally ended when Benegal met Karishma Kapoor, the reigning Bollywood star of the time. Exceptionally talented and beautiful, Karishma was tiring of the run-of-the-mill films that she had to make in the

Zubeidaa *poster.*

commercial industry. She signed for the film at a price much lower than what she usually commanded, as both the role and the opportunity to work with Benegal would give her career a fresh turn.

The little boy Riyaz in *Mammo* was told his mother died in an accident. Riyaz grows up to be a journalist and, with much enterprise, tries to find his mother's story. Like Sardari, Zubeidaa's life is constructed from multiple sources – her diary entries, letters and interviews with people who knew her at various stages of her life. The film opens with Zubeidaa's funeral in 1952; as the little boy Riyaz (Parzaan Dastur) looks at his mother's grave, a red scarf floats down from the sky. The scarf is a visual metaphor for the dead mother who is the recipient of the child's dreams and memories. The boy's fantasy about his dead mother filters his search for her as an adult. In fact, the first glimpse of Zubeidaa is afforded through the boy's mind as he dreams of his mother singing a lullaby. The soft-focus lighting around the child's bedroom as he sees his mother as a fairy princess sets the tone for the film. The past is in fact created through a different look (in terms of light, lens and period sets), while the present is treated in a more realistic tone. The present is set in 1980, the now adult Riyaz (Rajit Kapur) lives with his aged grandmother Fayyazi (Surekha Sikri) – these are the same characters and apartment we saw in *Mammo*. Riyaz is searching for his mother's story through multiple narratives.

The first half of the film moves in long flashback sequences to Zubeidaa's early life. It is Bombay in the late 1940s. Zubeidaa is a teenager in an upper-class Muslim household. Her father, Suleman Seth (Amrish Puri), is the owner of a film studio. Her mother, Fayyazi, is a submissive wife ruled by her husband. Zubeidaa wants to live her life freely, but familial and social pressures make this freedom elusive. She lives within a conventional male-dominated society, straining against the barriers set around her by her father, husband and, later, lover. As a young girl, she aspires to be a film star, but her father puts an end to these hopes by arranging her marriage to his friend's son. The old dance master who lives in the studio premises recounts how Zubeidaa was signed for her first film. The flashback sets up a film dance set with Zubeidaa singing a gypsy song. She is rudely pulled away by her father, who thinks that women from his family should not work in films.

Fayyazi's story recounts Zubeidaa's wedding. The reluctant Zubeidaa tries to kill herself, but ultimately accedes to her father's wishes. At first she refuses to suffer submissively like her mother, who has quietly accepted her husband's mistress, the Anglo-Indian actress Rose Davenport (Lillete Dubey). The wonderfully shot wedding scene is laid over a traditional marriage song; Zubeidaa's aunt Mammo (Farida Jalal) leads the wedding rituals. The song takes forward the drama of Zubeidaa's anger and attempted suicide; finally, the wedding is formalised. As Zubeidaa sets up her new life, another storm is brewing. Zubeidaa's father-in-law plans to leave for Pakistan. After Partition, he faces prejudice as a Muslim trader in Bombay. The far-reaching ramifications of Partition are felt even in this Muslim household in Bombay, a city which was not directly affected by the Partition riots. Soon after the birth of Riyaz, an argument between the fathers leads to a crisis in Zubeidaa's life. In long shot, the family are seen sitting in the

Zubeidaa (Karishma Kapoor) is jealous of her husband's (Manoj Bajpai) attention to his first wife Mandira (Rekha) in Zubeidaa.

drawing room, Zubeidaa clutching the baby in her arms, as her husband pronounces the divorce. Her husband loses all contact with her after returning to Pakistan. Avoiding sentimentality, Benegal evokes the inevitable tragedy in Zubeidaa's life as once again the elders make important decisions concerning her life. Once again she is the hapless victim.

The now aged actress Rose recounts to Riyaz how the royal romance blossomed. A tiny glimpse is offered into the actress's lonely life, the general fate of ageing, out-of-work actors in the industry. When Zubeidaa sinks into depression, the actress Rose takes her on social outings. As an Anglo-Indian, the English-speaking Rose is comfortable in the social circuit of clubs and parties. One day during a polo match, Zubeidaa meets the handsome prince Vijayendra Singh (Manoj Bajpai) from Rajasthan. Courtship and romance follow on the sets of ballrooms and elegant buildings. The previously married prince offers to take her as a second wife. Fayyazi relents to the Hindu–Muslim marriage on condition that Riyaz is left with her. Zubeidaa leaves for the state of Fatepur, hoping finally to break free of authoritarian control. She expresses her freedom as she dances in the hills. A stock song-and-dance sequence is invested with subjective meaning as she sings: 'Dheeme Dheeme Gaaon' ('I sing on softly, shake my anklets and dance for you my love'). Benegal shoots on the Western Ghats using a soft filter and authentic period costumes for the characters. The words of the song serve almost as an extension of dialogue; the scene is less a spectacle than an evocation of the characters.

Later, as Zubeidaa rides across the princely estates alongside the prince, she aspires to an equal role with her man. Such hopes prove short-lived when she enters the palace only to be told by her senior co-wife, Mandira (Rekha), that she must live according to the conventions of the royal family. The paradoxes of royal life are explored as the women imprisoned within four walls have access to Western sports, fashion and education. Zubeidaa exhibits emotions that are only human – she is possessive of her husband

and jealous of his co-wife. During a festival when commoners dance at the palace, Zubeidaa impulsively joins in, only to be rebuked by the senior queen. Zubeidaa storms out of the palace, refusing to live like an imprisoned bird.

Zubeidaa's life as a princess is recounted through her voice in diary extracts, responses from the senior queen, the royal aide and the prince's younger brother when Riyaz travels to Fatepur himself. The royal palace has been converted into a hotel and is overseen by the prince's brother. More narratives relate the course of events. As Zubeidaa finds brief happiness with the prince, larger political events again impact upon her life. The new nation is preparing for its first elections; the princely states are being integrated into the new nation-state. The prince and his first wife are away on election campaigns. Zubeidaa is increasingly isolated and faced with sexual advances by the prince's brother. She realises that, as a Muslim actress, she will find no one in the household who is willing to accept her. One fateful day, Zubeidaa insists on flying out with the prince. Shortly afterwards, both are killed in an air crash.

Much of Zubeidaa's story in the palace is recounted by the dignified Mandira as she looks back with fondness at those days when Zubeidaa entered the palace as a young, hopeful bride. She finally hands over to Riyaz old photographs and the missing reel of the film *Banjaran*. This is juxtaposed against the male narratives – the aide tells Riyaz that Zubeidaa was a concubine who drove the prince to his death. Finally, the prince's brother denies that there ever was a younger princess, pointing to the complete erasure of Zubeidaa from the pages of royal history. In the face of these negating voices, the sensitive Mandira hands over photographs of Zubeidaa and the prince. In the last scene, Riyaz and Fayyazi sit in a private cinema, watching the black-and-white footage of the gypsy song. Riyaz sees his mother come to life on the big screen – as the star she had aspired to be. A fragment of celluloid, multiple voices and confessional diary jottings reshape Zubeidaa for the viewer. Like the son our quest is also over.

Benegal was attracted to the theme for two reasons. First the sentimental ethos of the subject, the search of a son for the memories of his mother; how Riyaz decides to unravel the enigma that is his mother. He reads her diary, interviews people, searches for material (film, photos). The second was the challenge of recreating an era, which Benegal had handled masterfully in *Bhumika* and the television historical series *Bharat Ek Khoj* (*Discovery of India*). The timeframe of flashback in the movies is the 1950s. Benegal says: 'It was a turbulent time in Indian history, following Independence, for the princely states in India.'

Benegal has described *Zubeidaa* as an intense love story underscored by tragedy. It is mounted on a larger scale than other Benegal films, but the director claims that the film remains true to his sensibilities:

> Whatever the genre of cinema, you cannot go beyond or against your own creative sensibilities. The range of your vocabulary can be flexible, but you can't defy your sensibility. If something does not move you as a film-maker, it is unlikely to move the audience.

Zubeidaa holds all the seeds for a grand love story. Mounted on a bigger scale, dressed with songs and a great music score by A. R. Rahman, *Zubeidaa* can be read as a nostalgic look at princely life, a lifestyle that was lost after the 1950s in India. At the core of the film lies a central concern for Benegal, a woman's struggle for freedom during changing times. Benegal grounds his concern within a specific historic context. With Khalid Mohamed's well-wrought script, this is indeed melodrama on a large scale. The narrative deals with conflict: the love between a Hindu prince and a Muslim woman, the desire for a woman's freedom in patriarchal households and traditional norms, the choice between motherhood and love. Zubeidaa is a rebel who does not find a place. The framing of romance and royalty does not detract from the premise of conflict and the lack of choice. The family trilogy on Muslim women's stories privileges narratives that are underrepresented. Breaking from the tradition of mainstream Muslim courtesan drama (Kamal Amrohi's *Pakeezah*; Muzaffar Ali's *Umrao Jaan*), Benegal's trilogy addresses the crisis of communal and individual identity, the treatment of which ranges from journalistic docudrama to big-production melodrama. Exploring patriarchal control in an upper middle-class Muslim household, as well as conflict in the intercommunity marriage, is part of the continuing theme of Muslim identity in this trilogy. Another theme linking *Sardari Begum* and *Zubeidaa* is that of the quest, in which a dead protagonist's life is reconstructed through journalistic research through a collection of memories, individual and collective.

Commenting on the process of memory and reconstructing oral histories, Urvashi Butalia has commented that 'so much depends on who remembers, when, with whom, indeed to whom and how … the way people choose to remember an event, a history, is as important as what one might call the "facts" of that history'.[12]

Working within the cultural studies project of fragmented histories, Benegal destabilises the master narrative and problematizes the concept of a homogeneous nation, in order to configure pluralized identity. Giving the marginal a voice, exploring subaltern subjectivity, Benegals' protagonists negotiate with the centre from the periphery, his texts reexamine and rework the space between state–region, male–female, oppressor–oppressed.

Benegal demonstrates a willingness to understand the changing economics of film-making in Bombay and the significance of marketing, promotion and the music market. He signed top actress Karishma Kapoor, who brought the audience in and whose challenging role fetched her the *Filmfare* Critic's Award. He worked with the leading composer A. R. Rahman, discussing in detail the Western symphonic nature of the music score. The music proved to be very popular, and frequent television promotions created sufficient curiosity about the film. Cinematographer Rajan Kothari – who also shot *Samar* and *Hari Bhari* – comments on the room for manoeuvre that the bigger budget allowed:

> Shyambabu likes to use modern technique. We used a lot of crane and trolley shots. He is extremely good with *mise-en-scène*. We had four- to five-minute shots in single takes. We used filters to get the period look without looking dated. *Zubeidaa* does not look like it was shot in 50 days.
>
> He is extremely disciplined and gives precise instructions so there is no spillover. He is also very good at incorporating suggestions in his scheme of things. I do a lot of work in the mainstream industry, but doing a film with Shyam is like rejuvenation every time. Both Gulzar and he seem to have more energy than a lot of younger directors. They believe in what they are doing.[13]

The film-maker also participated willingly in the multimedia marketing of the film – several television promotions and interviews, and music releases. *Zubeidaa* had the biggest release, including a worldwide premiere, of all of Benegal's films to date. Yashraj Films (Yash Chopra's company) released it simultaneously in India, the United Kingdom, the United States and other international territories. In the United Kingdom, it ran for 12 weeks and grossed £175,000. The film has been featured at various film festivals, and it is available on VHS and DVD format on the international market.

8

Experiments with Truth

Suraj Ka Satwan Ghoda (*The Seventh Horse of the Sun*, 1992)

> I am fascinated by the idea of change because it is a measure of progress, of moving, like a shadow does with the movement of the sun.
>
> Shyam Benegal

For nearly 30 years, Benegal's work has revealed an interesting dichotomy. On the one hand, there have been the politically inflected melodramas about caste and gender oppression such as his first trilogy, *Ankur*, *Nishant* and *Manthan*. On the other hand, the film-maker has constantly surprised us with his search for narrative and the manner in which he wants to tell stories. Grounded squarely in experiential reality, the realist linear narratives call for the need for change in the social structure that his characters inhabit. In the more stylised films, Benegal plays with time and probability – he explores myths and dreams to push into past and present, to blur the lines between fantasy and reality (*Kondura*; *Manthan*; *Trikaal*). The two impulses – not wholly unrelated – have not developed as chronological stages, but have existed side by side from his early years of film-making. Blaze Films supported Benegal's early films, but he has also made films for the National Film Development Corporation (NFDC) and various state departments. His commitment to social development and media education has produced films such as *Samar* and *Hari Bhari*. Some have seen Benegal's choice of working with the state as a compromise to his artistic ideals. Many of his colleagues and critics believe that Benegal has taken his role as a communicator too seriously and curbed his cinematic potential to work towards films with a cause. Shabana Azmi, whose career and reputation is closely connected to Benegal's films, talks of the director's craft:

> Shyam has the director's eye. It cannot ever be that Shyam will place the camera wrongly. We would rehearse, find our spaces and Shyam would put his camera. There was never a frame which looked wrong. Shyam's strength is in exploring small moments of human drama, exploring human relationships in the micro picture as in *Ankur* and *Nishant*. A succession of 'cause' or message movies stifled his cinematic spirit in pragmatic projects. Making production easier and quicker prevented great films from being made.[1]

Benegal himself recalls with humour that, when he approached Shabana for *Hari Bhari*, she said to him, 'When will you stop making cause films and make a film?' It is Benegal's prolific body of work that has drawn criticism from some in his own circle who feel that his television work has had a negative impact on his cinematic vision. Critic Maithili Rao comments:

> Shyam Benegal reclaimed regional status for the Hindi language. Social concern has been part of his sensibility, it informed dramatic films like *Manthan*, but the recent *Hari Bhari* underlines its message in a cluttered fashion. He is a master of the *mise-en-scène* and has used new narrative styles in *Suraj* and in *Zubeidaa* – you see a director confident of his craft. Many new wave film-makers have remained one or two film-making wonders; Shyam on the other hand has been overproductive and sometimes in a hurry. It is the unevenness of his work that has bothered me. I see him as a successful film-maker with flashes of greatness. He has been far more prolific than contemporaries like Adoor Gopalakrishnan, although the latter is a greater film-maker. At his best, Shyam's films span an extraordinary range of human relationships, and there are powerful women-dominated stories (*Ankur*, *Bhumika*, *Mandi*). I think Shyam has not always allowed himself to remain true to his sensibilities.[2]

In 1993, Shyam Benegal made the film I view as his masterpiece, an adaptation of Dharamvir Bharati's celebrated Hindi novella which he had been to keen to make for a long time. Benegal's restlessness with the narrative voice had been increasingly evident in earlier efforts such as *Mandi* and *Trikaal.* More and more, the film-maker seemed inclined to depart from linear storytelling and explore other, more complex modes. He has spoken of the influence of magical realism (Gabriel García Márquez and Milan Kundera's novels) and Chinese opera which was evident in *Trikaal*, of the relevance and reproduction of epic archetypes in *Nishant* and *Kalyug*, of black humour and satire in *Mandi.*

In *Suraj Ka Satwan Ghoda*, Benegal most openly questions the very causal truth that forms the basis of most of his films. He explores relativity and finds for himself a narrative mastery that re-energises his film-making practice. Benegal goes to the very foundation of narrative experience, the perennial form of oral storytelling which by its very nature has a free-flowing flexibility to it. The structure of different stories told from shifting

Amrish Puri and Neena Gupta in Suraj Ka Satwan Ghoda.

perspectives and the narrative device of commenting on the stories invest it with a self-reflexive irony, very postmodern in its approach. The audience constantly evaluates the narrator's role and his storytelling techniques, leading to different approaches on the same material. The story is set in an old residential quarter of Lucknow, a muhalla, where, over three afternoons, Manek Mulla (Rajit Kapoor) regales a group of college students with stories about love and romance. His young friends listen and respond with conclusions, probabilities and moral and ethical questions.

The interlinked lives of Jamuna (Rajeshwari Sachdev in her debut role), Lily (Pallavi Joshi), Satti (Neena Gupta) and Tanna (Virendra Saxena) are approached from different points in time and narrative space. The narrator Manek's own life is involved with all of these characters. He is both a witness and a participant to events that he juggles around wilfully for his eager audience. One of the college students, Shyam (Raghubir Yadav), becomes a writer whose memory of the muhalla is triggered when he sees an exhibition of paintings which remind him of that locality in Lucknow. The camera zooms in on a canvas that shows a crowded neighbourhood, houses and people. Shyam's voice-over takes us into the Allahabad muhalla with its narrow streets (recreated in Chandivli Studios) which is the setting for Manek's stories. He evokes a not-so-remote past when idle college students would argue about politics and love. Their love for stories draws them magnetically to the raconteur Manek, who, as a clerk in the railways, has a lot of spare time on his hands. Manek lives alone in his ancestral house. He appears worldly wise and argues with the younger men about the futility of love and sentimentality. Is love governed by socioeconomic factors? What is romance? Are true love stories those of fulfilment or failure? Here Benegal evokes more recent archetypes from literature and film, the persona of Devdas, the tragic hero who drank himself to death after the failure of his love. Saratchandra Chattopadhyay's literary hero and his cinematic avatars in films made in the 1940s and 1950s (and remade yet again in 2002) have held a profound grip on the collective consciousness. This effete, self-destructive hero has been considered a symbol of the ineffective middle-class male psyche.[3] Both the novel and the films harbour intertextual references to male behavioural codes. Benegal treats romantic love with deep irony – it was the accepted norm that a young man in love was unable to do much about this in real life. More often than not, he would watch helplessly as the woman of his dreams was married off to someone her family thought suitable. Manek narrates the first story, which he witnessed as a gawky schoolboy. Tanna is the nervous son of a dominating and bullying father, the merchant Maheshwar. Tanna is in love with his neighbour Jamuna, but cannot do anything about it. Jamuna confides in Manek and sometimes fantasises that he is her lover. Jamuna is soon married off to a rich widower, and she sinks into a comfortable life. Her old husband is impotent, and she soon has a son by the coachman who becomes the estate manager after her husband's death. Maheshwar marries Tanna to a rich girl, Lily, while his eyes are on Lily's mother and her wealth. The independent Lily returns to her mother soon after her child is born. She does not need men in her life. It is later revealed that Lily was in love with the young Manek, who heroically gives up his claims on her, reminding her of the legendary Indian lovers who are never really united. Manek and Lily sing a love duet visualised as a tribute-cum-parody of stock Bollywood love situations (the lovers walk in the rain). After each narrative, Shyam and his friends comment on the story and critique Manek's style. One boy carries out a Marxist analysis of the love stories. Shyam has grotesque visions and bizarre dreams, and the third teenager asks about morals in the story. Benegal deconstructs the narrative form by returning to Manek Mullah's room after every episode.

Characters meet and separate, and often refer to other characters who become the primary players in the next narrative. The third story is about the low-caste girl Satti, who is sold by her uncle to Maheshwar, who rapes her one night. Satti trusts Manek and asks him for help. Manek proves a coward when put to the test and gives in to his brother, who will finance his further studies. Satti and her uncle disappear from the neighbourhood. When the last story is over, Manek leaves for work. As he stands at the tea stall, Satti appears with her child and surprises Manek. The fictitious character comes to life, reminding the viewer that stories are after all about real life. Wispy imaginative talk suddenly becomes hard reality. Manek disappears suddenly, like the characters he would evoke every evening. Shyam later becomes a writer and records these stories. His voice-over brings us back to the present. Scriptwriter Shama Zaidi wrote the adaptation from the novella:

> I worked on several drafts of the script – designed Manek as the narrator in the story and Shyam as the frame narrator. The challenge was to see how to deal with simultaneous events (like in Kurosawa's *Rashomon*): from where do you look at the action? It was also exploring the post-Independence era of the 1950s in a small town ambience – looking at the archetypes that have remained – Devdas as a doomed lover ...'[4]

The camera remains on the three women depicted on the painting's canvas, reminders of the three stories from Manek's life. *Suraj Ka Satwan Ghoda* is a celebration of oral storytelling using postmodern techniques with a double narrative framework, deconstructive analysis, differing perspectives, intertextuality, irony and pastiche. It is a film about reality and imagination, about the elusiveness of truth, a morally complex story. The masterful ease with which the stories unfold belies the densely layered structure of the narrative. In questioning the relativity of truth, *Suraj* operates on the same premise as Akira Kurosawa's *Rashomon* (1950), creating a modern myth about the tentativeness of life. The same story is approached from different angles and with different interpretations. Later sections fill in well-crafted narrative gaps, always investing fresh layers of meaning. Manek remains largely impassive himself, while peopling his stories with quickened action in compressed time. For me, this is the closest any film-maker comes to using narrative irony in exploring the contradictions between intent and action. Maithili Rao writes:

> Benegal displays a wonderful, even self mocking, assurance while he combines the pleasure of literary allusion, realistic *mise-en-scène* that turns expressionist at times and a charming gravity to which he passes from the initial engaging humour. *Suraj Ka Satwan Ghoda* is a tour de force.[5]

Shyam Benegal creates a rich framework of reference using Bharati's fiction and Ghulam Mohammad Sheikh's paintings, weaving in literary and cinematic echoes of the perennial archetype of Devdas, the tragic lover. Shifting points of view cut, shape and recreate a piece of linear narrative exploring notions of love and romance, and the evanescence of human relationships. The female characters in the film are the most intriguing and dynamic, manipulative and rebellious, with aspects that they hide and reveal as under a Venetian shutter.[6] On a realistic level, *Suraj Ka Satwan Ghoda* recreates a small-town atmosphere in which a group of youths vicariously enter the lives of Manek's characters. On the philosophical level, the film raises profound questions about life experiences. Each fictitious character is defined by his or her social background, and the film opens up broader questions of cultural definitions of masculinity and femininity. Manek's responses to the three women in his life differ according to his age in the narrative time. The stories are told at the same time, they are set in the same neighbourhood and they deal with varying experiences of love. With Jamuna, however, Manek is an adolescent, with Lily the young lover, and with Satti the indecisive young adult unable to handle the demands of real life. At strategic points of his life, Manek remains ineffective and inactive. He looks on as Jamuna is married off to an old man. He advises Lily to marry Jamuna's lover, Tanna, and he fails to save Satti when she asks for his help.

Benegal indicates that the seeds of non-linear narrative were sown with *Mandi* and extended in *Trikaal*:

> At some stage, film-makers wonder if a story can be articulated in a way that's different from the traditional narrative. In cinema, everything is phenomenalised, a story is caught in the warp of space and time. On the other hand, music and literature leave you free to make different interpretations. And so you start wondering, why can't cinema do this as well? Why must it be merely like carpentry making a chair with four legs? Ninety per cent of film-making follows such a set definition. I felt it would be more exciting to go beyond this fixed point. Besides telling a story, a film-maker has to evolve new forms, discover the limitless possibilities in his mind. I got an opportunity to do this with the TV series *Bharat Ek Khoj*, which was like making 52 different films in 18 months. I didn't worry about the kind of form I was adopting for each episode and drew liberally from folk, Western and classical theatre. It was an exercise in loosening up. It is about how each one of us perceives love. I was seduced by the idea of making a love story perhaps because through it I could also answer the question, what is the creative act? The raconteur tells different stories which are open to different interpretations. It's exciting to try and place your finger on the pulse of a story, to distinguish between fact and fiction. What the three stories finally reveal is life itself – the moments of rapture and betrayal.[7]

With a brilliant screenplay by Shama Zaidi, atmospheric camerawork by one of India's greatest cinematographers, Piyush Shah, and memorable performances by a repertory cast, Benegal achieves a densely layered drama that moves at an elegant pace. He gives the three stories different looks and colour palettes experimenting with light and decor. With *Suraj Ka Satwan Ghoda*, Benegal takes his work into broader vistas of human imagination and creativity, an effort he himself will find hard to surpass. The title is also a clue to the film. The seventh horse of the sun is the youngest; he moves perpetually towards the future, towards light. The title itself signifies the concept of time with the Hindu myth of the sun god riding in his chariot driven by seven white horses. Man will constantly be drawn towards love and imagination; lives will always be lived and stories will always be told.

Nehru (1983)

In a career spanning 20 feature films so far, Benegal also has a formidable body of documentary films to his credit. These range from cultural anthropology (*Indian Youth*, 1968) and problems of industrialisation (*Steel: A Whole New Way of Life*, 1971) to Indian classical music (*Raga and the Emotions*, 1971). The best known of these are the Indo-Soviet coproduction *Nehru* and the Films Division production *Satyajit Ray*. In his two long documentaries, Benegal has designed a deceptively simple approach to two extraordinary men of India. These films are not chronological statements with exterior commentary or conclusions. In both cases, Benegal lets the man speak in his own words.

Nehru is a three-hour documentary film on the life of Jawaharlal Nehru (1889–1964), made in three parts: 'The Awakening', 'The Struggle' and 'Freedom'. The film traces the evolution of Nehru from his early years, necessarily tracing the history of the nationalist movement and post-Independence India until 1964. The Indian Ministry of Broadcasting and Information commissioned *Nehru* as a coproduction between Indian Films Division and the Soviet Union. The script uses a first-person narrative (Saeed Jaffrey's voice-over) and is sourced from Jawaharlal Nehru's own writings (*Discovery of India*, *Glimpses of World History*, *Selected Works*, *Letters and Speeches*). Both *Glimpses* and *Discovery* were formative influences on Benegal when he read them as a young boy.[8]

He went on to make a mammoth 52-part television series *Bharat Ek Khoj* (1989–94) based on *Discovery of India*, which can be unarguably considered the most definitive educational programme on Indian history. Nehru's concern for an egalitarian society and his socialist vision of development are, to a large extent, mirrored in Benegal's concerns as a film-maker. Given Nehru's influence on his thinking, it seemed inevitable that Benegal would be asked to make the film. The density of the richly layered material makes *Nehru* resemble a visual text. The film is an excellent example of documentation, using photographs, objects, letters and colonial documents, but it is much more than that. This material alternates with four grand, orchestrated movements in colour capturing contemporary India, her people, landscapes and architecture. Nehru's political thoughts and his reflections are also visualised in different styles. Benegal the director stands back and allows Nehru's own words and thoughts to construct the persona for the viewer.

The film opens with a preface by Indira Gandhi, who speaks to camera about her father, saying, 'He was the humanity in a human being.' She also points to the inherent conflict in Nehru, which arose from the seeming unchanging nature of society, as well as the conflict in himself as a poet and politician. 'The Awakening' traces the birth of Nehru in Allahabad, the son of prosperous lawyer Motilal Nehru. The context is set with the founding of the Indian National Congress in 1885 and a brief history of the British Empire in India, including the handing over from the East India Company to the British Crown after the 1857 Mutiny. This is illustrated with sketches, etchings and black-and-white stills.

Archival footage of nineteenth-century London illustrates Nehru's first trip to England, and photographs support his subsequent years of education at Harrow and Trinity College, Cambridge. After studying law, Nehru returns to India to find the Congress 'an English-speaking upper-class affair'. His marriage to Kamala in 1916 is followed by World War I footage and the Russian Revolution led by Lenin. Nehru's growing interest in world history brings into context his increasing involvement with Indian politics. He talks of Gandhi as a 'powerful element of fresh air who seemed to emerge from the millions of India', accompanied by footage of the non-violent movement and police atrocities against the satyagrahis (members of Gandhi's non-violent resistance movement). Nehru at this time came into close contact with peasant life, and he realised how urban culture ignored the poverty and degradation of the masses. His disapproval of class differences firmed his intention of ridding India of poverty and oppression. Gandhi's leadership made the Congress a more agrarian organisation, and Nehru himself felt the thrill of influencing the masses with his speeches. Just before the visit of the Prince of Wales, all important nationalist leaders were put into jail. The next sequence is shot in the Lucknow jail cell which housed Nehru, the first of those reflective phases which produced his great books on Indian and world history.

Extensive footage of Soviet Russia illustrates Nehru's deep admiration for the socialist structure of the state and his hope that a similar pattern could be used in India. An exchange of letters demonstrates the close relationship and differences between Gandhi and Nehru. The latter emerges as a staunch but critical disciple of Gandhi, arguing against capitalist exploitation, 'I am a socialist and a republican, no believer of princes and industrialists.' In fact, the widening perspective of his world view leads him to observe that 'nationalism is a narrow, indefinite creed'. Footage of the civil disobedience movement shows brutal oppression by the British forces and Gandhi on his Salt March to Dandi. Over the next few years, Nehru is in and out of jail, while Gandhi travels to London to meet the British ministers. Nehru is discharged from jail to visit his ailing wife Kamala, at which time he admits not fully understanding his wife, having thrown himself completely into the freedom movement. Personal events and the intensified nationalist movement are set against larger world events: the collapse of Western civilisation in the world war and the setting up of a socialist structure in Russia.

The second part of the documentary, 'The Struggle', starts with Nehru immersing himself completely in the people's movement after his return to India from Switzerland, where Kamala died in 1935. Nehru returns with the conviction that socialism is the only solution to curing India's woes. His growing concern about communalism in Indian politics comes to a head when the Muslim League leader Jinnah propounds the two-nation theory. The debate on coexisting religions in India which ensued is followed by a letter to Jinnah, in which he writes, 'Thinking of communal groups functioning politically, is to think in terms of medievalism.' Viewing this section after the communal violence of the 1990s (and even as it continues today in India) and the rise of right-wing politics – sharply underlines the collapse of the secular beliefs and ideals which Nehru propagated for the new India.

This period of turbulence in the Indian freedom movement is set in a global context with footage of Hitler and Mussolini, Nazi processions and war footage in Russia, India, Burma and Singapore. Nehru is enraged at the manner in which reluctant Indians had to fight in both world wars as part of the British Army. In his letters to his daughter Indira, Nehru writes of the conflict between the ideal of nonviolence and the surrounding violence of World War II. Disturbing footage of police violence in the Do or Die resistance movement as well as the horrific wartime famine in Bengal is followed by Nehru's reflective thoughts about Indian civilisation and the rich heritage of culture. A richly layered montage includes the Buddhist caves in Ajanta and Ellora, Rajasthani painting, temple architecture (Madurai and Konark), the golden temple in Amritsar, Qutb Minar, Benaras and Muslim artisans and weavers at work. This sequence, at once lyrical and powerfully suggestive, evokes the rich matrix of India's people and their history. Benegal demonstrates his deep understanding and knowledge of Indian history and a tolerant culture. This juxtaposition of the specifics of history (as in the freedom movement) with more profound observations about a culture – and stylistic variations for both strands – is what makes *Nehru* a monumental work, sharply relevant in today's context for the Indian viewer.

This section ends in 1947 with Indian Independence. Partition footage is offset by a heavy-hearted Nehru delivering the famous freedom speech: 'At the stroke of the midnight hour... India will awake to life and freedom.'

Part three is entitled 'Freedom' and opens with a marvellous colour montage of buildings and people to the strains of the morning Raaga Lalit (sung by Bhimsen Joshi). The golden hues of this dawn of freedom are veiled by footage of the refugee trains, murder and arson in the Punjab. Nehru's conflict within himself and the need for accountability set an urgent tone. A series of significant events follow, illustrated by more recent film footage: Gandhi's assassination, the signing of the constitution and the momentous task of building a new India. Nehru's ideal of peaceful coexistence ('peace is essential to our growing') and Jaffrey's voice-over announcing 'Violence cannot lead to any solution – democracy and socialism are but the means to an end', with a pan over the Bombay skyline and the Ganapati immersion, today seem invested with an ironic edge.

The footage which follows concentrates on Nehru's role as the first prime minister of independent India, as he lays the foundation for rapid national development in agriculture, industry, science and technology. Nehru's strategic role in the non-aligned movement again demonstrates his lifelong belief in world peace. Russian footage of Nehru's visit to the Soviet Union records the popularity he enjoyed with the people of that land. The most remarkable footage in this section shows a worried, stressed and agitated Nehru holding a private meeting with the Indian Army commanders in chief during the Sino-Indian war. In an interview, he talks to camera and speaks of 'the satisfaction of fitting in one's thoughts with one's actions'. The film ends with Nehru's death and funeral ceremony, after which his ashes are scattered in the Ganges and over the fields. Prominent in the mourning ceremony are his daughter Indira and grandsons Rajiv and Sanjay. Both Indira Gandhi and Rajiv Gandhi were assassinated while holding the office of prime minister.

The film was codirected by Benegal and Yuri Aldokhin. Aldokhin says:

> Nehru's character interests the entire world, especially the Russians. There is a Russian proverb that says, 'Tell me who your friend is, and I will tell you who you are!' We are extremely proud to have Nehru as a friend. As a director, I was doubly proud to make the film.[9]

Nehru's views on socialism, India's friendship with the Soviet Union and the high regard Russians had for Nehru offered a premise to use extensive archival footage from Soviet Russia (the revolution, the two world wars, Nehru's visits to the Soviet Union) from the Centre for Film Archives. The subsequent collapse of Soviet Russia and any related analysis bring a cutting edge to the film. The colour sections specially shot for the documentary by ace cameraman Subrato Mitra (Satyajit Ray's cinematographer) capture and often transcend the spirit of Nehru's vision. It is both the relevance of Nehru's ideals and the departures from his world that invest a dynamic tension in the reading of this text. *Nehru* offers the viewer not just a personality, but a national history framed in the larger context of turbulent world history. More importantly, it offers glimpses into a heritage and culture, and ideals of peace and equality which seem so far removed from today's reality in India. When *Nehru* was screened at the NFT in London, the film was described as follows:

> As much a history of India itself as of the complex, sometimes insecure statesman who led his country through so many years of turmoil. If the exigencies of co-production result in a degree of political wariness, it does not impair the flow of historical material. Essential viewing for social historians and India watchers.[10]

Even today, *Nehru* remains a definitive educational documentary which deserves to be revisited by every student of history and

Benegal checking the print of Nehru *in Moscow with co-director Yuri Aldokhin.*

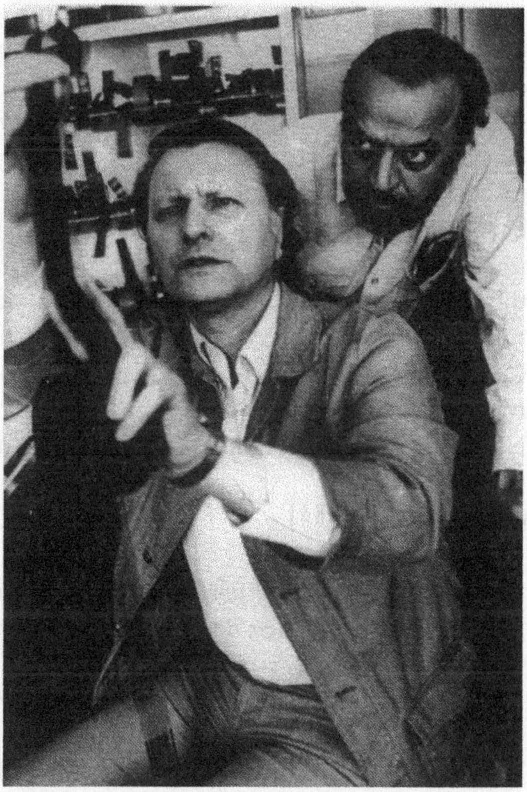

film. It remains one of the most important films from Benegal's oeuvre that merits a DVD release.

At one point in the film, Nehru writes, 'Buddha, Marx and Gandhi appealed to me.' All three figures have had their deep influence on Benegal as well, equally as has Nehru's writings and philosophy. It was Nehru's talk on the subliminal effect of cinema that inspired the young Benegal to consume everything that he could read about the medium. Benegal started his career with a self-conscious socialist view of contemporary society (*Ankur* and *Nishant*). His *Manthan* has been read as a document of the Nehruvian developmental model. The *Encyclopaedia of Indian Cinema* states: 'This work provided an early aesthetic articulation of what would soon become government policy towards the rural areas via the SITE programme.'[11] Benegal has consistently worked as a critical voice within state machinery (the state commissioned *Bharat Ek Khoj*, *Samar* and *Hari Bhari*). He has often been criticised for compromising aesthetic standards to work with the state to make films with a cause. He has also been influential with regard to film policy organisations. Most importantly, Benegal has consistently made films to communicate the need for change and to strive for the ideals of equality and freedom. The film-maker was part of the National Integration Council (1986–89) and the National Council of Art. His repertoire could even be seen as a cinematic equivalent to Nehru's writings on Indian politics and history.

Satyajit Ray (1984)

> Seeing some new wave films of today, you realize that Benegal is the pioneer of new cinema – he has blazed a trail for others to follow. Shyam Benegal is to the new generation of filmmakers what Satyajit Ray was, and is, to Benegal's generation.[12]

While discussing Satyajit Ray as one of the formative influences in his life as a film-maker, Benegal says:

> One can categorise Indian cinema in two periods: before Ray and after Ray. He did serve as an inspiration to a whole genre of film-makers who came after him. I was interested in making a film on him because I have strong opinions on his work – and I have been an admirer of his work ever since I began making films.... I have tried making the definitive film about Ray, not just impressions about him.[13]

Benegal's documentary on Satyajit Ray opens with the auteur on the set of *Ghare Baire* (*The Home and the World*) capturing Ray at work, talking to his art director and directing his actors, Jennifer Kapoor, Victor Bannerjee and Swatilekha Sengupta. Ray is in turn

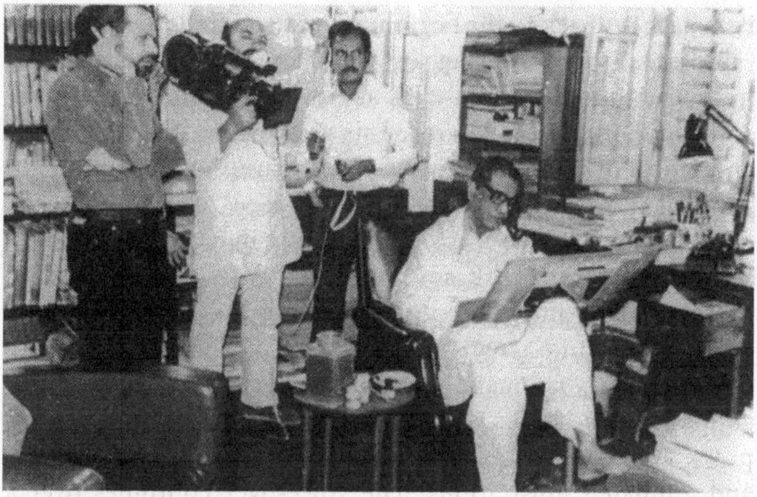

Shyam Benegal and Govind Nihalani shooting for the documentary on Satyajit Ray. Ray in his study, seated on his familiar leather couch

relaxed, humorous, intense and thoughtful before he disappears below the black screen to operate the camera. Govind Nihalani's camera unobtrusively captures the master in his space, Ray in his familiar study or at his piano. The two-hour documentary is structured as a freewheeling conversation between Ray and Benegal. Benegal leads without imposing on his subject's thoughts, and the result is one of the most generous tributes from one film-maker to another. This is considered the most comprehensive interview given by Ray, in which he discusses all the influences and thought processes that have gone into his grand oeuvre. In his introduction to the script of the documentary, Samik Bandopadhyay writes:

> Ray, we have been told, would have liked this film to be more Benegal than Ray, more of an evaluation of or response to his entire corpus. I recall Benegal thinking aloud on the same lines after a spell of shooting. I have never asked him why he changed his thrust. Was it the sheer clarity of Ray's articulation that took over at a certain point and shaped the film the way it is now?[14]

Benegal goes back to the beginnings of the man, a period which represents the flowering of the Bengal renaissance. The interview unfolds as Ray talks about his childhood memories and early influences. Ray recounts growing up in a rich family ambience of music, literature and painting, extending to Santiniketan and Indian art, Western classical music, commercial art, the first film society in Calcutta, Renoir, Pudovkin and Cherkasov, children's literature and an increasingly complex political setting in Bengal. Family photographs and actual shots of Ray's old house and school illustrate Ray's fascinating account of his early days. Ray talks about his grandfather Upendra Kishore's writings and printing press, and also of his father Sukumar Ray's nonsense rhymes and animated illustrations. The voice-over continues over a clip from Ray's children's film *Goopy Gyne Bagha Byne* (1968), the chiaroscuro ghost dance as the king of the ghosts grants three boons to the heroes.

Shots from the South Calcutta school and Presidency College illustrate Ray's account of his school and college days. Nihalani's camera captures striking scenes of Santiniketan (the university founded by Rabindranath Tagore) where Ray studied art. Sunlight spills through the stained-glass prayer house, children sit on the grass for outdoor classes in the mango grove, choral voices emanate from the music department. As Ray talks about his discovery of a vigorous art aesthetic in Santiniketan, several paintings by the Tagores and other artists melt into the frame. Ray's book jacket illustrations are displayed as he talks about his days in advertising and publishing. While designing the jacket for *Aam Athir Bhepu* (*The Mango Shell Flute*), a children's adaptation of Bibhutibhushan Bandopadhyay's *Pather Panchali*, Ray was inspired to make a film of Apu's story. This was the genesis of the Apu trilogy which placed both Indian cinema and Ray on the world map.

There are striking similarities in the thinking of Ray and Benegal. Benegal was so discontented with the state of Indian films in general that he lacked the conviction needed for making a film such as *Ankur*. *Pather Panchali* revived his hope about making the sort of film in which he believed. In this documentary, Benegal asks Ray what view he had about the state of Indian cinema when he started to make films. Ray answers:

> Well, we were certainly very strongly critical of the Bengali films of that period. In fact, that's one of the things that we did at the film society. We were studying foreign films – we were having seminars on things on the Indian cinema of that period. We were always strongly critical. We found most of our stuff very false, unrealistic and shoddy, commercial in a bad way. That sort of thing. They were very theatrical.

A discussion on Hollywood films is laid over stills of Hollywood stars, including Greta Garbo, Marlene Dietrich and Clark Gable. Ray states that his main interest in films as a schoolboy was in stars, an interest sustained by magazines such as *Picturegoer*, *Photoplay* and *Film Pictorial*. As a college student, he became more interested in the directorial aspect of film-making and started reading up on people such as John Ford, William Wyler, Ernst Lubitsch and Frank Capra. Over stills and posters, Ray's voice-over continues:

> I saw whatever John Ford films I could get to see and then, even later, the early forties or late thirties, Hollywood comedies and the Hollywood thriller. Very hard-edged films like the Billy Wilder of the early forties – *Double Indemnity, Lost Weekend* – and comedies like *Major and Minor*, Lee McCarey's comedies with Cary Grant and Irene Dunne, which were very fine. And I have re-seen them on television, and they are still marvellous. And the Frank Capra films of the thirties like *It Happened One Night* and *Mr Smith Goes to Washington* and all the others.

In close-up, Ray continues, 'So they were very, very well crafted films, so my education really is based on these extremely well-written, well-directed, well-shot, well-acted films of the thirties and forties.' Over a clip from Jean Renoir's *The Southerner* (1945), Ray explains how the film looked completely different from American films and how he recognised a completely new approach, a new style of film-making, from looking at American films made by a French director. Ray was influenced by Italian neo-realism and Cartier-Bresson's naturalistic photographic style. Commenting on Ray's visual style, Benegal initiates the following conversation:

> Benegal: You set a certain kind of photographic style when you made your first film, because Indian films used to rely a great deal on what one might call a manufactured kind of feel and look, which was highly cosmetic, and did a great deal for the main actors, you know, to make them look good, and so on. And you changed it. Was there a very conscious attempt on your part?
>
> Ray: It was very, very conscious. It was something I discussed with my cameraman right at the start of the shooting. We were great admirers of Cartier-Bresson and we believed in available light, the source of light for photography, I mean maintaining the sources as far as possible.... Well, for location you chose certain times of the day to shoot certain scenes ... we made some experiments with 16 mm camera shooting and all kinds of light conditions, and we found that everything came out. So we decided to do the realistic kind of photography.

Ray discusses the problems of filmcraft he encountered when making *Pather Panchali* when he was experimenting with a totally new unit, with various cameras and lenses. Benegal points to Ray's powerful use of detail to express emotions or relationships between people. Benegal chooses to illustrate his point with the sequence in which Apu and Durga discover their dead aunt and her brass pot rolls into the water. The battered brass pot dances in the water as a plaintive song in the aunt's voice is heard in the background. A very engaging discussion continues on Ray's use of sparse dialogue, minimal information scenes and unique use of ambient sound. The influence of Ray's thoughts on Benegal's own style are indicated in the following response from Ray:

> You must have the feeling of doing the right thing in the right circumstances. And that comes from observation, your personal experience ... and there may be incidents which you have not experienced personally, directly. There is this thing like logic in a story which makes your story ring true, whatever you make happen on the screen, you make ring true.

Ray continues, stating that he is more interested in the subject than in the form:

> What interests me is density. How much you can tell, how telling you can make your images and how much you can pack in your films without gimmicks or whatever you wish to call them...the attempt is to achieve clarity with a group of characters, with a group of situations which don't follow a normal normative pattern.

Benegal illustrates with the long memory game sequence from *Aranyer Din Ratri* (*Days and Nights in the Forest*, 1969), as he reads the only piece of commentary in the film:

> Mr Ray has often referred to the influence of Western classical music on his work, Mozart's operas in particular. The ability of the individual characters to maintain their individuality through elaborate ensembles. He says the memory game in *Days and Nights in the Forest* attempts this. The game itself is the ground base over which the six characters play out their individual roles in word, look and gesture.

Benegal's own treatment of ensemble films (*Mandi*, *Trikaal*, *Suraj Ka Satwan Ghoda*) adheres very much to the structure that he describes above.

At one point Benegal says to Ray, 'You have always been an observer of, let's say, reality, if I might use the term, and whatever statements you have had to make have always been oblique.' Ray answers, 'By temperament I think I am a film-maker who likes to be oblique, if such a thing is possible or valid in relation to the subject.'

The illustrated clips from *Apur Sansar* (*The World of Apu*, 1959) and *Charulata* (1964) are highly charged erotic scenes, but Ray exploits the sexual frisson rather than broad overtures. The sequences are strong reminders of Benegal's treatment of sexuality in *Manthan* and *Bhumika*, in which the director exploits the tension below the surface instead of using overt sex scenes. Ray's Apu trilogy captured the entire sociopolitical change that resulted in migration to the city. But only when this economic canvas starts to shape and affect Apu's destiny does it hold narrative interest for the viewer. The progressive values of education and mobility are later replaced by a harsh and unrelenting view of crass commercialism in the nightmare world of the city. In his Calcutta films, Ray makes oblique comments on the corruption of values by blatant market forces. Like Ray, Benegal has also probed historically determined situations and basic human relationships at the heart of them in his films – in *Ankur*, *Bhumika*, *Mandi*, *Kalyug* and *Mammo*, to name a few. Benegal asks Ray: 'Would you say that you knew that the environment was changing around you, and there was the effect of that on you?' Ray replies, 'That did happen towards the end of the sixties, the early seventies. I could describe that as a period in which you strongly felt certain changes taking place. Almost in the day-to-day existence, you felt it, and you felt that without that you couldn't make a film.'

With *Pratidwandi* (*The Adversary*, 1970) and the later 1970s films, Ray explored the problems of middle-class society in Calcutta, casting an increasingly harsh eye on the decadent bourgeois value system. Benegal points to the core concern in Ray's films (which is equally true of his own work) when he tells Ray:

> … most of your films have dealt with change actually. Your characters, your main characters are usually coping with or adapting to this change. It starts with your trilogy and carries all the way through to *Jana Aranya* (*The Middleman*, 1975).

Benegal's economy of film-making, manner of locating, use of minimal dialogue, density of ambient sound, richness of details and leitmotifs, fascination with the past – all these areas seem to bear Ray's strong influence. Critics in the West have hailed Benegal as the upholder of Ray's legacy. Some refer to the senior film-maker as Benegal's mentor. As far as the history of parallel cinema is concerned, Benegal did initiate a larger movement by breaking away from the conventions of commercial Hindi cinema in the 1970s. The groundwork had been laid, however, two decades earlier by directors such as Ray and Ritwik Ghatak, as they challenged the theatricality of Bengali cinema.

Ironically, the two film-makers discuss the same idea in the following conversation:

> Benegal: Your status in Indian film has been, as one might call it, one of splendid isolation. You have been quite alone in what you have been doing and with the kind of concern you show in your films. Now, has that affected you in anyway, because there hasn't been enough of a kind of bouncing board to react against or to place yourself in the milieu?

> Ray: Well, this is not something of my creation. I mean I would have wanted, for instance, to start a trend, a whole new trend or something like that.… In any case, film-making has so many hassles that … so problematic here to get a film done one stops to think whether you are creating a school or whether others are following in your footsteps.… You just keep on working because after all it's also a living and you make a living, and you express yourself at the same time crossing many obstacles on the way.

Ray's body of work – like Benegal's later – represents a liberal humanist perception of the history of modern India. The interview makes use of extensive clips from Ray's films, sometimes as illustrations and sometimes as interesting counterpoints. For the uninitiated viewer, the documentary offers a scintillating overview of Ray's oeuvre, his craft and the critical responses of a film-maker who has studied this formidable body of work very closely. Samik Bandopadhyay concludes:

> In his long interview, Ray opens up in a manner in which he has not opened up before, and that would perhaps be the greatest compliment for Benegal, who has treated Ray more as an elder colleague and fellow worker than as a master.[15]

Conclusion

A highly respected film-maker in his country, Benegal is one of the few Indian directors who enjoys an international reputation as a new wave film-maker. Following the overwhelming success of his first trilogy and his trips to various festivals all over the world, Benegal at one point had become a cultural ambassador for India. While Benegal's best films remain outstanding cinematic achievements, almost all his work is a vast cultural document – an insider's view of the contemporary nation, its history, its heroes and underdogs, its women and outcasts. Prominent economist Amiya Bagchi refers to Benegal's early films as 'the best articulation of the dialectics of social change in Indian cinema. Of showing economic structures and power balance in a pared down story.'[16]

Samik Bandopadhyay, film and theatre critic, wrote the post production film scripts for *Manthan* and *Satyajit Ray* for publication (see Bibliography). In the 1980s, when video tapes were not generally available, film students had to fall back on scripts as tools for film studies. He comments:

> Shyam Benegal found a place with credible narratives and working within the parameters of government project commissioning. Benegal has been

> the only one to pursue the project of using films for a social purpose. His films are anti-establishment, grappling with intricacies and complexities of a changing reality. As opposed to the facile films made in the name of pure cinema, Shyam's sophistication and artistry has been consistent in using people, locations, textures, cool quiet handling of the media. His films also have this internal lyricism in cinematic terms, which he allows to surface without holding back – it is quite exceptional.

Considering Benegal's vast oeuvre, his choice of subjects, his interventions and negotiations in the changing map of Indian cinema, writer and programme-maker Nasreen Munni Kabir compares him to the French director François Truffaut:

> Shyam's wide range of narratives and the manner of engaging with his characters reminds me of Truffaut's style. Shyam, like Truffaut, also had to defend his success. I had programmed Benegal's *Bhumika* at the Pompidou Centre, Paris, in 1983. The French loved the film and Smita. In fact, *Bhumika* has been recently acquired by a French distributor. Benegal represents the whole world in which a character belongs. A foreign audience enters that story, gets involved with the character and is willing to go on the journey. In India, he is considered a think tank. He was very influential in formulating Doordarshan [state television] policy about how the government defined culture.[17]

Benegal is one of the most respected men in the film and television industry, a godfather to many talented actors and technicians. However, despite consistent work of very high standards, it is true that international awards have eluded him. *The Making of the Mahatma* did not prove to be the international crossover film he had hoped for, something which was due more to the failure of the NFDC marketing strategy than any failings in the film. Nor has he set the cash registers jingling with his kind of films in an increasingly global market. As Derek Malcolm has analysed:

> All over the world, it's becoming more and more difficult for independently minded directors to make films that are not going to make money in the popular sense. It's true in England, it's true in France, it's certainly true in America. The Shyam Benegals of this world have had a very very rough deal in the last ten years. Very few of them have succeeded at the box office. All over the world the quality market has contracted. It's rather like an industry. More and more corporations are springing up which have hundreds of businesses under their wing. Everything is becoming more and more controlled by fewer and fewer people. Filmmakers and artists in general are under the wing of commercial artists. Culture is becoming more and more homogenised. It's the McDonalds culture whereby everybody sees the same things all over the world.[18]

After a teaching term at Northwestern University in Chicago in Spring 2002, Benegal has returned to pre-production on a feature based on the life of the Indian nationalist leader Subhas Chandra Bose. The Sahara Group, an Indian corporation, will produce the film, which is to be shot in India, Burma, Hungary and Germany. The project will take the film-maker back to the world of another prominent Indian whose controversial life has fascinated him since he was a child, when his uncle fought in the Indian National Army, set up by Bose. This talented film-maker's career seems to have no end in sight, as he tirelessly explores and reworks important social and historical issues in cinematic form.

Benegal admits he would like to go on making films that he believes in:

> I'd like to go on making films, I don't think I can do anything as well, I'm not even sure if I do this well enough .... India continues to inspire with a variety of different subjects to work on. I love doing films on the temperature of society and capture the transition of this amazingly diverse structure of our nation. But I need to be driven by the subject, to be completely possessed by it.

Appendix: Reflections

Shyam Benegal's reflections

On the language of commercial cinema
Whatever the genre of cinema, you cannot go beyond your own sensibilities. Your sensibilities determine your subject and its treatment, you cannot do things you are not convinced about. You can extend your vocabulary but not change your sensibility.

I think some popular films like *Sholay* (1975) are great fun. I have no quarrels about the spectatorship of Bombay cinema. My films are all about conflict; in mainstream cinema, the values projected are status quo. Hindi commercial cinema constantly tells you that change is not possible!

On cinema as a tool for social reform
I don't know if cinema can actually bring about change in society. But cinema can certainly be a vehicle for creating social awareness. I believe in egalitarianism and every person's awareness of human rights. Through my films I can say, 'Here is the world, and here are the possibilities we have.' It is difficult to define the purpose of my art. ... [E]ventually it is to offer an insight into life, into experience, into a certain kind of emotive or cerebral area.

On his own oeuvre
It is very difficult for me as a film-maker to talk about my own films – I make one and move on to the next. Films have their own life – they are like children. Once they grow into adults, the connection is no longer there with the maker. At that stage, the film develops a relationship with the audience, which is even more significant than the relationship with the maker.

On his contemporaries

Other film-makers interested me all the time. There was no overt influence – you internalise a lot. When it comes out, it is your own voice. I don't imitate. I never have felt the need to imitate anyone's work. Even the biggest influence, *Pather Panchali*, was so internalised that I never thought of imitating any scene or sequence or adapting anything from Ray's film. The impact of *Pather Panchali* was so great that it convinced me that I could make the film I wanted to make. There was no question of that. It was an important conviction for myself that I didn't have to toe anyone's line.

Adoor Gopalakrishnan had made his first film before *Ankur*, soon after he came out of the Film Institute. I made it a point to see films from different parts of India. I wasn't particularly pleased with *Swayamvaram* (1972), but his work in the late 1970s was so unbelievably good. He was probably one of the most original voices in Indian cinema. Ketan Mehta and Saeed Mirza came later. I liked *Mirch Masala* (Mehta, 1986) very much, it would be hard put to equal that film even till today. Saeed hasn't fully realised his potential. Saeed is capable of making much better films than what he has already produced. His scripts are wonderful and ideas are wonderful. His films don't seem fully realised. Kundan Shah made *Jaaney Bhi Do Yaaro* (1983), which was a fully realised film. Kundan hasn't been able to match that film with anything else later. Basu Chatterjee – I was very impressed by his first film, *Sara Akash* (1969). He never equalled that film. Mani Kaul's *Uski Roti* (1970) came at the same time. I started to like Mrinal Sen's Calcutta trilogy and also *In Search of Famine* (*Akaler Sandhaney*, 1980), his best film. *Calcutta 71* (1971), also Ray's *Pratidwandi* (1970). Also Mrinal's films after *Calcutta 71*.

[The] post-Emergency scene resulted in the strident hero – the angry young man. I never really related to Bombay films in the 1970s, although *Deewar* (1975) was a very accomplished film. Then I can never really relate to these films very much. My experience was never extended nor could I relate to them in any way. Of course, for a lark I loved the films of Manmohan Desai. My daughter Pia, for her birthday, we had to get *Amar Akbar Anthony* (1977) for her – it was the best film she had seen.

On his cast and crew

I was casting for *Nishant*, and I couldn't find an actor to play the part of Rukmini. I was thinking of another Marathi actress, Bhakti Bharve, who died recently in a road accident. One day I was watching the news on television, and I took notice of this very attractive newsreader [Smita Patil]. The camera was really loving her – she had great presence. I asked my sound recordist Hiten Ghosh, who had just started with me fresh from the Film Institute. He said he knew her, and he spoke to the family. Smita's mother had seen *Ankur* and was very interested in her daughter working with me. Smita, of course, was most reluctant. She did not want to have anything to do with films. She came to see me twice, once with her father who was then minister of the Maharashtra cabinet. I finally managed to persuade her to act in *Nishant*. She was not a trained actress, to see what her acting capabilities were I put her in *Charandas Chor*, a children's film made for the Children's Film Society. She was very good. She was absolutely first class. There was no question after that that she would be ideal for *Manthan*. Shabana at that time was riding very high, and she said no to *Manthan*, so I took Smita, and there was no question in my mind that she was to be in *Bhumika*. Until the time we did *Bhumika*, Smita still was not sure that she wanted to be an actress. For *Nishant*, the problem more than her was her principal of St Xavier's College. He refused to let her go for the shoot because it was close to exams. For the missionary padres, film was just a vulgar obscenity, so I had to meet him and convince him.

With the National Award for *Bhumika* she found her métier, she knew she wanted to be an actress. She was as successful as Shabana. People were starting to talk about her in the same way.

They were the new breed of actresses working in the realist genre.

Naseeruddin Shah was noticed quite a lot for *Manthan*. He started getting all kind of roles in mainstream cinema after *Manthan*. He, of course, considers *Manthan* to be the least successful of his performances. Whatever he does he gives it his best. His commitment to acting is total. There is no other thing on his mind except to give the best possible performance. But he does not have the sense of humour that Om Puri has. Also Om has a great deal of compassion as a human being. Naseer was too focused on his own self. Om is a more affable human being.

More or less by now I had my own repertory cast members – Shabana Azmi, Smita Patil, Naseer, Girish Karnad, Kulbhushan Kharbanda. Girish was never serious about acting – he concentrated on writing. He is one of the best playwrights we have produced in recent years. His acting came second to that. I think he made a pretty handsome livelihood as an actor. Mohan Agashe goes back to his theatre days in Theatre Academy. But I haven't cast him after *Bhumika*, which is almost 25 years now. I was taking graduates from the National School of Drama.

Govind was my cameraman for eleven films and seven documentaries. After that Ashok Mehta came in and other cameramen. Rajan Kothari has worked for the last three films. My editor Bhanu Divkar fell ill and eventually died, after which there have been various editors until recently – Asheem Sinha has worked as editor for the last four films.

I had V. K. Murthy [Guru Dutt's cinematographer] for one feature film plus all of *Bharat Ek Khoj*; Vanraj Bhatia as music director. *Mandi* – I used classical Urdu poets and Majrooh Sultanpuri, also in *Bhumika*. Kaifi Azmi wrote the dialogues for *Manthan* and won the National Award for that. Javed Akhtar has written the songs for *Sardari Begum* and *Zubeidaa*. Gulzar wrote the song for *Mammo*.

Reflections on Benegal

Govind Nihalani – Benegal's cinematographer and film-maker
Film-makers like Shyam got with them a world view. He took a position vis-à-vis the reality that he depicted – as a director he had a taken position. My political education began in his company. A fine combination of passion and the cerebral, he is one director who struck a balance between personal experience and ideology in his films. Shyam's contribution has been immense, he made films without government support, did not succumb to mainstream formula, gave viewers an intelligent choice of films, also proved that art films can be economically viable. Shyam gave his kind of films a place of tremendous respect – these films became part of people's conversations. Raising questions, suggesting choices, initiating debate was very important. As a person he is a very fine human being, with no rancour, helpful even to his worst critics. The guy is a good man!

Shyam was well exposed to international cinema. The Film Society movement was a major contributing factor in the evolution of shooting styles. As an ad-film-maker, constant innovation became part of his style. He was open to new ideas and believed the cameraman can realise his vision. This served as the foundation of our working relationship. At that time, the Czech cinema movement was a great stimulating factor. Breaking out of indoor style of shooting and new technology (enabling synch-sound) brought a sense of liberation.

The concentration was on character, aesthetics were utilised to project the character with maximum impact – human beings were at the centre of the story, centre of the predicament. Visually, full importance was given to characters as human beings who come across as real. Characters make the film seem real. Having made an average of one film per year, Shyam kept the parallel cinema going into so many years. If you look at his filmography, here is a cinema of Indian history.

Shama Zaidi – researcher, scriptwriter and long-term collaborator

It was always comfortable working as a team, production was a collaborative effort, people could give suggestions which Shyam would take on board. He places a lot of importance to research, I have gone on several research trips for films like *Antarnaad*, *Aarohan*, *Hari Bhari* [which was based on case studies of Muslim women]. For *Bhumika*, Mr Kamat Ghanekar was consulted for the black-and-white sequences. I researched for the period setting – sets, costumes, old films, photographs, old properties.

With Blaze Productions, Shyam did creative, imaginative and even aggressive marketing for his early film. There was also enough audience for what you call parallel cinema. Now private producers are fewer for this type of cinema, NFDC funds are insufficient, television channels offer good marketing potential, but these channels have to be tapped into.

Shabana Azmi – actor

Shyam Benegal is my reluctant guru. He has not allowed me to be worshipful, but he is my mentor and adviser. He wears his wisdom very lightly and has always challenged me to be his equal. That doesn't come easily to people. As a film-maker, he is deeply connected to life. An avid reader, loves music, theatre, painting – he is somebody that I would like to be.

There are two aspects to my personality – my international side and my traditional Muslim side (my culture) – I could have tilted either way. It was because of Shyam, Jennifer and Shashi Kapoor that I developed my international side – their world views and ideas ... The way I look at a city was shaped by Shyam. When I went to Cannes with Shyam, he would ask about the history of the place, about its architecture, its people. At 21, I was more interested in shopping and such. He would discuss and plan all the films that I should watch at the festival. In Paris, he would take me to the most authentic food joints.

It became a pattern to accompany him on location hunts. I would go with him; he would talk about the character with rich details and back stories. I would absorb everything because during the shoot he would not have the time to say all this again. On location in the villages, Shyam would build toilets, build badminton courts, arrange for carrom sets, so the unit could be fit and relaxed. Shyam has the director's eye. He had this brilliant team of actors who would learn their lines quickly. We would rehearse, find our spaces, then Shyam would place his camera – never a frame which looked wrong. After the day's shoot, Shyam would be the big father figure to his unit – discussing their love life, personal problems etc.

Much later his total involvement with 'cause' films has been a problem. Now the scripts are not as dramatic, production has been made easier, thus preventing great films from being made. With the script for *Hari Bhari*, I had felt there was some stereotyping of the Muslim community (they are poor, have too many children, etc.). As UN goodwill ambassador for population, I also thought that was politically incorrect. But Shyam is very open to suggestions and will never make ego an issue at all. I had suggested some changes in the script about my character Ghazala, which were taken very easily. Ghazala stitches clothes to earn some money at her mother's home; she then encourages her daughter to study.

Om Puri – actor

Shyam has been productive for three decades and has introduced new talent in actors, scriptwriters, editors, art directors. What is most outstanding is Benegal's sense of history, of film and history in general.

Benegal's films in Hindi are an immense contribution to national cinema, unlike Satyajit Ray, whose films were known in Bengal and abroad, but not in other regions of India. Shyam is not just a feature film-maker, he is an activist with films on various subjects, always trying to tell a story, using narrative devices to underscore an issue. His early script collaborators did a fine job in balancing the drama and issues in each film.

There was great sense of camaraderie in Shyam's units. During the shoot for *Mandi*, we would all play volleyball outside the sets till each one was called in for his or her shot. For *Susman*, I spent two weeks with the weavers of Pochampally to learn weaving for my part. I actually wove 40 metres of cloth which I gave to Shyam, Nira, Shabana and Govind.

I find his sense of history astounding, not just history of film, but of life in general. Like Neena Gupta said, Shyam has the answer to every 'why' under the sun – even the history of the safety pin. I treat him like a walking encyclopaedia on various subjects. After Ibrahim Alkazi, my teacher in the National School of Drama, Shyam is the strongest influence in shaping my personality.

Shyam shies away from passion or emotion (unlike Govind Nihalani). In this manner he is like Ray. Perhaps his intellect does not allow the display of raw emotions – we see an effort to distance from overdramatised scenes, quick cuts from emotional scenes. However, this is not wholly true of *Ankur* or *Bhumika*.

The problem with distribution of Shyam's films can be attributed to the fact that Benegal has not followed up marketing like other commercial directors. The production budgets had no investment in public relations. Also the present scriptwriters are of no comparable standard to his earlier collaborators.

An extremely disciplined man, he is in his office at 10 every morning. He works in the office half a day even when he is not into production.

Khaled Mohamed – scriptwriter
When I started film journalism in 1976 there was a strong polarisation between commercial cinema and uncompromising cinema. I fiercely believed in the pure cinema of Mani Kaul and

found Benegal's early films very cosily constructed. I wrote harsh reviews of his films. But I have moved from criticism to collaboration. When we met for the script of *Mammo*, it is to his total credit that there was never any articulation of past friction.

Shyam's forte is his compassion and warmth for people. He works best with three or four characters in frame – in interpersonal conversations. In the department of scriptwriting he has been a mentor to me, teaching me how to subdue melodrama and sentiment. *Zubeidaa* is a wish movie from a son, I had romanticised her as a mother. Shyam retained the spirit and substance but dignified the whole thing by putting the story in a historical context.

Shyam has taught me how to give space to performers, it has been a journey of progression as a writer from *Mammo* to *Zubeidaa.* My experience as a scriptwriter concretised the job of director when I made *Fiza* soon after.

Notes

Introduction

1. The Film Finance Corporation project turned realism into a national project. This policy of low-budget art films is referred to as the beginning of the new cinema movement in India. It included film-makers as varied as the avant-garde Mani Kaul and Kumar Shahani, the realistic Mrinal Sen and Basu Chatterjee, and several first-time directors whose realisation never matched intent. The terms 'parallel cinema', 'new wave cinema' and 'alternative cinema' are freely interchanged and flexibly used in the following chapters.
2. In subaltern studies in historiography, attention is drawn towards the powerless and voiceless, focusing on them as subjects and their narratives. Ranajit Guha's manifesto on subaltern subjects challenges the master narrative with one of fragments, validating marginal voices. See Ranajit Guha, *Subaltern Studies: Writings on South Asian History and Society*, (Delhi and London: Oxford University Press, 1982), especially chs 1 & 6.
3. *Guardian* Lecture by Shyam Benegal, National Film Theatre, October 1988. Chaired by Derek Malcolm. Transcript from archival tape held at the BFI Library, London.
4. Ibid.
5. Vijaya Mehta talks about Shyam encouraging her to direct her own films. Kalpana Lajmi talks about how her world views were shaped by Benegal, leading her to the bold themes in her films such as *Ek Pal* (1986). Aparna Sen refers to Benegal's humanistic vision, which she emulates in *Yugant* (1995).
6. See Peter Cowie (ed.), *International Film Guide* (London: Tantivy, 1979).
7. For more information on these directors, see Nasreen Munni Kabir, *Guru Dutt: A Life in Cinema* (Delhi and London: Oxford University Press, 1996); Rinki Bhattacharya, *Bimal Roy: A Man of Silence* (New Delhi: Indus, 1994); Bunny Reuben, *Mehboob, India's DeMille: The First Biography* (New Delhi: Indus, 1994); Bunny Reuben, *Raj Kapoor, The Fabulous Showman: An Intimate Biography* (New Delhi: Indus, 1995).

8. The Indian People's Theatre Association (IPTA) was an avant-garde leftist theatre movement launched to defend 'culture against Imperialism and Fascism'. The IPTA's impact on cinema was marked by the collective efforts of Khwaja Ahmad Abbas's *Dharti Ke Lal* (1946) and Chetan Anand's *Neecha Nagar* (1946); the actors Balraj Sahni, Shambhu Mitra and Prithviraj Kapoor; dancer Uday Shankar; musician Ravi Shankar; writers Krishan Chander and K. A. Abbas; and directors such as Raj Kapoor and V. Shantaram.
9. M. Madhava Prasad, *Ideology of the Hindi Film: A Historical Construction* (Delhi and Oxford: Oxford University Press, 1998), p. 197.
10. Satyajit Ray, 'Four and a Quarter', in *Our Films, Their Films* (Bombay: Orient Longman, 1976), p. 103.
11. Rachel Dwyer, *Yash Chopra* (London: BFI Publishing, 2002).
12. Shyam Benegal, 'Making Movies in Mumbai', in Lalit Mohan Joshi (ed.), *Bollywood: Popular Indian Cinema* (London: Dakini, 2001), p. 178.

1 – Parallel Cinema in India

1. Chidananda Dasgupta, 'The New Cinema: A Wave or a Future?', in Aruna Vasudev and Philippe Lenglet (eds), *India Cinema Superbazaar* (New Delhi: Vikas, c. 1983), p. 41.
2. See Ashis Nandy, 'Indian Popular Cinema as a Slum's Eye View of Politics', in Ashis Nandy (ed.), *The Secret Politics of our Desires: Innocence, Culpability and Indian Popular Cinema* (London: Zed, 1998).
3. Ashish Rajadhyaksha and Paul Willemen (eds), *Encyclopaedia of Indian Cinema*, 2nd edn (London: BFI; New Delhi: Oxford University Press, 1999), p. 27.
4. See Sunil Khilnani, *The Idea of India* (London: Hamish Hamilton, 1997).
5. See Sumita Chakravarty, *National Identity in Indian Popular Cinema, 1947–1987* (Austin: University of Texas Press, 1993), p. 235.
6. Ibid, p. 240.
7. Ranajit Guha, *Subaltern Studies: Writings on South Asian History and Society* (Delhi and London: Oxford University Press, 1982), p. 4.
8. Rajadhyaksha and Willemen (eds), p. 27.
9. *Guardian* Lecture by Shyam Benegal, National Film Theatre, October 1988. Chaired by Derek Malcolm. Transcript from archival tape held at the BFI Library, London.
10. Aruna Vasudev, *The New Indian Cinema* (Delhi: Macmillan, 1986), p. 40.
11. Rajadhyaksha and Willemen (eds), p. 416.
12. Derek Malcolm, *Guardian* Lecture, October 1988.
13. Satyajit Ray, 'A New Indian Cinema?', in *Our Films, Their*

Films (Bombay: Orient Longman, 1976), p. 93.

14. Shyam Benegal, 'Making Movies in Mumbai', in Lalit Mohan Joshi (ed.), *Bollywood: Popular Indian Cinema* (London: Dakini, 2001), p. 202.
15. See Sanjit Narwekar, 'Shyam Benegal: International Recognition', in *Filmworld*, vol. 13, no. 1, January 1977.
16. Chakravarty, p. 240.
17. See chapter 3.
18. Girish Karnad, 'Amitabh Did It', *Book Review*, vol. 23, no. 12.
19. See my documentary *The Way I See It: Women Film-makers in India* (1999).
20. Govind Nihalani, 'Contemporary Cinema in India', transcript of talk delivered at the Nehru Centre, London, 11 November 2001.
21. Plus Channel was funded by the Piramal and had several arms such as Plus Music, Plus Films, Plus Events, etc. The corporation lost money and, by 1997, Piramal withdrew its backing. Plus Channel was later bought out by Reliance. Amitabh Bachchan Corporation Limited was floated with much fanfare, but suffered from poor management and vision. It was declared bankrupt in 1998, leaving Bachchan with huge debts to clear. Bachchan recovered with the hit television show *Kaun Banega Karorpati*, and ABCL is in production once again (*Aks/Reflections 2001*).

2 – The Formative Years

1. The Nizam of Hyderabad refused to accede to the Indian Union and actively encouraged the Razakars (members of the fundamentalist Ittehad-ul-Muslimen) to terrorise and oppress the peasant population.
2. See Nasreen Munni Kabir, *Guru Dutt: A Life In Cinema* (Delhi and London: Oxford University Press, 1996).
3. See Filmography.
4. Uday Shankar was the pioneer of modern dance in India and his younger brother Ravi Shankar is the legendary sitar player who composed music for Ray's *Pather Panchali* (1955) and other films. He became a prominent world music figure, particularly after teaching George Harrison and his subsequent association with the Beatles. Guru Dutt learnt dance at Uday Shankar's school and began his career in Bombay as a dance director.
5. Wadia Movietone was established in 1933 by Vinci's father, J. B. H. Wadia. Homi Wadia was best known for his Fairbanks-inspired stunt films featuring Fearless Nadia. He directed Nadia in these films and later married her. Wadia Movietone was also known for documentaries and World War II newsreels.
6. Interview with author, London, 8 February 2002. Karnad's first film as scriptwriter and actor was *Samskara* (1970), and his first as

director was *Vamsha Vriksha* (1971, co-directed with B. V. Karanth). His best-known film, *Kaadu* (1973), placed him alongside Benegal in new cinema with its consideration of rural India.
7. The video series of *Bharat Ek Khoj* (1988) is marketed by the National Film Development Corporation (NFDC), Bombay.

3 – The Rural Trilogy: Winds of Change

1. Jasodhara Bagchi, 'Shyam Benegaler Panchkanya' ('Shyam Benegal's Five Women'), *Mahanagar*, 1982 (in Bengali).
2. Ashish Rajadhyaksha and Paul Willemen (eds), *Encyclopaedia of Indian Cinema*, 2nd edn (London: BFI; New Delhi: Oxford University Press, 1999).
3. M. Madhava Prasad, *Ideology of the Hindi Film: A Historical Construction* (Delhi and Oxford: Oxford University Press, 1998), p. 196.
4. Lalit Mohan Joshi (ed.), *Bollywood: Popular Indian Cinema* (London: Dakini, 2001), p. 43.
5. *Cinema Vision India*, vol. 1, no. 3, 1980.
6. Rajadhyaksha and Willemen (eds), *Encyclopaedia of Indian Cinema*, p. 387.
7. Prasad, *Ideology of the Hindi Film*, p. 197.
8. Maithili Rao, *Director in Search of a Narrative*, festival brochure for Shyam Benegal Retrospective (Bombay: Prabhat Chitra Mandal, 1998), p. 9.
9. Behroze Gandhy, 'Interview with Shyam Benegal' in *Framework*, issue 12, December 1979.
10. Sudhir Nandgaonkar, 'Director's Perspective', in Ashok Rane (ed.), *Shyam Benegal Film Festival Brochure* (Bombay: Prabhat Chitra Mandal, 1998).
11. Satyajit Ray, '*Our Films, Their Films* (Bombay: Orient Longman, 1976).
12. Interview with author, Bombay, May 2001.
13. *Financial Times*, 6 September 1976.
14. Derek Malcolm, *Guardian*, 5 February 1976.
15. See Kishore Valicha, *The Moving Image: A Study of Indian Cinema* (Orient Longman, 1988).
16. Prasad, *Ideology of the Hindi Film*, p. 205.
17. Ibid., p. 206.
18. The Nehruvian vision was one of modernising villages and rapid industrialisation, a development proposal manifest in the five-year plans model.
19. Anand Dairies produced Amul butter and other Amul dairy products, enjoying a virtual market monopoly.
20. Prasad, *Ideology of the Hindi Film*, p. 210.
21. Ibid., p. 214. Jim Pines and Paul Willemen (eds), *Questions of Third Cinema* (London: BFI Publishing, 1989), p. 2.
23. Ibid., p. 4.
24. Ibid., p. 2.

25. Teshome H. Gabriel. 'Towards a Critical Theory of Third World Films' in *Questions of Third Cinema*, p. 35.
26. Sunday Review, *Times of India*, 2 August, 1998.

4 – The Woman's Voice: Bhumika and Mandi

1. Hansa Wadkar, *Sangtye Aika* (Pune: Rajhans Publication, 1970) (in Marathi).
2. An extract of the autobiography has been translated in Susie Tharu and K. Lalitha (eds), *Women Writing in India: Vol. 2 The Twentieth Century* (London: Pandora, 1993), p. 188.
3. London Film Festival Programme, 1978. Held at BFI Library, London.
4. The legendary actor Prithviraj Kapoor joined Imperial in 1929 and starred in India's first talkie, *Alam Ara* (1931).
5. See Tharu and Lalita, *Women Writing in India: Vol. 2 The Twentieth Century*, p. 188.
6. Wadia Brothers of Wadia Movietone made B-grade films in the Hollywood stunt mode, the best of which starred Fearless Nadia, the stuntwoman famous for her films *Hunterwali* (1935) and *Diamond Queen* (1940).
7. This was the introduction of colour in Indian films.
8. Jasodhara Bagchi, 'Shyam Benegaler Panchkanya' ('Shyam Benegal's Five Women'), *Mahanagar*, issue 1, 1982 (in Bengali).
9. See Sumita S. Chakravarty, *National Identity in Indian Popular Cinema, 1947–1987* (Austin: University of Texas Press, 1993), p. 300.
10. Dnyaneshwar Nadkarni, '*Bhumika*: Myth and Reality', *Times of India*, 30 April 1978.
11. See *Filmworld*, May 1977.
12. See Shobha Kilachand, 'Interface with Shyam Benegal', *Illustrated Weekly of India*, 30 October 1983, p. 35.
13. See Chakravarty, *National Identity in Indian Popular Cinema*, p. 301.
14. See Aijaz Ahmed, *In Theory: Classes, Nations, Literatures* (London: Verso, 1992), p. 117.
15. See Chakravarty, *National Identity in Indian Popular Cinema*, p. 304.
16. Quoted in NFT programme notes for Shyam Benegal retrospective, London, October 1988.
17. Interview with author, Bombay, June 2001.
18. 'The Benegal Interview', *The Telegraph*, 22 December 2000.

5 – Histories and Epics

1. Ashish Rajadhyaksha and Paul Willemen (eds), *Encyclopaedia of Indian Cinema* (New Delhi: Oxford University Press; London: BFI, 1994), p. 407.
2. See '*Junoon*: Critics Obsession', *Economic Times*, 8 April 1979; Khalid Mohamed, '*Junoon*: A Hollow Obsession', *Times of India*, 2 April 1979.

3. *Nishant* has been read as a reworking of the Ramayana myth. See chapter 3, p. 77.
4. Iqbal Masud, 'The Epic as Trap', *Indian Express*, 3 August 1979.
5. Gyanendra Pandey, *Hindus and Others: The Question of Identity in India Today* (New Delhi: Viking, 1993), p. 24.
6. Sumita S. Chakravarty, *National Identity in Indian Popular Cinema, 1947–1987* (Austin: University of Texas Press, 1993), p. 252.
7. R. Krishnamoorthy, '*Trikaal*: Benegal's Trials with Time Element', *Indian Express*, 21 September 1986.
8. Mohan Bawa, 'Bringing back Goa's Past', *Sunday Observer*, 5 May 1985.
9. Derek Malcolm in NFT programme notes for Shyam Benegal retrospective, London, October 1988.
10. Chidananda Dasgupta, 'Shyam Benegal's *Trikaal*', *Express Magazine*, 27 October 1985.
11. Maithili Rao, interview with author, Bombay, May 2001.
12. Leela Naidu to Sheila Vasunia, '*Trikaal* Is a Joyous Experience in My Life', *Cinema India International*, July–September 1985.
13. Interview with Sunil John, Filmotsav 86, *Deccan Chronicle*, January 1986.
14. Shyam Benegal's interview with Anil Dharkar, *Debonair*, February 1986, quoted in *Monograph on Shyam Benegal* (Bombay: NFDC, 1980).

6 – Subaltern Voices

1. Bikram Singh, 'To the Rescue of Threatened Species', *Sunday Observer*, 22 June 1986.
2. Interview with author, Bombay, May 2001.
3. M. Rahman, 'A Rich Tapestry', *India Today*, August 1986.
4. Interview with author, Pune, May 2001.
5. *Manthan* was made through the auspices of the National Dairy Development Board (NDDB). See chapter 3, for more details.
6. For details of the Bengal land reform movement, see Partha Chatterjee, *The Present History of West Bengal: Essays in Political Criticism* (New Delhi and Oxford: Oxford University Press, 1997).
7. Meenakshi Shedde, 'A Tale with a Twist', *Times of India*, 9 May 1999.
8. Saibal Chatterjee, 'An Indian *Samar*', *Outlook*, 23 August 1999, p. 58.
9. Hasina's story is an interesting counterpoint to popular films such as *Hum Aapke Hain Koun …!*, in which the heroine is almost married off to her brother-in-law after her sister's death. The divine intervention that finally unites the lovers is as much a Hindu fantasy as the Bollywood notions of sugary romance. The film was a runaway hit and a milestone in the success of romantic musicals of the 1990s. It was an uneasy indicator of growing Hindutva (pertaining to Hindu identity)

sensibility and the continual idealising of the family. Against the culture of the big picture, Benegal continues to tell realistic stories of people who inhabit a community or nation.

10. Interview with Shyam Benegal, *Movies*, 28 July 1999 – www.rediff.com/entertai/1999/july/28shy.htm>

7 – The Last Trilogy: Search for Identity

1. Sangeeta Datta, 'Globalisation and Representations of Women in Indian Cinema' *Social Scientist*, vol. 28, nos 3 & 4, March 2000.
2. Shyam Benegal, 'Making Movies in Mumbai,' in Lalit Mohan Joshi (ed.), *Bollywood: Popular Indian Cinema* (London: Dakini, 2001), p. 175.
3. Ibid., p. 183.
4. Ruth Vanita, 'Marriage as a Metaphor: *Bombay*, *Mammo* and the Conventions of Popular Cinema', *Manushi*, no. 89, 1996.
5. Ritu Menon and Kamla Bhasin, *Borders and Boundaries: Women in India's Partition* (New Delhi: Kali for Women, 1998), p. 9.
6. Urvashi Butalia, *The Other Side of Silence: Voices from the Partition of India* (Delhi: Viking, 1998), writes about women's histories of partition as a process 'sometimes painfully so, of the need to fold back several layers of history (or of what we see as fact) before one can begin to arrive at a different more complex "truth".'
7. Ruth Vanita, 'Marriage as a Metaphor: *Bombay*, *Mammo* and the Conventions of Popular Cinema'.
8. The thumri was performed, rather than merely sung, and was enacted through hand gestures or the kathak style of classical dance. The songs were about love and desire, and often had a vaguely erotic subtext. Today, thumri is considered a dying art form, as patronage – formerly drawn from kings and feudal lords – declined rapidly after Independence.
9. In middle-class Indian society, deep suspicion about the performing woman and her trade exists. The thumri had moved from the royal courts to the kothas (salons); the courtesan had moved to the marketplace as a baijee (who sold her art as well as her body).
10. Vaishali Honawar, 'The Right Direction', *Telegraph*, 21 April 1996.
11. Menon and Bhasin, *Borders and Boundaries*, p. 8.
12. Urvashi Butalia, *The Other Side of Silence: Voices from the Partition of India*. See chapter 1.
13. Interview in Bombay, July 2001.

8 – Experiments with Truth

1 Interview with author, Bombay, May 2001.
2. Interview with author, Bombay, May 2001.
3. See Ashish Nandy, 'Invitation to an Antique Death', in Rachel Dwyer and Christopher Pinney

(eds), *Pleasure and the Nation: The History, Politics and Consumption of Public Culture in India* (New Delhi and Oxford: Oxford University Press, 2001), pp. 139–60.

4. Interview with author, Bombay, May 2001.
5. Maithili Rao, *Director in Search of a Narrative*, festival brochure for Shyam Benegal Retrospective (Bombay: Prabhat Chitra Mandal, 1998).
6. See Sangeeta Datta, *Cinema in India*, May 1993.
7. The Many Faces of Love, *Times of India*, 21 February, 1993.
8. Jawaharlal Nehru, *Glimpses of World History*, Delhi, 1951. Jawaharlal Nehru, *The Discovery of India* (Calcutta: Signet Press, 1946). S. Gopal (ed.), *Selected Works of Jawaharlal Nehru 1889–1964*, (Delhi: Jawaharlal Nehru Memorial Fund, distributed by Oxford University Press distributors, c. 2001).
9. See *Sunday Observer*, 8 July 1984, p. 18.
10. NFT programme notes for Shyam Benegal retrospective, London, October 1988.
11. Ashish Rajadhyaksha and Paul Willemen (eds), *Encyclopaedia of Indian Cinema*, 2nd edn (London: BFI; New Delhi: Oxford University Press, 1999), p. 57.
12. Anil Dharkar, Review in *Gentleman*, July 1981.
13. See *Monograph on Benegal* (Bombay: NFDC, 1980).
14. Samik Bandopadhyay, 'Introduction', *Satyajit Ray: A Film by Shyam Benegal*, (Calcutta: Seagull, 1988), p. v.
15. Ibid., p. viii.
16. Interview with author, Calcutta, January 2002.
17. Interview with author, London, October 2001.
18. Quoted in Lalit Mohan Joshi (ed.), *South Asian Cinema*, vol. 1, no. 1, February 2001, p. 18.

Bibliography

Further reading

Ahmad, Aijaz, *In Theory: Classes, Nations, Literatures* (London: Verso, 1992).

Altman, Rick, *Film/Genre* (London: BFI Publishing, 1999).

Banerjee, Shampa, *New Indian Cinema* (New Delhi: NFDC, 1982).

Benegal, Shyam, 'Making Movies in Mumbai', in Lalit Mohan Joshi (ed.), *Bollywood: Popular Indian Cinema* (London: Dakini, 2001).

Benegal, Shyam, 'Popular Cinema', in *100 Years of Cinema* (Calcutta: Nandan, 1995), pp. 3—20.

Bhattacharya, Rinki, *Bimal Roy: A Man of Silence* (New Delhi: Indus, 1994).

Breckenridge, Carol (ed.) *Consuming Modernity: Public Culture in a South Asian World* (Minneapolis and London: University of Minnesota Press, 1995).

Butalia, Urvashi, *The Other Side of Silence: Voices from the Partition of India* (Delhi: Viking, 1998).

Chakravarty, Sumita S., *National Identity in Indian Popular Cinema, 1947–1987* (Austin: University of Texas Press, 1993).

Chatterjee, Partha, *A Possible India: Essays in Political Criticism* (Delhi and Oxford: Oxford University Press, 1997).

Chatterjee, Partha, *The Nation and Its Fragments: Colonial and Postcolonial Histories* (Princeton, NJ: Princeton University Press, 1993).

Chatterjee, Partha, *The Present History of West Bengal: Essays in Political Criticism* (New Delhi and Oxford: Oxford University Press, 1997).

Cooper, Darius. *The Cinema of Satyajit Ray: Between Tradition and Modernity* (Cambridge: Cambridge University Press, 2000).

Das, Gurcharan, *India Unbound: From Independence to the Global Information Age* (London: Profile, 2002).

Das Gupta, Chidananda, *Talking about Films* (New Delhi: Orient Longman, 1981).

Deep, Mohan, *Simply Scandalous: Meena Kumari* (Bombay: Magna Books, 1998).

Dwyer, Rachel, *Yash Chopra* (London: BFI Publishing, 2002).

Dwyer, Rachel and Christopher Pinney (eds) *Pleasure and the Nation: The History, Politics and Consumption of Public Culture in India* (New Delhi and Oxford: Oxford University Press, 2001).

Guha, Ranajit, *Subaltern Studies:*

Writings on South Asian History and Society* (Delhi and London: Oxford University Press, 1982).

Guha, Ranajit (ed.), *Subaltern Studies II: Writings on South Asian History and Society, vol. 2* (Delhi: Oxford University Press, 1994).

Hood, John W., *Chasing the Truth: The Films of Mrinal Sen* (Calcutta: Seagull, 1993).

Hood, John W., *Time and Dreams: The Films of Buddhadeb Dasgupta* (Calcutta: Seagull, 1998).

Jaffrelot, Christophe, *The Hindu Nationalist Movement and Indian Politics, 1925 to the 1990s* (London: Hurst, 1996).

Joshi, Lalit Mohan (ed.), *Bollywood: Popular Indian Cinema* (London: Dakini, 2001).

Kabir, Nasreen Munni, *Guru Dutt: A Life in Cinema* (Delhi and London: Oxford University Press, 1996).

Kakar, Sudhir, *The Colours of Violence* (New Delhi and London: Viking, 1995).

Kakar, Sudhir, *The Indian Psyche* (Delhi: Oxford University Press, 1996).

Menon, Ritu and Kamla Bhasin, *Borders and Boundaries: Women in India's Partition* (New Delhi: Kali for Women, 1998).

Mishra, Vijay, *Bollywood Cinema: Temples of Desire* (New York and London: Routledge, 2002).

Nandy, Ashis, *The Intimate Enemy: Loss and Recovery of Self under Colonialism* (Delhi and Oxford: Oxford University Press, 1983).

Nandy, Ashis (ed.), *The Secret Politics of Our Desires: Innocence, Culpability and Indian Popular Cinema* (London: Zed, 1998).

National Film and Development Corporation (NFDC), *Cinema in India*, vol. 4, no. 3, March 1993.

National Film and Development Corporation (NFDC), *Cinema in India Yearbook* (Bombay: NFDC, 1993).

National Film Theatre, 'Shyam Benegal: Style and Passion', NFT Programme, (London: NFT, 1988).

Pandey, Gyanendra, *Hindus and Others: The Question of Identity in India Today* (New Delhi: Viking, 1993).

Pandey, Gyanendra, *The Construction of Communalism in Colonial North India* (Delhi: Oxford University Press, 1990).

Pines, Jim and Paul Willemen (eds), *Questions of Third Cinema* (London: BFI Publishing, 1989).

Prasad, M. Madhava, *Ideology of the Hindi Film: A Historical Construction* (Delhi and Oxford: Oxford University Press, 1998).

Rajadhyaksha, Ashish and Paul Willemen (eds), *Encyclopaedia of Indian Cinema*, 2nd edn (London: BFI; New Delhi: Oxford University Press, 1999).

Rane, Ashok (ed.), *A Shyam Benegal Film Festival* (Bombay: Prabhat Chitra Mandal, 1998).

Ray, Satyajit, *Our Films, Their Films* (Bombay: Orient Longman, 1976).

Reuben, Bunny, *Mehboob, India's DeMille: The First Biography* (New Delhi: Indus, 1994).

Reuben, Bunny, *Raj Kapoor: The Fabulous Showman* (New Delhi: Indus, 1995).

Robinson, Andrew, *Satyajit Ray: The Inner Eye* (London: Deutsch, 1989).

Sarkar, Sumit, *Writing Social History* (Delhi: Oxford University Press, 1997).

Tharu, Susie J. and K. Lalitha (eds), *Women Writing in India: Vol. 1 600 BC to the Early Twentieth Century* (London: Pandora, 1991).

Tharu, Susie J. and K. Lalitha (eds), *Women Writing in India: Vol. 2 The Twentieth Century* (London: Pandora, 1993).

Tiwari, Shriram (ed.), *Patkatha: Special Series on Shyam Benegal, vol. 12, 1991* (in Hindi).

Vasudev, Aruna, *Frames of Mind: Reflections on Indian Cinema* (Delhi: UBS Publishers, 1995).

Vasudev, Aruna and Philippe Lenglet (eds), *India Cinema Superbazaar* (New Delhi: Vikas, c.1983).

Vasudev Aruna, *The New Indian Cinema* (Delhi: Macmillan, 1986).

Film scripts

Benegal, Shyam *Satyajit Ray* (Calcutta: Seagull, 1988).

Benegal, Shyam, *Manthan (The Churning)* (Calcutta: Seagull, 1978)

Hauff, Reinhard, *Ten Days in Calcutta: A Portrait of Mrinal Sen* (Calcutta: Seagull, 1987).

Articles

Bagchi, Jasodhara, 'Shyam Benegaler Panchkanya' ('Shyam Benegal's Five Women'), *Mahanagar*, issue 1, Calcutta, 1982 (in Bengali).

Benegal, Shyam, 'The Many Faces of Love', *Sunday Times of India*, 21 February 1993.

Benegal, Shyam, 'We All Want Our Films to Run', *Sunday Observer*, 8 July 1984.

Datta, Sangeeta, 'Globalisation and Representations of Women in Indian Cinema', *Social Scientist*, vol. 28, nos 3 & 4, 2000.

Datta, Sangeeta, 'Smiles and Tears: Portrayal of Women in *Rudaali* and *Suraj Ka Satwan Ghoda*', *Cinema in India*, vol. 4, no. 5, May 1993, pp. 25–9.

Datta, Sangeeta, 'Women's Stories: Shyam Benegal's *Suraj Ka Satwan Ghoda*,' Sunday Review, *Times of India*, 6 February 1994.

Dharkar Anil, 'Shyam Benegal: Five Best Directors', in Peter Cowie (ed.), *International Film Guide* (London: Tantivy, 1979).

Jain, Madhu, 'Shyam Benegal: Renaissance Man', *India Today*, 30 November 1999.

Joshi, Lalit Mohan, 'Shyam Benegal's Second Coming', *South Asian Cinema*, vol. 1, no. 1, February 2001.

Karkaria, Bachi, '*Manthan*' *Illustrated Weekly of India*, 11 September 1977.

Karnad, Girish, 'Amitabh Did It', *The Book Review*, vol. 23, no. 12, December 1999.

Kilachand, Shobha, 'Interface with Shyam Benegal' *Illustrated Weekly of India*, 30 October 1983.

Malcolm, Derek, Review of *Ankur*, *Guardian*, 5 February 1976.

Mulvey, Laura, 'Visual Pleasures and Narrative Cinema', *Screen*, vol. 16, no. 3, 1975.

Naidu, Leela, 'Trikaal Is a Joyous Experience', *Cinema India International*, July–September 1985.

Narwekar, Sanjit, 'Shyam Benegal: International Recognition', *Filmworld*, vol. 13, no. 1, January 1977.

Parihar, Rohit, 'Master and the Princess', *India Today*, 27 December 1999.

Singh, Bikram, '*Mandi*: A Triumph of Good Taste', *Sunday Observer*, 9 October 1993.

Spivak, Gayatri Chakravorty, 'Can the Subaltern Speak?', in B. Ashcroft, G. Griffiths and H. Tiffin (eds), *The Post-colonial Studies Reader* (London: Routledge, 1995).

Filmography

Ankur (The Seedling, 1974)
Screenplay: Satyadev Dubey
Cinematography: Govind Nihalani
Editing: Bhanudas Divkar
Music: Vanraj Bhatia
Cast: Shabana Azmi, Sadhu Meher, Anant Nag, Priya Tendulkar, Kadar Ali Beg, Aga Mohmad Husen
Produced by: Blaze Film Enterprises, Lalit M. Bijlani, Freni Variava
Awards: Best Hindi film and two other National Awards, 1974
Recognition: Received 43 international awards. Also nominated as an Indian entry in the film festivals of Berlin, Stratford and London. Selected for foreign film section of the Oscars, 1974
Running Time: 137 minutes
Language: Hindi
Colour

Charandas Chor
(Charandas the Thief, 1975)
Story/Screenplay: Shama Zaidi, Habib Tanvir
Cinematography: Govind Nihalani
Music: Nandkishor Mittal
Lyrics: Nandkishor Mittal, Gangaram, Swarkumar
Cast: Smita Patil, Anjali Paigaonkar, Sadhu Meher, Habib Tanvir, Lalu Ram, Madanlal, Bhakalaram, Ramnath, Thaurram, Malabai, Bhidabal, Ramratan, Hiraram
Produced by: Children's Film Society, Lalit M. Bijlani, Freni Variava
Running Time: 176 minutes
Language: Hindi
Black and White

Nishant (Night's End, 1975)
Story/Screenplay: Vijay Tendulkar
Dialogue: Satyadev Dubey
Cinematography: Govind Nihalani
Editing: Bhanudas Divkar
Music: Vanraj Bhatia
Lyrics: Mohamad Kurla, Kutub Shah
Cast: Smita Patil, Shabana Azmi, Girish Karnad, Anant Nag, Amrish Puri, Satyadev Dubey, Kulbhushan Kharbanda, Savita Bajaj, Sadhu Meher
Produced by: Blaze Film Enterprises, Mohan J. Bijlani, Freni Variava
Awards: *World Magazine*'s award for best film, best director and best supporting actress. Bengal Film Journalists also judged it as best film and Shyam Benegal as best director. Received National Award for best Hindi film, 1976
Recognition: Invited to appear in 1976 Cannes Film Festival and London Film Festival, and Melbourne Film Festival in 1977.

Won Golden
Plaque at Chicago Film Festival
Running Time: 145 minutes
Language: Hindi
Colour

Manthan (The Churning, 1976)
Story: V. Kuriyan/Shyam Benegal
Screenplay: Vijay Tendulkar
Dialogue: Kaifi Azmi
Cinematography: Govind Nihalani
Editing: Bhanudas Divkar
Music: Vanraj Bhatia
Lyrics: Niti Sagar
Playback singer: Preeti Sagar
Cast: Smita Patil, Girish Karnad, Sadhu Meher, Naseeruddin Shah, Anant Nag, Amrish Puri, Kulbhushan Kharbanda, Mohan Agashe, Savita Bajaj, Abha Dhulia, Anjali Paigaonkar
Produced by: Gujarat Co-operative Milk Marketing Federation, Sahyadri Films
Awards: National Award for best Hindi film and best screenplay, 1976
Recognition: Shown at London, Los Angeles, Melbourne and Hong Kong film festivals. Indian entry for the best foreign film section of the Oscars
Running Time: 135 minutes
Language: Hindi
Colour

Bhumika (The Role, 1977)
Story: Based on autobiography of Hansa Wadkar (*Sangtye Aika,* 1970)
Screenplay: Shyam Benegal, Girish Karnad, Satyadev Dubey
Dialogue: Satyadev Dubey
Cinematography: Govind Nihalani
Editing: Bhanudas Divkar
Music: Vanraj Bhatia
Lyrics: Majrooh Sultanpuri, Vasant Dev, Raja Mehndi, Ali Khan
Playback singer: Preeti Sagar
Cast: Smita Patil, Amol Palekar, Anant Nag, Amrish Puri, Naseeruddin Shah, Sulabha Deshpande, Kulbhushan Kharbanda, B. V. Karanth
Produced by: Blaze Film Enterprises, Lalit M. Bijlani, Freni Variava
Awards: National Award for best Hindi film and best actress, 1977
Recognition: Shown at Kartigue, Chicago and Algerian film festivals
Running Time: 145 minutes
Language: Hindi
Colour

Anugraham (The Boon/The Sage from the Sea, 1977)
Story: Based on Marathi novel *Kondura* by Khanolkar
Screenplay: Arudra, Girish Karnad and Shyam Benegal
Dialogue: Arudra
Cinematography: Govind Nihalani
Editing: Bhanudas Divkar
Music: Vanraj Bhatia
Lyrics: Arudra
Cast: Anant Nag, Smita Patil, Vanisree, Raogopalrao, Venu, A. R. Krishna, G. Nirmala, Sulabha Deshpande
Produced by: Raviraj International
Running Time: 137 minutes
Language: Telugu
Colour

Kondura (The Boon/The Sage from the Sea, 1977)
Story: Based on Marathi novel *Kondura* by Khanolkar
Screenplay: Shyam Benegal, Arudra, Girish Karnad
Dialogue: Satyadev Dubey
Cinematography: Govind Nihalani
Editing: Bhanudas Divkar
Music: Vanraj Bhatia
Lyrics: Vasant Dev
Produced by: Raviraj International, K. Venkatarama Reddy
Cast: Smita Patil, Vanishree, Anant Nag, Shekhar Chatterjee, Satyadev Dubey, Sulabha Deshpande, Amrish Puri, Venu Sidhesh, Seshat Raju, Nirmala, Jaya Vani
Recognition: Participation in London, Montreal, Los Angeles, Berlin and New Delhi film festivals
Running Time: 138 minutes
Language: Hindi
Colour

Junoon (Possessed, 1978)
Story: Based on Ruskin Bond's 'A Flight of Pigeons'
Dialogue: Satyadev Dubey
Cinematography: Govind Nihalani.
Editing: Bhanudas Divkar
Music: Vanraj Bhatia
Lyrics: Yogesh Praveen, Kabir Sant, Jigar Muradabadi, Amir Khusro
Cast: Shashi Kapoor, Shabana Azmi, Jennifer Kapoor (née Kendal), Naseeruddin Shah, Jalal Agha, Kulbhushan Kharbanda, Benjamin Gillani, Tom Alter, Pearl Pedamsee, Nafisa Ali, Ismat Chugtai, Sushma Shreshth, Deepti Naval
Produced by: Filmvallas, Shashi Kapoor
Running Time: 141 minutes
Language: Hindi
Colour

Kalyug (The Machine Age, 1980)
Story/Screenplay: Shyam Benegal, Girish Karnad
Dialogue: Satyadev Dubey
Cinematography: Govind Nihalani
Editing: Bhanudas Divkar
Sound: Hitendra Ghosh
Music: Vanraj Bhatia
Lyrics: Balwant Tandon
Cast: Shashi Kapoor, Rekha, Anant Nag, Raj Babbar, Kulbhushan Kharbanda, Victor Bannerjee, Vinod Doshi, Vijaya Mehta, Sushma Shresht, Supriya Pathak
Produced by: Filmvallas, Shashi Kapoor
Running Time: 163 minutes
Language: Hindi
Colour

Aarohan (The Ascent, 1982)
Screenplay: Shama Zaidi
Dialogue: Niaz Hyder
Cinematography: Govind Nihalani
Editing: Bhanudas Divkar
Sound: Hitendra Ghosh
Music: Purnadas Baul
Cast: Om Puri, Shrila Majumdar, Victor Bannerjee, Rajen Taraphdar, Gita Sen, Pankaj Kapoor
Produced by: Department of Information and Culture, Government of West Bengal
Awards: National Awards for best

Hindi film, best actor, best editing, 1982
Running Time: 147 minutes
Language: Hindi
Colour

Mandi (Market Place, 1983)
Screenplay: Shyam Benegal, Satyadev Dubey, Shama Zaidi
Dialogue: Satyadev Dubey
Cinematography: Ashok Mehta
Editing: Bhanudas Divkar
Sound: Hitendra Ghosh
Music: Vanraj Bhatia
Lyrics: Mir Taki Mir, Bahadur Shah Jaffar, Insha, Moshram Mohiddin, Talwar Danda, Ila Arun
Cast: Smita Patil, Shabana Azmi, Amrish Puri, Naseeruddin Shah, Kulbhushan Kharbanda, Saeed Jaffrey, Om Puri, Shrila Mujumdar, Harish Patel, Neena Gupta, Soni Razdan, Ila Arun, Gita Siddharth, Aditya Bhattacharya
Produced by: Blaze Film Enterprises, Lalit M. Bijlani, Freni Variava
Awards: National Award for art direction, 1983
Recognition: Shown at London, Los Angeles and Hong Kong film festivals and in the Panorama section of Mumbai Film Festival
Running Time: 162 minutes
Language: Hindi
Colour

Trikaal (Past, Present and Future, 1985)
Screenplay: Shyam Benegal
Dialogue: Shama Zaidi
Cinematography: Ashok Mehta
Art Director: Nitish Roy
Editing: Bhanudas Divkar
Sound: Hitendra Ghosh
Music: Vanraj Bhatia, Remo Fernandes
Lyrics: Ila Arun
Cast: Leela Naidu, Naseeruddin Shah, Neena Gupta, Anita Kunwar, Dilip Tahil, Soni Razdan, Sushma Prakash, K. K. Raina, Keith Stevens, Kulbhushan Kharbanda, Maqsoom Ali
Produced by: Blaze Film Enterprises, Lalit M. Bijlani, Freni Variava
Awards: National Award for best direction and best costumes, 1985
Recognition: Participation in London and Lisbon film festivals and Indian Panorama
Running Time: 137 minutes
Language: Hindi
Colour

Susman (The Essence, 1986)
Screenplay: Shyam Benegal, Shama Zaidi
Cinematography: Ashok Mehta
Art Director: Nitish Roy
Editing: Bhanudas Divkar
Sound: S. W. Deshpande
Music: Vanraj Bhatia
Cast: Shabana Azmi, Om Puri, Neena Gupta, Kulbhushan Kharbanda, K. K. Raina, Anu Kapoor, Harish Patel, Mohan Agashe, Ila Arun
Produced by: Association of Co-operatives and Apex Societies of Handloom
Recognition: Participation in Indian

Panorama 1987 and London, Chicago, Sydney and Melbourne film festivals
Runnung Time: 140 minutes
Language: Hindi
Colour

Antarnaad (Inner Voice, 1991)
Story: Based on Pandurang Shastri Athawale's Swadhyaya movement
Screenplay: Shama Zaidi, Sunil Shanbaug
Cinematography: V. K. Murthy
Editing: Bhanudas Divkar
Music: Vanraj Bhatia
Lyrics: Vasant Dev, Ila Arun
Produced by: Suhetu Films
Cast: Shabana Azmi, Kulbhushan Kharbanda, Om Puri, K. K. Raina, Ila Arun, Dina Pathak, Pavan Malhotra, Anang Desai, Virendra Saxena, Kishor Kadam, John David
Running Time: 155 minutes
Language: Hindi
Colour

Suraj Ka Satwan Ghoda (The Seventh Horse of the Sun, 1992)
Story: Dharamveer Bharati
Screenplay: Shama Zaidi
Cinematography: Piyush Shah
Editing: Bhanudas Divkar
Art Director: Nitish Roy
Sound: Ashwin Balsawar
Lyrics: Vasant Dev
Music: Vanraj Bhatia
Cast: Amrish Puri, Neena Gupta, Ila Arun, K. K. Raina, Pallavi Joshi, Rajeshwari Sachdev, Raghuvir Yadav, Prakash Dhar, Anang Desai, Virendra Saxena, Rajit Kapur
Produced by: National Film Development Corporation (NFDC), Doordarshan
Awards: National Award for best film in 1993. Best film at Singapore Film Festival 1994. Participated in London, Chicago, Cairo, Washington, San Francisco and Los Angeles film festivals
Running Time: 128 minutes
Language: Hindi
Colour

Mammo (Grandmother, 1994)
Story: Khalid Mohamed
Screenplay: Khalid Mohamed, Shama Zaidi
Dialogue: Shama Zaidi
Cinematography: Prasanna Jain
Editing: Asim Sinha
Music: Vanraj Bhatia
Sound: Ashwin Balsawar
Produced by: National Film and Development Corporation (NFDC), Doordarshan
Cast: Farida Jalal, Amit Phalke, Surekha Sikri Rege, Rajit Kapur, Himani Shivpuri, Shiv Vallabh Vyas
Awards: National Award for best Hindi film and best supporting actress, 1994
Running Time: 130 minutes
Language: Hindi
Colour

The Making of the Mahatma (1995)
Story: Fatima Mir
Screenplay: Fatima Mir, Shama Zaidi, Shyam Benegal

Cinematography: Ashok Mehta
Music: Vanraj Bhatia
Cast: Rajit Kapur, Pallavi Joshi, Amrish Puri, Keath Stevens, Stimy Pillai, Charles Pillai, Siraj Khan
Produced by: National Film Development Corporation (NFDC), Doordarshan
Running Time: 170 minutes
Language: Hindi/English
Colour

Sardari Begum (1996)
Story: Khalid Mohamed
Dialogue: Shama Zaidi
Cinematography: Sanjay Dharankar
Art Director: Sameer Chandra
Editing: Asim Sinha
Sound: Ashwin Balsawar
Music: Vanraj Bhatia
Playback singer: Asha Bhonsle
Lyrics: Javed Akhtar
Produced by: Plus Films
Cast: Kiron Kher, Smriti Mishra, Amrish Puri, Rajit Kapur, Surekha Sikri Rege, Rajeshwari Sachdev
Awards: Best Urdu film, best supporting actress, special jury award at National Awards, 1996
Running Time: 126 minutes
Language: Hindi
Colour

Samar (Conflict, 1998)
Script: Ashok Mishra
Cinematography: Rajan Kothari
Editing: Asim Sinha
Sound: Ashwin Balsawar
Music: Vanraj Bhatia
Cast: Rajit Kapur, Rajeshwari Sachdev, Kishore Kadam, Seema Biswas, Raghuvir Yadav
Produced by: Ministry of Social Justice and Empowerment
Awards: Best film at National Awards in 1998
Running Time: 125 minutes
Language: Hindi
Colour

Hari Bhari (2000)
Dialogue/screenplay: Shama Zaidi
Cinematography: Rajan Kothari
Editing: Asim Sinha
Music: Vanraj Bhatia
Sound: Ashwin Balsawar
Cast: Shabana Azmi, Nandita Das, Surekha Sikri, Rajit Kapur, Rajeshwari Sachdev
Produced by: Ministry of Family Welfare
Awards: Best film on family welfare at 1999 National Awards
Running Time: 146 minutes
Language: Hindi
Colour

Zubeidaa (2000)
Script: Khalid Mohamed
Cinematography: Rajan Kothari
Editing: Asim Sinha
Music: A. R. Rahman
Playback singers: Lata Mangeshkar, Kavita Krishnamurthy
Sound: Ashwyn Balsawar
Art Director: Sameer Chanda
Costumes: Pia Benegal
Cast: Karishma Kapoor, Rekha, Manoj Bajpai, Rajit Kapur, Surekha Sikri, Amrish Puri
Produced by: Firoz Rattansi
Distributors: Yashraj Films
Awards: Best Hindi film at 2000 National Awards

Running Time: 150 minutes
Language: Hindi
Colour

Documentaries

Nehru (1983)
Script: Shyam Benegal, Vladimir Zimlanin, Yuri Aldokhin, Aleksander Gorev
Cinematography: Subrata Mitra, Konstantin Orozaliev
Editing: Somnath Kulkarni, Valeria Konovalova
Sound: Hitendra Ghosh, Alexei Kozlov
Music: Vanraj Bhatia
Running Time: 180 minutes
Language: English
Colour

Satyajit Ray (1984)
Script: Shyam Benegal
Cinematography: Govind Nihalani
Sound: Hitendra Ghosh
Music: Vanraj Bhatia
Credits design: Satyajit Ray
Running Time: 133 minutes
Language: English
Colour

Index

Films and other works indexed by title are by Benegal unless otherwise indicated
Italicised page numbers denote illustrations; those in bold indicate detailed analysis
n = endnote (indexed only for background information, not citations).

சிந்தனைகள் மூலம் செல்வந்தன் ஆகு

நெப்போலியன் ஹில்

உலகெங்கும் சிறப்பாக விற்பனையாகும் *சிந்தனைகள் மூலம் செல்வந்தன் ஆகு* என்ற நூலின் எழுத்தாளர் நெப்போலியன் ஹில், பல சுய உதவி நூல்களின் ஆசிரியர் மற்றும் தொழிலதிபராக இருந்தவர். நார்மன் வின்சென்ட் பீல் முதல் டொனால்ட் ட்ரம்ப் வரை உலகம் முழுவதிலும் உள்ள பல்வேறு மனிதர்களின் வாழ்வில் சிறப்பான தாக்கத்தை தன் வேலைகள் மூலம் இவர் உருவாக்கியுள்ளார். பிறப்பால் ஏழையாக இருந்தாலும் பலதரப்பட்ட தொழில்களை துவங்கி வண்ணமயமான வாழ்கையை இவர் வாழ்ந்தார். அமெரிக்க ஜனாதிபதியான வுட்ரோ வில்சன் போன்ற பிரபலமானவர்களை சந்தித்து அவர்களுக்கு ஆலோசனைகள் வழங்கினார். இறுதியில் ஹில் ஊக்கமளிக்கும் பேச்சாளராக பரவலான வெற்றி பெற்றார். வாழ்கையில் வெற்றி காண்பது எப்படி என்பது குறித்து பல புத்தகங்கள் எழுதி சுய உதவி என்னும் இலக்கியநடையை உருவாக்கினார் என்றே கூறலாம்.

RUPA

First Published by
Rupa Publications India Pvt. Ltd 2024
7/16, Ansari Road, Daryaganj
New Delhi 110002

Sales centres:
Bengaluru Chennai
Hyderabad Jaipur Kathmandu
Kolkata Mumbai Prayagraj

P-ISBN: 978-93-6156-808-4
E-ISBN: 978-93-6156-554-0

Second impression 2025

10 9 8 7 6 5 4 3 2

Printed in India